FIST FROM
THE SKY

THE AMERICAN CIVIL WAR

Cavalry Raids of the Civil War
Pickett's Charge
Witness to Gettysburg

WORLD WAR II

Armor Battles of the Waffen-SS, 1943–45
Australian Commandos
The B-24 in China
Beyond the Beachhead
The Brandenburger Commandos
Bringing the Thunder
Coast Watching in World War II
Flying American Combat Aircraft of World War II
Forging the Thunderbolt
Germany's Panzer Arm in World War II
Grenadiers
Infantry Aces
Luftwaffe Aces
Messerschmitts over Sicily
Michael Wittmann and the Waffen SS Tiger Commanders
of the Leibstandarte in World War II, Vol. 1
Michael Wittmann and the Waffen SS Tiger Commanders
of the Leibstandarte in World War II, Vol. 2
On the Canal
Packs On!
Panzer Aces
Panzer Aces II
Surviving Bataan and Beyond
The 12th SS, Volume One
The 12th SS, Volume Two
Tigers in the Mud

THE COLD WAR / VIETNAM

Flying American Combat Aircraft: The Cold War
Land with No Sun
Street without Joy

WARS OF THE MIDDLE EAST

Never-Ending Conflict

FIST FROM THE SKY

JAPAN'S DIVE-BOMBER ACE OF WORLD WAR II

Peter C. Smith

STACKPOLE
BOOKS

Published in paperback in 2006 by
STACKPOLE BOOKS
5067 Ritter Road
Mechanicsburg, PA 17055
www.stackpolebooks.com

Printed in the United States of America

10 9 8 7 6 5 4 3 2 1

FIRST EDITION

Cataloging-in-publication data is on file with the Library of Congress and
the British Library.

ISBN-10: 0-8117-3330-0
ISBN-13: 978-0-8117-3330-4

'Whenever the Imperial Japanese Navy won a battle, there always, was Egusa!'
Professor Samuel Eliot Morison, Ph D

'Lieutenant-Commander Takashige Egusa was a prominent dive-bomber pilot, great leader and brilliant warrior'
Suma Tomioka

Dedication

Commander Sadao Seno, JMDF, Rtd; historian, and friend
with gratitude for your friendship and your counsel down the years

Contents

Publishers note:
Research has brought to light many contemporary and rare photographs of varying quality. They are reproduced and have been enhanced as far as possible.

Acknowledgements

The Author would like to acknowledge the help of many friends and colleagues in Japan; first and foremost of noted historian Sadao Seno, JMSDF (Rtd). Both during my various research visits to many offices, facilities and individuals in Japan he has guided me and acted as the perfect diplomat, opening doors for me that others have not even knocked upon. My debt to him is enormous. I would also like to express my gratitude for the courtesy and helpfulness I have received from the many Japanese people consulted during the long research for this book, in particular:

Professor Toshimasa Egusa, Kobe City, for permission to reproduce photographs of his father and mother from the family archives and to quote from private letters and also from his mothers autobiography, *Futatsu no Jidai: Otto wa 'Kanbaku no Kamisama' to iwarete (The Two Ages);* Historian and Author Mitsuharu Uehara, for permission to use photographs from his own book *Kambaku Taicho Egusa Takashige (Life of a Front Line Commander of Carrierborne Dive-Bomber Group);* Vice Admiral Kazunari Doke, Commandant, Kure District, Japan Maritime Self-Defence Force, Hiroshima; Rear Admiral Sadayoshi Matsuoka, JMSDF, Superintendent, Officer Candidate School, Etajima; Rear Admiral Kazuo Takahashi, JMSDF, Chief of Staff, Commandant Kure District, Hiroshima; Captain Masato Shimada, Deputy Superintendent, Officers Candidate School, Etajima; Lieutenant Commander Zenji Abe, IJN (Rtd) famous dive-bomber ace, for memoirs and recollections of Egusa and of Etajima; Lieutenant Takeshi Maeda, IJN (Rtd), Tokyo, former pilot of Nakajima 'Kate' aboard *Kaga,* now Honorary President, Unabarakai; Rear Admiral Taemi Ichikawa, IJN (Rtd), Matsudo City, former assistant communications officer carrier *Akagi* for kind hospitality in his home; Lieutenant Commander Iyozo Fujita, Zero ace aboard carrier *Sōryū,* and his family, for their hospitality in their home; Kumio Kosemoto for permission to reproduce the photo of Ford Island under attack taken by Petty Officer Miki Ishii; Richard Watanabe, a font of knowledge on the IJN's naval affairs for wise advise and assistance; Ryunosuke Valentine Megumi, JMSDF (Rtd), Okinawa, for our extremely and informative discussion in London, and for information from his study into Commander Shuhaku Kudo, commander of the destroyer *Ikazuchi (Thunder)*; Colonel Shogo Hattori, JASDF (Rtd) and Commander Noritaka Kitazawa, JMSDF (Rtd), formerly of the Military History Department, National Institute for Defence Studies, Tokyo, for much assistance down the years; Professor T Kamei, Kyoto City, son of Rear-Admiral Y Kamei, for permission to reproduce some photographs of the 521st Air Group; Mitsutoshi Okano of the Mitsubishi Komaki South Plant, Nagoya, for permission to examine the preserved Zero-Sen fighter there and research its radio equipment and communications equipment; The men of the 74th Classmate of Imperial Naval Academy for welcoming me to their reunion and lunch on 9 November 2005 and many memoirs; Shinawa, Tokyo; Lieutenant Commander Sadamu Takahashi, IJN (Rtd) for permission to quote from his book *Hishogumo (Flying Clouds);* Akira Nakamura for permission to quote from his book *Dai Toa Senso Eno Michi (The route to the Great East Asia War);* Kohji Ishiwata, Honorary President, and founder *Ships of the World* Magazine, Kaijinsha Corporation; Tohru Kizu, Editor in Chief/Director, *Ships of the World*, Kaijinsha Corporation, Tokyo; Mr Hitoshi Hasegawa, staff writer of the *Kojinsha,* for advising me via Commander Seno down the years; Miss Misa Matsugi, Sapporo City, Hokkaido, daughter of Mr Fujio Matsugi, for permission to reproduce many of her father's splendid photographs of the Imperial Naval Academy at Etajima activities in the 1930's; Mr Tetsuya Nakama, Hankyu Toho Group, of the Dai-Ichi-Hotel, Tokyo and Hanku Hotel, Kure for making my visits a pleasure; Mr Shuzo Inaba, who treated me to a ceremonial tea service in his home at Kure, and to Gill Richardson, at Crécy Publishing for her instant sanctioning of my original idea at the London Book Fair and subsequent encouragement of this project.

Peter C Smith
Riseley, Bedfordshire
October 2005

Facing page: The memorial statue to the pilots of the Imperial Japanese Navy during World War II in place outside the Museum building of the Yasakuni Jinja in central Tokyo. *(Peter C Smith)*

Glossary

Anjin	The Pilot. (William Adams, the first Englishman to set foot on Japanese soil in 1600hrs was given this honorary title. His shrine is still revered above Yokosuka)
Bakudan	Bomb
Bobi Senta	Local Defence Flotilla for protection of ports etc. Comprised of net-layers, dam-layers, minelayers and formed from mainly old warships and auxiliaries
Bobi tai	Any small mainly mobile unit of garrison port defence troops, used for anti-aircraft defences, fire-fighting, observation etc
Botaoshi	Pole-downing (Etajima game)
Bu	Division
Buntai	Basic air unit, three (normally) aircraft
Buntaishi	Assistant Divisional officer – Junior Lieutenant, Ensign or Warrant Officer
Buntaicho	Divisional officer (normally) Lieutenant
Buntaikanji	Officer in charge (Lieutenant or Lieutenant-Commander)
Chakkan Shidoto	Carrier Landing Guidance light
Chusa	Commander (rank)
Chu	Medium, Intermediate
Chui	Lieutenant, junior grade (jg)
Chujo	Vice Admiral
Chusa	Commander
Chutai	Medium size unit. In dive-bomber *Kokukantai*, a temporary division of aircraft nine (normally) aircraft
Chutaicho, Chutai	Commander
Daii	Lieutenant
Daikodo	Great Hall
Daisa	Captain

Daitai	Large unit. In dive-bomber *Kokukantai, normally* a sub-division of 27 aircraft or three *Chutai*
Daitaicho, Daitai	Commander
Fukkan	Bursar of Naval College
Gensui	Admiral of the Fleet
Gocho	Head cadet
Gocho-ho	Second cadet
Gun	Fighting forces (Army or Navy)
Guntai	Fighting man (sailor or soldier)
Gunkan	Major fighting ships (battleships, battle-cruisers, heavy and light cruisers and aircraft carriers)
Hachiman	War-God
Hikōchō	Air Officer
Hikōtaichō	Commander/Leader
Han	Smallest air unit (two aircraft)
Heika ikan	Combatant Personnel
Hentai	Formation
Hiko	Fly, flying, flight
Hiko Buntai	Administrative term. The flight section of combat *Kokutai*, detached to work from neighbouring bases. Replaced as a term by *Hikoitai (op cit)*
Hiko Jikken Bu	Flight Research Division
Hikokitai	A formation of an unspecific number of aircraft (Tactical)
Hikoitai	Carrier Air Unit (two *Buntai* minimum) the flight sections of combat *Kokutai*, previously termed as *Hiko Buntai (op cit)*
Hiko Gakusei	Flight Course Student
Hiko Taicho	Air Group commander (normally) Lieutenant-Commander or Senior Lieutenant
Hikochō	Air Operations Officer
Hikotai-cho	Wing Leader
Honka Renshusei	Pilot candidates
Hōjutsu-ka	Gunnery personnel

Ikan	From Warrant Officer to Lieutenant
Itto Hikohei	Naval Aviation Pilot, First Class (NAC 1/C)
Johriku	Landing
Jukenjitsu	Bayonet practice
Junshoku	Killed in Action (or *Senshi)*
Kaigun Byo-i	Naval Hospital
Kaigun-ku	Naval District. 1st – Yokosuka; 2nd Kure; 3rd Sasebo; 4th Maizuru
Kaigun-guntia	Soldiers of the Sea – Sailors (*not* Marines!)
Kaigun Musen Denshinsho	Naval Wireless Museum / Naval Telegraph Office
Kaigun Shoi Kohosei	Midshipman (lower ranking than a Warrant Officer but higher than a Chief Petty Officer
Kaigun Koku Honbu	Department of Naval Aeronautics
Kaigun Koku Honbu Shusshi	Naval Air Command / Attendant, Naval Air Command
Kaijyo Goei Sotai	General Escort Command. Formed to protect the convoy routes between mainland Japan and the southern conquests, under enormous threat from American submarines from 1943 onward. Equipped with new corvettes, auxiliary escorts and old torpedo boats
Kan	Ship
Kancho	Battleship, aircraft-carrier or cruiser captain (Rear Admiral or Captain)
Kanjo Bakugekiki (*Kanbaku*)	Carrier-based Dive-bomber
Kanjo Kogekiki (*Kanako*)	Carrier-based Attack/Torpedo bomber
Kanjo Sentoki (*Kansen*)	Carrier-based Fighter aircraft
Kanpan	Deck

Kantei	Intermediate fighting ships (destroyers, submarines, minelayers,escort, minesweepers, which did not carry flotilla staff, surgeons,accounts staff or have facilities for them)
Keibifu	Lesser naval bases/HQ guarding strategically important straits or bays near major cities. Oh-Minato (Tsugaru Strait); Ma-King (Pon-Fu Islands, west of Formosa; Chinkai (Chin-He Bay near Pusan, Korea); Osaka (Mercantile Convoy Control); Kainan (Hai-Nan Island, off southern China)
Keibi Senta	Local Defence Squadron. Coastal convoy protection work and patrol
Keibi tai	Similar to *Bobi tai* but more a static land defence unit to defend a specified area
Ki	Machine (thus *Hikoki* is aircraft, ie flying machine)
Kichi Koku Butai	Base Air Group
Kidū Butai	Carrier Strike Force
Kidū Kantai	1st Action Fleet formed March 1944 to enable Vice Admiral Ozawa, commander of 3rd Fleet to help operate 2nd (battleship) Fleet as 1st Fleet had been disbanded
Kikan Chujo	Vice Admiral (Engineering)
Kikan Daisa	Captain (Engineering)
Kikan Shoi-Kohosei	Midshipman (Engineering)
Kikan Shosho	Rear Admiral (Engineering)
Kôkai-ka	Navigation personnel
Koku	Aeronautics, aeronautical
Kōkūbūtai	Naval Air Force
Kokujutsu Gakusei	Aircraft operation Course Student
Kokukantai	Air Fleet (in wartime Allied definitions, although size varied. The original 1st Koku Kantai was formed in April 1941 for the concentrated use of the carrier forces; 11th and 21st were HQ units for land based aircraft. Subsequently the 2nd, 3rd, 5th, 10th, 12th, 13th and 14th were raised as land based fleets later in the war

Kokusentai	Carrier-based or Land-base Air Division. A two-carrier force with assigned destroyers for escort and aircrew ditching recovery ships (these destroyers were termed 'Dragonfly Catchers' in the fleet). In 1941 two or more naval air groups operating together were also so termed. Carrier groups were numbered in the range 1-9; seaplane tenders in the range 10-19 and ground based units 20 upward
Koku Kushu Butai	Air Attack Force
Kokuki Jikken Bu	Aircraft Research Division
Koku Musen Bu	Aviation Radio Division
Kokusho Kokutai (Sensuitai, Rikusentai etc)	Air Arsenal Land-based Naval Air Group. Initially included aircraft, aircrew and ground crews. Later specialist wings established with either aircrew or ground crew. The latter were named after their bases, the former were given numeric titles
Konkyochitai	Port Maintenance forces to operate captured ports for naval use
Kuchiku Kancho	Destroyer captain (normally) Commander or Lieutenant-Commander)
Kyokan	Instructor
Kyudo	Archery
Musen Bu	Radio Division
Randori	Contest
Rengo Kantai	Combined Fleet. From 1924 formed from 1st and 2nd fleets, working under 1st fleet command, and made permanent in 1933 with its own overall GHQ
Rengo Koutai	Combined Air Group. First formed in 1937 from two carrier air groups operating together. Changed in 1941 to Air Squadrons but airfield maintenance and training units organised and named thus in war
Renshu Kokutai	Training Wing for pilot training
Seitokan	Cadet Quarters

Seitotai-kanji   Cadet commander

Sensui Kancho   Submarine captain (normally Commander or
                         Lieutenant-Commander

Sensui Sentai   Submarine flotilla, Depot ship and four divisions
                         of four submarines totalling sixteen boats

Sentai   Squadron

Shina homen   China Theatre Fleet. Coastal defence and escort
  Kantai   force subordinated to GHQ

Shiki   Ceremonies

Shirei   Captain or Commander

Shirei Chokan   Commander (normally) Admiral or Vice Admiral
  Kantai

Shirekan   Commander (normally) Vice Admiral or Rear
  Sentai   Admiral

Sho   Small, lesser

Shotai   Small unit

Shoi   Sub-Lieutenant, 2nd grade

Shoi-Kohosei   Midshipman (Also, *Shoi-Shiho*, *Shoi-Ho* or *Shoi-
                         koho sei* – the rank just below Ensign)

Shosho   Rear Admiral

Shosa   Lieutenant-commander

Shotai   In dive-bomber *Kokukantai*, a temporary section
                         of three (normally) aircraft

Shotaicho, Shotai   Commander

Shukei Shoi   Midshipman (Paymaster)
  Kohosei

Sotantei   All boats out (inspection)

Suirai-ka   Torpedo personnel

Suirai Sentai   Destroyer Squadron. Equivalent to a British
                         Destroyer Flotilla (in its pre-1921 form.)
                         Consisted of a light cruiser flagship and four
                         destroyer divisions of four ships each. The six
                         premier units comprised the latest destroyers
                         equipped with the 'Long Lance' long-range
                         heavy torpedo for attacks on enemy heavy ships

Taisa	Captain (rank)
Taisho	Admiral
Tai	Lieutenant. Also a unit, or division. Usually two to four combat ships or aircraft, (*Kantei*) formed a division, with an assigned commander in addition to the flagships captain
Tokusetsu Kantei	Requisitioned (usually) or converted mercantile ship used by the IJN as depot ships, minelayers, minesweepers and other auxiliary functions, but only if manned by regular navy personnel. Continued to carry the suffix *Maru* (Circle) of all merchant vessels even when in IJN service
Tsuki	Thrust
Yoka-Ren	New pilot training programme introduced in 1930
Yokobu	3rd Class Naval bases/HQ's for smaller ports
Yokokan	Naval cadets club

Introduction

This is the biography of a fighting man. A straight-forward statement, but how curiously unfashionable it has become to record, let-alone respect, courage and bravery in combat, in the Britain of the twenty-first century. Let that man be a foreign serviceman, and more, a man from a nation that is still reviled in many quarters and vastly misunderstood in many more, and such a history almost seems provocative! Add to this heady mix a man brought up to believe his Emperor was 'Divine', and an audience, in Britain if not in America, secular in the main and sceptical, if not scornful, of any religious commitment, and the gap of incomprehension is almost total.

And yet Egusa fought with enormous dedication and great skill for that Emperor, and for his nation, against enormous odds, and went knowingly into combat for the last time almost certain he would die, thus pre-dating the *Kamikaze* attacks by his equally dedicated countrymen that were to follow. To try and understand the motivation of such warriors it is essential to know their background, traditions and upbringing. Not too long ago Great Britain shared many of these concepts, now but fading memories, and it would have been easier to understand him. Today, in Britain anyway, such qualities are mocked and scorned by the popular media, and by whole generations of citizens, quite apart from millions of immigrants who, may have little knowledge or conception of traditional British values or history. Since most people obtain their sketchy versions of history from the TV and radio nowadays, they are as much the victims of their culture, as Egusa could be said to have been in his own particular beliefs. In the United States, fortunately, their fighting men are, generally, still honoured and respected still, and so understanding will be greater, despite the fact that Egusa was their feared enemy for many years.

Egusa was essentially a simple man, born and raised in the countryside. He was not sophisticated or urbane, but, despite his lowly birth, his nation respected his worth and gave him the opportunity to become a valued citizen and a skilled and able officer. In return for his dedication, intelligence and bravery, he became an icon and a hero to his people. But he was also a noble combatant, unsullied by the cruelty and extremism of a few of his countrymen.

He fought an especially old-fashioned war in that, as a dive-bomber pilot, he pitted himself almost man-to-man with his military opponents, almost face-to-face which, in a mechanised war of mass, in which thousands of Allied bombers pounded cities and civilians to pulp and huge land armies slaughtered each other in battles numbering millions of men, was a rarity.

Egusa's life was also influenced by many things; his religious upbringing in *The Saddharma Pundarika Sutra* decreed 'They are not defiled by worldliness, just as the lotus-flower is not defiled by water.' True and he lived his life by such tenets, yet, in the career he chose, the Navy, and the nation he served, there was much that, while not defiling him, influenced events and circumstances in which he moved and shaped the course of his life even though he was not a direct party to them. These are described here, not to censure his actions, but to help Western 21st century minds understand. Above all the martial skills, Egusa, like all young men of his age, was imbued with the belief, which no defeat by any outside enemy had yet challenged, that *Nihon Seishin* (the pure and unsullied Japanese spirit) would *always* prevail.

Egusa also showed humility and a tender side. His love for his wife and their young family, more and more fleeting as the contacts were as the war progressed, endured. His wife often wrote to me of her feelings toward her husband and his children still respond with deep affection to the memory of their father, who they hardly knew. As in all things, love, war, worship, fidelity and commitment, Egusa was a *Samurai* by action and deed, in the truest sense of the word. He was more; he was an *honest* man, who lived cleanly by his code. Who can hope to be more?

The statue of the famed *Samurai* warrior Masahige. His loyalty to the Emperor was absolute, and ultimately led to his sacrificing his life in obedience. This overriding reverence for the Imperial House was epitomised by this attitude, and, whatever a cadet's religion, it was subordinated to service to the Emperor, himself a direct descendant of Amaterasu, the Sun Goddess, and her grandson, the first Emperor, Jimmu. Cadets were taught that to die in battle for the glory of the Emperor was the acme of their existence. *(Peter C Smith)*

CHAPTER ONE

Egusa's Childhood

'When the general regards his troops as young children, they will advance into the deepest valleys with him. When he regards the troops as his beloved children, they will be willing to die for him.'
Sun Tzu – The Art of War.

On 29 September 1909, in Arima-mura village, Ajina County, in Hiroshima Prefecture[1], a baby son was born to Kyuemon and Kita Egusa. He was called Takashige. He was destined for great things. This is his story.

One of the most skilful and influential leaders in the field of dive-bombing was Takashige Egusa of the Imperial Japanese Navy. His fame became legendary, his units' achievements outstanding, their influence compared to their numbers, enormous. As the fine tip of the red-hot spear that was the Japanese Navy's Nagumo Task Force, it was Egusa and his dive-bomber crews who created the maximum havoc among the Western Allies in the first year of the Pacific War and gave the Japanese Emperor a unique succession of overwhelming victories against a numerically far-superior enemy. Egusa represents the great effect that one well-trained group of men could have on deciding the outcome of great campaigns.

Egusa's influence was exercised as much by inspiration as by example. He set standards that his men strove to equal and then achieved. His expertise was unchallenged, but his influence was even more effective in spurring others to great deeds. Takashige Egusa's wartime exploits, and the manner of carrying them out, was only equalled by his hero's death in action. His self-sacrifice epitomised all that was best of Japan's fighting Navy in World War II. At first, the Japanese Navy's dive-bombers followed the route of the German Stukas in the European War, and led the assault that broke every conventional defence with ease. However, also like Germany and Italy, Japan relied on a professional elite. Once those veterans began to fall, and it became a war of logistics, big battalions and industrial might, in which resources and numbers ultimately tipped the scales against any amount of individual skill, the balance rapidly shifted away from them. As the tide of war changed, the dive-bomber pilots found that, more and more, their own brand of perfection counted less and less in the scheme of things. This was particularly so in the case of Japan, which did not at that time possess the wide industrial base to compete in a long war against the enormous resources and populations of the United States, the Soviet Union and, to a lesser extent, the British Empire.

Takashige was born the second son of the local headman, one Kyuemon Egusa. His father's chief claim to fame was that he was renowned as a 'heavy drinker'; he liked and could hold his *sake* but he could also claim descent from a lord of a castle in the Izumo area (in the present-day Shimane Prefecture) during the time of the fabulous 'era of wars' 400 years earlier. The Egusas had traditionally been a powerful family in the Fukuyama area. In this modest parentage Egusa was in good company: the great Isoroku Yamamoto, the Japanese Navy's Commander-in-Chief, was himself the son of a schoolmaster.

The Egusa family were very powerful in their locality, and had provided the village headman for many generations. Takashige was the third son of Kyuemon and Kita, their first son being Kazumi, and the second son, Shizuo. For many years, the Egusa family were farmers, but their line was an illustrious one for their distant ancestor, Izunokami-Mototada Egusa, was the enshrined deity Sakurayama (Cherry Hill) Shrine, which is in the grounds of the Kibitsu Shrine, close to the Egusa family residence. Izunokami-Mototada was a member of the Koretoshi Egusa who had built a castle in the area as a loyal subject to the Emperor Godaigo. He was a close associate of the famed loyalist general Kusonoki Masashige, who fought in battle at Minatogawa, Kobe for the Emperor's cause and who killed himself rather than face defeat, of whom more later. However, the bloodline of the farmer's young baby boy was already steeped in that of a great warrior and perhaps his future and fate was thus already pre-ordained to a degree.

Life was hard for the youngster and this was reflected in the youth himself. He grew up as a taciturn, self-possessed and stout-hearted adolescent, but it is recalled also that he was gentle and thoughtful in both manner and deed.

Kyuemon and Kita were to be blessed once more, with a fourth son, Yoshimasa, some twelve years after Takashige's birth. No doubt thanks for a further strong pair of arms to tend the farm were made for the Egusas were strong in the Buddhist faith. The Egusas were followers of the Sutra of Lotus, Hokekyo, and had been from generation to generation. They had always kept strictly to this Buddhist path to preserve the purity of their sect. Many years later Toshimasa told the historian Mitsuharu Uehara:

> 'All the Egusa children used to bear their feet being paralysed by the tatami mats for more than an hour at a time, while the priest chanted sutras in the Buddhist Memorial Service for the ancestors, listening intently to the spirited sound of the drum.'

When questioned in the late 1980s that old priest, Nichigyo, chief monk of the Egusa family temple, explained how he felt this tied in with Takashige's subsequent career.

> 'Carrier-borne dive-bombers went straight and true to attack the enemy ships, without any fear of death. I think that Takashige probably reached that state of purity where he did not fear his death, by the steadfast influence of the *sutra* of the Lotus Hokekyo.'[2]

Buddhist ideas had spread to Japan from mainland Asia with travellers in the 7th century and had quickly taken root in all the many manifestations of the basic Mahayana strand then current in China and Korea, like Jodo, Shingon and Tendai. This, despite the existing native Shinto religion. But many Japanese did not abandon the old faith but embraced the new as a complementary religion, aided by the fact that in many ways the two overlapped. It was the Japanese monk Nichiren Shu, who initially had followed the Tendai path. He founded one school of Buddhism unique to Japan. The Nichiren Shu based his belief on the Lotus *sutra* (Sanskrit texts or Scriptures, written as if spoken by the Buddha himself), claiming that he 'took refuge in the wondrous Sutra of the Lotus.'

Because Shinto, 'the way of the Gods', is more a religious experience than a fixed doctrine or set of firm beliefs, it melded with the preaching of Nichiren. In Shinto, nature is the focus, the *Kami*, which are the spirits that concentrate nature and embraced animals, birds, plants as well as seas and mountains, while *Kami* also resides in one's ancestors.

With the beauty of nature itself as its basis Shinto required little to mark out its shrines, other than the *torii* entrance gates, which

framed the natural setting, as at Itsukushima on the Inland Sea.
Therefore *kami* could be taken as the local manifestations of
Buddhas and it is perfectly acceptable for its temples to exist
alongside, or in some cases even inside existing Shinto shrines and
for the Buddhist monks themselves to participate in Shinto festivals.
Both beliefs worshipped the seven gods of good fortune also making
their complementary adoption simple to embrace.[3]

The Shinto Shrine at Etajima. The *torii*, a simple ceremonial entrance gateway,
marks the entrance. It is a fact that, in theory anyway, the Japanese Constitution in
the 1930s granted total religious freedom, thus tolerating Buddhism, Christianity
and Shintoism. In truth, however, it was the latter that had taken on the role of the
official state religion following its separation, in the mid 1870s, from the former.
With the placing of all the Shinto shrines under the Department of Home Affairs in
1900, this elevation was given official sanction. Under it, the deification of the
Royal House was total. *(Cecil Bullock)*

For many years nothing of the Buddha's sayings was written
down, but was handed on by word of mouth. Because of this all
sutras commenced with the phrase, '**THUS** have I heard.' When
Buddha expounded the *sutra* of the *Mahayana* (Great Vehicle)
entitled the Lotus Flower of the Wonderful Dharma, to the assembled
gods, rich and poor humans and beasts, birds and fishes alike, from
the top of the Mount Gradharkuta (Mountain of the Sacred Eagle) in
Rajgir, Behar, India, it was as a sacred spoken emission.

In this strand of Sakyamuni Buddha's teachings, from the Hokke-Nehan Period during the final eight years prior to his death at the age of eighty, the Lotus symbolised purity. Just as the beautiful lotus flowers are never soiled by muddy water, so devoted followers should never be influenced by a bad environment. The onus of responsibility is on the individual and others should never be blamed for one's own errors. In conforming to both these strictures Egusa's own life was to be a clear example. The laws of cause, causation and effect are also typified by this flower because at the time of its blooming it already holds the seeds of new life within itself.

The basic concepts in Buddhism are the Four (Noble) Truths, which explain the causes of suffering and the way to free oneself from them. These are:

1: All existence is suffering.
2: The cause of suffering is illusion and desire.
3: Nirvana is the Realm free from sufferings.
4: The ways for the attainment of Nirvana are to practice the eight-fold paths of Right View; Right Thought; Right Speech; Right Conduct: Right Livelihood: Right Endeavour; Right Mindfulness and Right Meditation.[4]

Takashige's life was shaped by this.[5] But there were other influences that made him the man he was to become; his family history and traditions, his nation's history and circumstances and, the Imperial Japanese Navy's history and legacy. Let us examine them.

The feudal warlord Mizuno Katsunari had established Fukuyama in 1619 as a castle town in the Bingo region. Growth was slow but by 1889, the area had achieved town status, being renamed Fukuyamacho. The arrival of the Sanyo Main Railway spurred more rapid expansion. By 1916, the town had become Fukuyama City and ten adjoining villages were annexed into its boundary twenty years later. Its main industrial base at this time was textiles.

Japan itself had likewise grown in the late nineteenth century into a major power, not least a major sea power, and her Navy was a force to be reckoned with in the Far East.

In 1638, the Japanese forbade their people from going abroad, declaring outside influences were harmful. The Spanish had already been expelled in 1624 and the Portuguese followed in 1638, while two years later all Europeans were banned. Japan's splendid isolation, a consciously and deliberately-taken decision had cut the country off

from almost all outside contact with the world, other than a few
Dutch traders restricted to Deshima, for two-and-a-half centuries.
Although the strictness of these edicts had been partly relaxed by the
early eighteenth-century, isolationism had not been finally broken
until 1853 when an American naval squadron under Commodore
Matthew Calbraith Perry, USN, steamed into Japanese waters.
Following this, almost constant pressure was made on the Shogun to
open her ports to outside trade. Exhorted by the Americans, French,
Russians and British for five years, the Japanese gave way.

The tomb of Wiliam Adams, the Gillingham-born pilot of the Dutch ship *Liefde*
who was the first Englishman to set foot in Japan when his ship was washed ashore
on the beach of Usuki town, Bungo (the present day Oita Prefecture), Kyushu on
19th April 1600hrs. The right tower marks Adams tomb, that on the left that of his
Japanese wife. The shogun of Japan, Tokugawa Leysau, highly valued Adams, and
gave him the estate of 'Samurai' with a domain in the Miura peninsula. Adams was
called *Miura Anjin*, (The Pilot of Miura). He was appointed a political and
diplomatic advisor to Leyasu. Later Adams was engaged in trading with Siam
(Thailand) and became an owner of a *Goshuinsen* (Overseas Trading Vessel)) and
voyaged to Annan (Cambodia) and Tonkin. Adams died of sickness at the age of 55
on 15th May 1620. His tomb stands on the hillside at Hemi-mura (the present
Tsukayama Park) his previous Miura home, overlooking Japan's largest naval base,
Yokosuka. It faces East being true to his last request, 'Bury my remains in the high
land overlooking the capital (Edo, present-day Tokyo), in order for me to forever
return the Shogun's favour to me, in the other world.'
(Courtesy of the tourism division, Yokosuka City Hall)

In the British case, Admiral Sir James Sterling had obtained written permission for British merchant ships to dock at the ports of Hakodate and Nagasaki as early as October 1854. Less than four years later, in August 1858, these agreements had been expanded by Lord Elgin into the full-blown Treaty of Yedo, which the Japanese duly signed. Under the terms of Yedo, Britain despatched a Consul General, one Rutherford Alcock to represent her at the Imperial Court. He was upgraded to Envoy Extraordinary and Minister Plenipotentiary shortly afterwards, partly to meet the grand expectations suitable to the most powerful nation on earth in the eyes of the emerging Japanese.[6]

The treaty, which saw Japan admitted to the International Trading System, was signed with all these powers in 1858. This led to the end of the Shogunate (or Military Governor's rule) in 1867, when the Emperor began his ascent to the status of Deity and a whole new, and turbulent, chapter in the nation's history began. The Meiji Era lasted until 1912 and was marked by a rapid 'westernisation' of Japan.

Japan had lived in perfect peace and harmony for 250 years, troubling nobody and threatening no one. Now, having been coerced by the outside world to throw off her tranquil isolation, the nation set about closing the long gap between enforced medieval feudalism and the modern world, and she did it, (but not without compromise or without deep concern with the upholding of their own long-cherished and unique values)[7], and at an incredible rate. From shunning the 'progress' of the western world, Japan now sought to embrace all aspects of it[8], from shipbuilding to railways, industrialisation to engineering, from commerce to modern defence. No ocean-going ships had been constructed for more than 200 years, but now Japan embarked on a frenzied programme of absorbing ever facet of nineteenth-century sea power; and that included a modern navy.

The first *Kaigun Heigakko* (naval college) was established at Tsukiji, Tokyo, in 1873 when a British Naval Mission of thirty-four officers and men under Captain Lucius Douglas, RN, arrived to assist in its setting-up. The group, with periodical replacements from Great Britain, remained for many years. Even when the college was fully functional and running, the practice of employing at least two British officers continually, in order to '…teach our cadets what an English gentleman is and how he should behave'[9], was continued without a break from 1888 until 1938, when the last Royal Navy officer teaching English left and was not replaced due to the worsening situation.

The statue of Masujiro Omura (1824-1869) who, after a successful army career, became the first War Minister of the re-established Meiji dynasty, located near the entrance to the Yasakuni Jinja, on Kudan Hill in central Tokyo. Here the few surviving veterans of the 20th twentieth century wars, still meet to honour their fallen comrades and fulfill the warriors' promise, 'Let us meet again beneath the cherry trees of Kudan.' *(Peter C Smith)*

In 1888 the naval college had outgrown its original site and the decision was taken to move it lock, stock and barrel to 'Water-rice field island' (Etajima), a Y-shaped island lying to the south of the city of Hiroshima in the bay of that name and across a narrow strait from Kure, the principal naval base of the Imperial Japanese Navy at the southern end of Honshu. Among the earliest cadets was one young man later to rise through the ranks to become Viscount Admiral Makoto Saito, a Premier of Japan, whom militant army officers were brutally to murder in Tokyo fifty-seven year later.

Thus, abandoning many centuries of self-imposed isolationism and adopting the best in the fields of military thinking and equipment from the leading nations of the day, Japan grew mighty and self-confident. This new-found strength had been reinforced by a succession of victories, firstly over the Chinese Empire and them, more dramatically in its effect and lasting impression, over the old Russian Empire of the Czar, when the Japanese Admiral, Heihachiro Togo, won the overwhelming naval victory of the Tsushima Straits in 1904. Coupled with the mystic faith that the Japanese were a chosen race protected by divine intervention, and destined to lead Asia into a new golden age, these achievements were a heady influence on the Japanese youth of the time and the young Takashige was not immune to them.

How had this transformation come about in such a short time? Just as in all other areas, the newly-enquiring Japanese naturally chose the leading contender in each of the chosen fields of endeavour to copy, and despatched her finest minds to learn and adapt every modern technique. A new national army looked to France as her model (but the sensational outcome of the Franco-Prussian War changed that, and her French instructors were quickly booted out and replaced by Prussians). Naturally, for expertise in all aspects of naval power, Japan chose to model herself upon the Royal Navy, at that time the overwhelming and undisputed naval power of the age. Being a far from self-sufficient group of islands offshore a major continent, exactly like Great Britain, sea-power was supremely important to her in her new position in the world. It was the only way for potential enemies to reach her and it was the bridge for her to create and extend her boundaries. She quickly acquired both the warships and the know-how of a modern sea power, to carry out both tasks. Universal military service was introduced in 1872 and, two years later, an expedition to Formosa was mounted. Japan had begun to flex her newly rediscovered muscles!

As Japan examined her position in the world it was obvious that the Korean peninsular posed the greatest threat to her, being like a dagger thrusting southward from mainland Asia. Although initially herself posing no threat, being merely a small backward and impotent dynasty (the Joseon), Korea could be dominated by hostile powers, either China or Russia, which would substantially change the outlook. Japan's first principle of foreign policy toward the new world order into which she had been thrust was therefore to neutralise any such threat. Within a quarter of a century their worst fears appeared to be becoming manifest. The ruling Qing Dynasty in China started to emphasise the tributary state tradition upon Japan and sought to infiltrate the Joseon ruling caste with her own placements and fellow travellers. This although Japan had recognised Korea as an independent state since 1875. At first Japan strived for a peaceful solution to this threat, but the Chinese refused to vary from their course.

Matters were abruptly brought to a head in 1894. Following the murder of a pro-Japanese reformist, the Tonghak religious order rose up and China sent in troops to put them down. The Japanese also sent in forces to support the uprising and the Chinese Navy rashly took on the Japanese Navy in skirmishes at sea. Outright war was declared on 1 August, with Japanese forces already established in Seoul, the capital. The Japanese Army easily defeated the Chinese force and pushed on to capture the vitally strategic base of Port Arthur (Lushun) on the Darien peninsular. On 17 September the two fleets clashed off the mouth of the Yalu River and the Chinese suffered total defeat, losing eight of their twelve ships. The survivors fled to the anchorage of Wei-hai-wei, but were smashed at their moorings when the Japanese Army outflanked the defences on the Liaodong Peninsula early in February 1895. The Chinese were forced to admit defeat and the Treaty of Shimonoseki, signed in April, ceded this whole area, plus the islands of Taiwan (Formosa) and the Pescadores to Japan. Japan's influence over Korea was strengthened, her confidence in her armed forces enhanced and her territories expanded.

However, at the height of the celebration Japan was to learn a harsh lesson from other great powers. Russia (who had ambitions in the area herself and was building the Trans-Siberian railway to back them up); Germany (seeking to establish herself in the Pacific) and France (always seeking to expand her influence), pressurised Japan to give up most of her gains. Japan had little choice but to comply. To make matters worse, within a few years, with flimsy excuses, Germany seized Tsingtao for herself; Russia occupied Port Arthur and the Liaotung peninsula as well as Talienwan, while the French took Kwang-chow-wan south of Hong Kong. These transfers were sealed by the Second Treaty of Shimonoseki on 8 May 1895.

As Russell Grenfell stated:

'The feelings of the Japanese can be imagined. They had recently been intimidated into abandoning the most important of their legitimate conquests by a trio of powers uttering high-sounding phrases about the integrity of China and the peace of the Far East. It could now be seen for how much the integrity of China and the peace of the Far East had really counted with this trio. The Japanese had been not only despoiled but tricked.'

He added:

'... after their experience in 1898, the Japanese could not have been blamed if they reached the conclusion that, in matters of international politics, aggression and duplicity were by no means obsolete but, on the contrary, remained effective instruments in the use by the best people.'[10]

Nor was this the end of Russian expansion, for, following the Boxer Rising in 1900, she occupied Manchuria and refused to budge once the uprising had been crushed. Japan now had a major European army and navy on her doorstep and was most alarmed. She negotiated a non-aggression treaty with Great Britain, transferred the port of Wei-hai-wei to her new ally and began building up her fleet, ordering six first-class battleships from British shipyards. When the Russians began to exert political pressure on Korea, just as China had done earlier, the Japanese saw the writing on the wall.

Tension between the two nations became acute, but, despite all the warnings, the Russian Far Eastern fleets battleships lay at anchor outside Port Arthur, with no guns manned, and no torpedo nets out and lights on when the Japanese destroyers made a pre-emptive torpedo strike prior to a formal declaration of war on the night of 8 February 1904. Three battleships were badly damaged and put out of action, leaving just four to face the six Japanese when combat was joined the next morning. Just as this surprise attack was the forerunner to Pearl Harbor, and in similar conditions, so the Sino-

Japanese War proved to be the forerunner to the Russo-Japanese war. Although European nations were supposed to be superior to eastern nations in modern warfare, the Japanese Army defeated the Russian Army at Mukden in early March and Port Arthur was placed under siege and attack again. In December, the Russian defences were breached and then it was their turn to have their ships sunk at anchor inside the port. A second Russian fleet, despatched from the Baltic to lift the siege, was met by the Japanese fleet under the redoubtable Admiral Togo in the Straits of Tsushima off the southern coast of Korea, and totally destroyed. It was the most comprehensive naval victory since Trafalgar.[11]

The author and his wife, with leading Japanese naval historian Commander Sadao Seno, JMDF (Rtd) in front of the restored battleship *Mikuma*, flagship of Admiral Togo at the Battle of Tsushima, 1905. This total and comprehensive naval victory over the Russian Baltic Fleet sealed Japan's coming of age as a major naval power. *(Peter C Smith)*

The Treaty of Portsmouth, which followed this debacle ended for the moment Russia's Imperial ambition in the East and further enhanced Japan's standing in the world. Practically, she now had Port Arthur and Darien, a much stronger fleet and a good and friendly alliance with Great Britain. She also had the respect of the world, including the United States of America, which had brokered

The former Russian Fortress at Port Arthur, overcome in the great siege during the Russo-Japanese War of 1904-5. It symbolises Japan's emergence as a military power of note, having defeated a premier European nation in combat on both land and sea. *(Photo Album of the Fleet Training of Midshipmen, the Class of 1930, Naval Academy of the Imperial Japanese Navy via Richard Watanabe)*

the peace talks. Japan therefore soon felt emboldened enough to announce a protectorate over Korea on 18 November 1905, which led to the abdication of the Korean ruler two years later. This was but a step in the process and Japan announced her full annexation of Korea in 1910. Great Britain, by now fatally engaged in the life-or-death naval arms race with her German rival that was to end at Jutland, turned a blind eye to this aggression; but this step soured relations with both China and America. Japan cited the 'open door' principle, which allowed for equal trading opportunities for all nations in China. In fact, this was a political smoke screen and she was to adopt the exact opposite policy in the years that followed.

Behind the scenes Japan was plotting and intriguing in China, and was thought to be behind much of the unrest that led to the uprising of 1911 and the overthrow of the corrupt Manchu dynasty represented by the Boy Emperor. If Japan hoped to benefit by this turmoil she initially failed, for a Chinese Republic was set up headed by the very able and competent Yuan-Shih-Kai. Japan threatened to intervene militarily to restore the Manchus as incompetent rulership in China suited her better, but Great Britain warned her off, telling her to stay out of China's affairs. This led to the first cooling of the hitherto excellent relations between the two island states and naval powers.

Japan bided her time and continued her plotting and a second uprising took place in 1913, in the south of the country, nominally led by Sun-Yat-Sen, who was sponsored with money, arms and

direct assistance by Japan. The rising failed and Sun-Yet-Sen was
forced to seek sanctuary in Japan aboard a Japanese ship.

With the outbreak of the Great War in 1914, the two allies joined
together to oust Germany from her naval base at Tsingtao. This was
taken by an Anglo-Japanese force on 7 November. All well and good,
but far from handing this prize back to China, Japan instead secretly
presented the Chinese Government a list of requirements, that, when they
later became known to the rest of the world, were termed 'the twenty-one
demands.' These, if conceded, would amount to unprecedented Japanese
control of Chinese affairs. There were five separate groups. The first
covered Tsingtao, which Japan was to deal with directly with Germany,
while railway building in Shangtung was to be the exclusive right of the
Japanese and no other nation. The second extended the lease of Port
Arthur and two railways in Manchuria for ninety-nine years, while Japan
was to install 'military, political and financial advisers' in South
Manchuria and Eastern Inner Mongolia, which would in effect make
them Japanese vassal states. Group three granted Japan exclusive coal
and iron-mining concessions in the Yangtse valley, again at the exclusion
of all other nations. Group four ensured that no other nation would be
allowed to lease harbours, bays or islands on the Chinese coast. But the
killer blow was contained in group five and again ensured the Japanese
advisers controlled political, financial and military matters across the
whole of China, with certain vital police, army and naval forces
becoming subject to joint Sino-Japanese administration. Japan's aim was
clearly dominance, but also self-sufficiency. China was mineral-rich,
Japan was not but clearly saw her near-neighbour as a vast 'milch-cow'
for her present and future needs.[12]

It was, in all but name, the takeover of China by Japan. When
these demands leaked out to the wider world, to Japan's fury (but not
embarrassment), there was widespread alarm and both Great Britain,
her principal ally since 1902, and America, raised strong protests.
Ignoring these, Japan presented China with an ultimatum in May
1915. With the Great War concerning these powers more and more,
their original firm stand gradually weakened. Great Britain
eventually promised to support Japan's claims on Tsingtao in return
for more active support of her ally in the war, in particular Japanese
destroyers were sent to the Mediterranean to help fight the U-boats.
This was against the general trend in Japan which by now favoured
the German cause over the British, and indeed most Japanese Army
officers expected Germany to win the war and were most surprised

when she did not! The United States of America, long used to claiming the high moral ground and criticising others, followed the same line. Under the Lansing-Ishii agreement of 1917, almost all American objections to the demands were withdrawn or watered-down due to the fact, in Lansing's words, that 'territorial propinquity creates special relations between nations.' In truth expediency had overrode moral fortitude in the USA as elsewhere.[13]

Being an ally of the winning combination further enhanced Japan's position as she inherited almost all of the former German possessions in the Far East as mandated territories. With Great Britain, the United States, France and Italy, Japan was now elevated, by the virtual elimination of the German, Austro-Hungarian and Russian Navies, to major status. This position among the world's remaining navies was reinforced by the obsequious surrendering of Britain's 300-year old naval supremacy to appease American senators in Kansas, at the humiliating Washington Naval Conference and Treaty of 1921-2. While British strength was cut to the bone, American and Japanese ratios were increased pro-rata by this American *diktat*. The British Government, blind in its eagerness of placate everyone whatever the risk, ate humble pie and signed, and the speed of British naval decline was staggering. The Japanese, by contrast, still believed in their destiny as a nation on its way to the goal of *Sekai Dai Ichi* (first in the world) and therefore were outraged. The Japanese delegation took a lot of persuading that 60 percent of their potential antagonist's strength was what their fleet was to be frozen at, but, in truth, they and America gained while Britain lost.[14]

Therefore, by the end of the First World War in 1918 and the succeeding Washington Naval Conferences of 1922, Japan found herself elevated, with little effort on her part, to the position of the third naval power of the world, behind the British Empire and the rising power of the United States. Many of the young officers considered this ranking to be an insult to be overturned as soon as practical and avenged. In fact, Japan had been elevated to third ranking with little effort and the real loser at Washington had been Britain, who had caved in to the American demands again and again.[15] Certainly, the holding of Japan's battleship strength at two-thirds of that of her two main rivals, gave the Japanese a spur to develop carrier aviation as an alternative to help redress the balance. In this, she was helped by the fact that she was nominally still a close ally of Great Britain, which, at that time, led the world in naval aviation.

A British aviation mission, twenty-nine strong, led by the Master of Sempill, had been despatched to the *Rinji Kaigun Koku-jutsu Koshubu* (Temporary Naval Aeronautical Institute) at the new Kasumigaura air base at Japan's request in September 1921, under the auspices of the old alliance still in force.[16] Lord Sempill, William Francis Sempill, son of Lord and Lady Sempill of Fintray House, a distinguished Scottish family, had been an apprentice engineer in his youth, and, at the outbreak of the Great War, he had volunteered for the Royal Flying Corps. He had become a test pilot and later transferred to the Royal Naval Air Service, hence the Japanese Navy interest in him. Unfortunately for the Royal Navy, and ultimately the British war effort in the Second World War, the whole of the Royal

The Master of Sempill and his wife (front row, 3rd from left) in Japanese dress with the Geishas geishas of the Katetsurou Restaurant in Tokyo. This Scottish laird and wartime Naval naval aviator became part of the newly formed RAF in 1918. Under the auspices of the existing Anglo-Japanese Alliance, he headed up a mission of other former pilots and military aviation experts who spent time in Japan helping establish her fledgling naval air force in the 1920's. They were instrumental in bringing the most modern ideas on both maritime aircraft and aircraft carriers to Japan, including plans of the new British carriers *Hermes* and *Eagle*. Lord Sempill himself, despite many of his ideas being rejected established a strong rapport with his hosts, which continued long after the mission had returned home. *(Kagetsurou Restaurant, Tokyo)*.

Navy's flying arm had been compulsorily merged with the RFC and the new Royal Air Force in 1918, a retrograde step that retarded the growth and expansion of maritime air power in Great Britain to a huge degree. Japan, like the United States, wisely kept her naval air power with the navy and suffered no such wholesale neglect. Sempill retired as a Colonel, AFC, in the RAF in 1920 becoming an Air Ministry aeronautical adviser.

In Japan Sempill struck up a close *rapport* with his Japanese hosts, joining them in revels at the famous Kagetsurou Restaurant in Tokyo.[17] It would seem he might have perhaps become rather too overenthusiastic in adopting their cause for his own good.[18]

Regardless of this, in any event, some twenty years later the results of this seeding flowered dramatically in the South China Sea when the pupil taught their erstwhile master how much things had changed in two decades. In that same year of 1921 Japan launched the first purpose-built aircraft-carrier (*koku bokan*, mother ship for aircraft); the little *Hosho* and the Mitsubishi company employed another famous English naval aviator, Sqn Ldr F J Rutland, who had flown from a seaplane-carrier at the battle of Jutland, to help design special naval aircraft for them.

The Master of Sempill with the famous Japanese *restaurateur* Horikoshi. This Scottish laird and wartime Naval naval aviator became part of the newly-formed RAF in 1918. Under the auspices of the existing Anglo-Japanese Alliance, he headed up a mission of other former pilots and military aviation experts which spent time in Japan helping establish her fledgling naval air force in the 1920's. They were instrumental in bringing the most modern ideas on both maritime aircraft and aircraft-carriers to Japan, including plans of the new British carriers *Hermes* and *Eagle*. Lord Sempill himself, despite many of his ideas being rejected, established a strong rapport with his hosts, which continued long after the mission had returned home.
(*Kagetsurou Restaurant, Tokyo*).

The British Aviation aviation delegation is feted at the opening of the new Imperial Japanese Navy Aeronautical College at Kasumigaura. The eager pupils of the 1920's were to show their masters just how naval air power should be correctly applied scant twenty years later. *(Kagetsurou Restaurant, Tokyo)*

The Sempill mission also input their considerable technical expertise in the preparation of Japan's first aircraft-carrier, the 10,000-ton *Hosho*. Originally laid down on the stocks as a fleet oiler at the Asano shipyard at Tsurumi in December 1919, she was taken in hand for conversion prior to her launch and converted to a carrier at Yokosuka navy yard, finally being completed in December 1922. It is said that Sempill brought with him plans of the British carrier *Argus*, the first flush-deck carrier, and the *Eagle*, designed before *Hosho*, but which took so long to convert from a Chilean battleship hull, that *Hosho* beat her into commission.[19] The British continued their tuition and the very first pilot to land aboard the *Hosho*, on 22 February 1923, was a civilian pilot, Mr W J Jordan.

Herbert Smith from the British Sopwith company was also brought over to Japan to specifically design, with the Mitsubishi company, suitable aircraft to work from the *Hosho's* 519ft deck. This collaboration resulted in the 2MT triplane; shipboard reconnaissance and torpedo-bomber aircraft and 442 were built. They began to enter service in 1925 as the Type 13 Torpedo Bomber although this proved too heavy. Further refinements followed and this aircraft remained in service until 1933.

As early as 1921, the Imperial Japanese Navy had approached the Gloucester Aircraft company in Great Britain, and purchased ninety Nighthawk aircraft, the rights having been acquired by that company the year before to manufacture the French Nieuport fighter. Fifty of these machines were modified for use as naval aircraft, and the remaining forty were shipped out in component form to the Yokosuka Air Arm to be assembled as trainers. These machines were initially named as the Mars II, and later adopted the name Sparrowhawk, and all had arrived in Japan within six months of the order being placed. However, the aircraft Sopwith designed were tailor-made for the job.

Thus the ground was prepared for the upending of the old world order in the Far East.

CHAPTER TWO

Early Naval Life

'The few are the ones who prepare against others; the many are the ones who make others prepare against them before.'
Sun Tzu – The Art of War.

The young Egusa's childhood and early adolescence was lived with the events thus described as a backdrop. They did not consciously affect his life. Takashige grew up a strong, pious youth, thoughtful and calm of nature.

In order to become a fully accepted member of the Buddhist community, at a certain age the young men were taken to their local monastery. Here their heads were ritually shaven by the monks who then presented them with an alms bowl and ceremonial robe. The lads remained at the monastery for several days, praying and fasting before returning home, not as boys any more, but as accepted adults.[20]

In April 1916, aged six, Egusa entered the Arima Primary School. It was only 500 metres from his house and he already knew it well. His particular schoolboy chum from these days, Rikuichi Sasaki, remembered his determination had been set on a martial career very early, in an interview conducted many years later:

'Takashige was very strong at *Sumou* (Sumo) wrestling. He was also a boy with a very strong will, stronger than he was at *Sumou*. He used to question me even then. Once, when we met at our special place by a bridge he asked me, "Which do you think better, for me to enter the naval academy or the army academy, because I have passed the entrance examinations of both?" I replied that he should enter the naval academy, but he seemed to have already made his mind up on a naval career before he even asked me my opinion. He clearly showed his determination to achieve what he had already decided. This proved to be my last farewell with him.'[21]

Another of his closest friends from Takashige's primary school years was Kunio Kajita, who later graduated to the sixth high school and majored in shipbuilding at Tokyo Imperial University. Kunio later became an engineer in warship construction and followed his pal's naval career accordingly. He recalled:

'Takashige was, above all, a man of strongly-built body and iron nerves. His voice was deep and his words were precise and clear. He was physically powerful and used to turn somersaults in the school corridors during rest periods. Responding to the cheers and claps of his classmates and their urgings for more, he would gather desks and chairs at the front of the classroom and make a small space. He could make many aerial turns with no need for a long run-up. His demonstrations of aerial turns made a deep impression on us for the strength they indicated.'[22]

He took this strength and dexterity into middle school, which was situated, in the neighbouring town of Fuchu, when he moved on in April 1923. A fellow pupil who remembered him there was Kunio Kajita who recalled with nostalgia that:

'Takashige's reflexes and nerves were superb.'

The Fuchu Middle Schoolhouse at the time that Egusa and his classmates graduated. This was then a modern stone building, whose design was particular to the latter period of the Taisho era. *(Dr Toshimasa Egusa)*

Due to the pernicious effects of the Washington Naval Treaty of 1921, which cut back the much-cherished expansion and size of the Imperial Japanese Navy dramatically, forcing her to abandon the '8-8' plan, many surplus naval officers were forced to retire prematurely from their careers. They found employment as school teachers in such middle schools. One such former naval commander, Tokitaro Shirai, arrived at the Fuchu Middle School as a sports instructor in 1923, specialising in *Kendo* (Japanese fencing) and archery. Takashige took lessons in both sports from Shirai and progressed rapidly through the various grades. Encouraged by his skills and praised by his instructor for his abilities, this yet further determined Egusa on a naval career. Another factor that influenced his choice of such a path was that the naval academy was situated in the same Prefecture, Hiroshima. It was important to the young man, with his strong family ties. Thus, the inland coasts of Hiroshima Prefecture were the shores most noteworthy in connection with the famous *Murakimi Suigun* (Naval Force), which expanded Takashige's dream of becoming a naval officer.

繁 隆 草 江

The young Egusa. *(Dr Toshimasa Egusa via Mitsuharu Uehara)*

Takashige Egusa had clearly set his heart on a naval career. Late in 1925, when he was fifteen, he passed the public entrance examination for the famed (and feared) naval academy at Etajima. This was the normal age of entry for the four-year course, the entrants being exclusively fourth-year middle school pupils. Unlike Britain, where a plethora of privileged entrants from public schools led to a whole strata of snobbery, all Japanese boys, rich or poor, attended the middle schools and therefore applicants were much more representative of national life, and all who sat stood an equal chance.[23] Ability, rather than wealth or connections, was the keystone to success. Thus dedication and application were essential. In Japan the sons of poor families were not deterred from applying, for once they had passed the entrance exam the state took over their well-being. Every expense was paid for, weekly pocket-money allocated and even free rail fares home at holiday times were catered for.

The down side was these young cadets became officers without having served in the ranks, and thus there was still a gap between officers and ratings in service, although good officers sought to overcome this.[24]

However, the competition was still fierce. Only one in thirty applicants made it through the selection. Where brain power and ability might be more than adequate, the hurdle of medical fitness was a high and daunting one where most rejections took place.

So, while he was still in the fourth year of middle school, Takashige applied for entry to Etajima.

For entrance examination to the naval academy, the date and location were notified some weeks in advance. Despite the Navy's expansion plans, there were still only a limited number of places available at this period, and only the best applicants stood any chance at all. The physical examination took place first, from 0800hrs, and was stringent.

Unsuccessful candidates were turned away at once, while the successful candidates, Egusa among them, were handed a single sheet of paper. This document contained the schedule for the academic examinations which were to follow a few days later.

The academic examination started at 0900hrs, with mathematics. Then came English language which started at 1230hrs. On completion of both these examinations, the candidates were left cooling their heels until 1800hrs, while the papers were being marked and evaluated. Those that had failed one or both written tests were unceremoniously handed back their admission cards and photographs and that was that!

The imposing college buildings at Etajima. Behind it can be seen the brooding bulk of Mount Furutaka, up which cadets and first year students who had finished their entrance schooling climbed, guided by the instructor of their class on the first Sunday. Mount Furutaka changes its appearance depending on the four seasons and thus was said to reflect the growing minds of the cadets. *(Egusa family)*

Egusa came through and faced a second day of exams. At the start of the day two the first exam was geometry which again started at 0900hrs and this was followed at 1230hrs by physics. Once more the same procedure was followed by the authorities and with the handing back of more photos, the *cadre* shrunk yet further, with only the successful applicants surviving for yet a third day's ordeal.

On day three, Egusa and the other survivors sat Japanese history in the morning and this was followed by Japanese language in the afternoon. Here the procedure differed as all the remaining examinees were permitted to go forward to the interview, which was held on the fourth day. Meanwhile random checks were made of some of the candidates' families by Naval Shore Patrol (SP) officials. The main aim of this was to locate and weed out any candidate that had any Communist sympathisers in his family unit, an automatic bar from eligibility.

There followed another two-week wait before the IJN's examination committee sent out telegrams to each of the successful candidates, and this time Egusa *was* one of those selected. The candidates who at this stage wished to proceed on the path to become naval officers at this stage had to make their final decision, and respond accordingly by sending a telegram back to the committee expressing their desire to so proceed. Of course, there was *no* hesitation on Takashige's part.

He was full of confidence, having already passed the written exams and knowing he was an exceptionally fit and healthy person. He was due to enter the academy in March 1926, when, like a bolt from the blue, he received a rejection letter. The shock of such an unexpected blow must have been severe, but even more so was the diagnoses that led to it. An X-ray taken in the final medical examination was diagnosed at tuberculosis or TB. In the 1920s and indeed for another forty years, TB was a killer disease, indeed at the time of Egusa's report, it was widely regarded in Japan as a 'non-recoverable illness.'

It was a very heavy blow, but Takashige's reputation for stubbornness was not lightly earned. He refused to accept it and challenged the result. Refusing to even consider the prospect of death, or even of a change in his determined path to destiny, the young man stuck resolutely to his guns. Further diagnosis of the X-ray was carried out, and, to his great delight, it was confirmed that the judgement had been a mistaken diagnosis by the naval medical officer.

Elated by this, Takashige still had to resit the entrance exams all over again; such were the very strict rules for the academy. He sat the exam for the second time in the summer of 1926 and once again passed with flying colours.

After another brief wait, the IJN sent Egusa a formal letter advising him 'you are to be adopted by the Imperial Japanese Navy' and notifying him he was to report to Etajima Naval Academy, his one-way rail ticket being paid.

Another Fuchu middle school boy, Zenichi Sato, also passed at the same time and both entered Etajima together on 1 April 1927.[25] Thus, thanks to his stubbornness, Takashige passed into the 58th Class of Etajima, along with 133 fellow cadets, and a further four years of intense study and training.

Built on the tough traditions of the warrior-caste and on similar adopted principles to the Royal Navy's Whale Island Gunner School, where discipline was paramount and harshness inbuilt, Etajima either made you or broke you.

At the time of his entry Etajima was well established. The college was built below the southern slopes of Mount Furutaka (Old-Hawk mountain)[26] in the northernmost segment of the island, and facing the almost land-locked bay of Etauchi facing south-west. The dominating building was the *Daikodo* (Great Hall) a large white stone building. Inside was the main hall, used for all ceremonial (*Shiki*) and routine assemblies, including the passing-out assembly. This large room was dominated by the Emperor's throne on a raised dais on the platform, used during royal visits.

Etajima *Kaigun heigakko*, (naval college), showing the *daikodo*, or Great Hall. Inside is audience seating, and opposite the main doors, a dais with waiting rooms behind on each side. Beyond this building, on the lower slopes of Mount Furutaka, were the two houses used during ceremonial visits by the Emperor and the Imperial Princes. Nowadays all connection with the Royal Family is banned constitutionally, although private visits are still allowed. *(Peter C Smith)*

An avenue of cherry trees led down to the main college gates, while, to its northern side, were the cadets quarters *(Akarenga-Seitokan)* built of red brick.[27] This had been started in June 1891 and completed in June 1894, when cadets moved out of their quarters aboard the training ship *Tokyo Maru* and into the hall itself. In Egusa's time it contained the student's dormitories, study rooms, the main dining hall, bath-houses, kitchens etc. and was entered via a central doorway surmounted by the Imperial Emblem of the Chrysanthemum. There were two large marble tablets on the walls of the gallery, which commemorated the names of every naval

The impressive main entrance to the *seitokan*, or main cadet building, which contained the dormitories, study rooms, dining hall and administrative offices. Built in the style of Dartmouth, the traditional story is that it was built using red bricks imported from England especially for the job. However recent investigations by Japanese building experts have revealed that the bricks were made in Japan and shipped via Kure to the island, misleading locals to think they had been imported. In Egusa's time the portal was embellished with the 16-petalled chrysanthemum, (below) symbol of the Imperial House of Japan and although this has been replaced since 1945, the original has been preserved inside the museum. *(Peter C Smith)*

officer who had laid down his life for the Emperor in battle. A separate room leading off from this imposing gallery contained the relics of Japan's greatest naval heroes.

The oldest building on the site, and the first built in the English style when the college was relocated from Tokyo. Still in use today as a store house and kept in immaculate style. *(Peter C Smith)*

Brand-new in Egusa's time, and quite apart from the heroes' room, the college had erected its own naval museum, built from subscriptions from all the officers and men of the Imperial Navy. Apart from commemorating Japan's naval heroes and victories, a room was dedicated to outstanding foreign naval personalities, the foremost of whom was, of course, Admiral Lord Nelson. Among the exhibitions here was a lock of Nelson's hair to match a similar trophy from Admiral Togo's head elsewhere in the museum.

Other auxiliary buildings included the usual administration blocks, a hospital, officers' club, various classrooms, engineering and maintenance shops, and a model ship house, along with a battery. There was a canteen, which was open all day, but the cadets were strictly forbidden to buy sweets, cake, chocolate or other such goodies! Various trophies were displayed around the facility, including a gun from a German U-boat captured by Japanese destroyers in the Mediterranean during the Great War, some Armstrong-built guns originally mounted aboard the armoured cruiser *Asama* and two Short Brothers built seaplanes and a flying-boat formerly used by the Navy.

Sport was represented by the a large playing field, which

contained several *Sumo* wrestling arenas, a 400 metres to the lap running track with a 200 metre straight track and room for other field events, an outdoor gymnasium, rugby and soccer pitches, a basketball court, and six tennis courts. Along the seawall that faced Etauchi were all the expected facilities for light boat work, with landing piers, signalling masts and boathouses. At the head of the parade ground was the reviewing stand, in fact the bridge structure of the despatch-boat *Chiyoda* of the Russo-Japanese War era. There were also separate *Judo* and *Kendo* halls and both sports were much practised.

On arrival at Etajima, Egusa and his companion freshmen were formally introduced to the senior cadets by their supervising officers, and these same officers also gave orientation to the cadets about the college, its location and its teaching programme as well as its rules and customs. The Entrant Ceremony followed this and the next day the whole class assembled for the class year group photograph.

At various times during the academic year *Judo, Kendo* (fencing Japanese-style) and *Sumo* competitions were held when both senior and junior cadets could compete together. The top winners of these events were rewarded with the presentation of a copper medal. Three copper medals could be exchanged for a single silver medal, a somewhat rare event.

A fellow cadet and classmate of Egusa at Etajima, later to become a commander in the IJN, remembered Takashige thus:

'He was good at studies and *Kendo*. Indeed, he was a first grade in *Kendo*, as was I. I later graduated to the third grade in the years after I left the naval academy and I think that Egusa would have done likewise, had he had the opportunity to continue his *Kendo* training.'[28]

Another classmate had a differing view. Masataka Chihaya told Mitsuharu Uehara:

'I can remember Takashige wore a green armband on his left arm sometimes, while we were fourth year cadets. This green armband was worn on the left arm of sick cadets as an indicator that they were to have reduced exercise regimes while ill. Yoshimitsu Oku was in the same *Buntai* (company) as Takashige. Oku was an all-round player of sports and very good at studies also. In the exercises of *Jukenjutsu* (bayonet drill), Oku would push over his opposition with an exultant

Traditional sports honed the young cadet's fitness and quick-responses to a high degree. Although western sports were also practiced to a large degree, the old ways were firmly to the fore. Pictured here are are a class of cadets assembled in full costume in the *Kendo* Hall, ready for fencing practice. The hall had its own shrine (to the right) and scrolls with inspiring messages hang from its entrance. *(Cecil Bullock)*

shout. I think that Takashige didn't stand out noticeably simply because Oku was in the same *Buntai* with him. Later it was a great surprise to me that Takashige who had put on a green armband some times, was the commander of the carrier dive-bombers in the Pearl Harbor attack, and that he made such great achievements in that, and later operations.'

Yoshimitsu Oku was later commissioned as an ensign. He was tragically killed during flying training, crashing into the western sea of Hokkaido in bad weather when he could not land on his training aircraft carrier. He died without the chance to realise his full potential. As Chihaya was to lament:

'Egusa of Carrier Dive-bomber; Shigeharu Murata of Torpedo-bomber and Oku of Fighter; three great air commanders would have originated from the 58th Class of Etajima if Oku had survived!'

The whole facility was overseen by the Admiral-President, a former serving officer and usually, in practice, a Vice-Admiral, The president answered directly to the Navy Minister. He had an ADC-cum-secretary-cum-manager, a commander, known as the *Fukkan,* to run the ordinary daily business affairs of the college. Under the Admiral-President was a Captain, the Vice-President who was in charge of the teaching organisation of the college. As would be expected the hospital (*Kaigun Byo-in*) was run by a Surgeon-Commander and the financial side was headed up by a Paymaster-Commander.

For the rest of the staff, some sixty specialist naval officers and thirty civilians were divided into departments, presided over by a commander. The cadets had English as the compulsory foreign-language course, with a very basic course in both German and French for the two latter years at the time Egusa attended.

The instructor of the 58th Class, Lieutenant Bunji Asakuara is remembered as teaching his charges with deep love and attention to their education and attached great importance to individual character development. The portrait was drawn by Cadet Susumu Sakai of the 8th Class. *(Dr Toshimasa Egusa via Mitsuharu Uehara)*

For seagoing training and experience an ancient despatch boat, the *Chihaya* was attached to the college as a tender; and a modern light cruiser was also allocated for the annual cruise, usually the *Oi*. These cruises varied in length according to the class year, the initial cruise being just to Kure naval base and Miyajima, close to Etajima. As the cadets gradually got their sea legs the *Oi* took them further afield with the final (4th) year cruise being to the Japan Sea and around Kyushu.

The cadets' quarters were spartan in the extreme, tiny and containing just a single iron cot (with optional mosquito net), a desk for study and a sea chest for personal effects. That and nothing more. There was nothing strange in this, traditional Japanese homes were equally basic, and Egusa's had known nothing better before. Also, Japanese warships were built to fight and crew comforts were minimal. This became even more marked around the 1920s and 1930s when, in an attempt to cram in more and more guns and armaments on the treaty-limited dimensions and tonnages of the new warships, crewing accommodation came second-best to Japanese warship designers.[29] Accentuating this trend was that contemporary Japanese warships were manpower heavy, compared to those in some other navies. This was all a matter of perspective. The Japanese viewed their accommodation as adequate and normal, while visiting British, American and French warships, the heavy cruiser *Berwick* or the French training cruiser *Jeanne d'Arc*, were considered luxurious, indeed almost *effete* by comparison and as examples of western decadence.

Naval cadets served for four years, arriving each year in March and, if successful, passing out before the winter holiday period four years later. The classes were numbered according to the year of entry, and Egusa joined the 58th Class of 1927. A class commander, known as *Gakunen-shido-kan* oversaw each year's activities. Each class varied considerably in numbers, generally rising sharply year-on-year from 1932 onward as the Naval Re-Armament Programmes got underway in earnest.[30] Each class was divided in divisions (*bu*), the number of *bu* depending on the overall class size. Bullock described it thus:

> 'The first cadet in merit is first in the 1st *bu*, the second is first in the 2nd *bu*, the third first in the 3rd, the fourth first in the 4th. Then the fifth is second in the 1st *bu*, and the sixth second in the 2nd, and so on down to the last cadet. In this way each *bu* is, as nearly as possible, equal to the others in general ability and attainments.'[31]

But, more than this system, for the ultimate goal of the college, the supply of young naval officers to man the expanding surface and air fleets, another system also applied. This was based on the *Buntai*, of which there were sixteen. Each of the sixteen *Buntai* was under the command of a Lieutenant or Lieutenant Commander (termed for this purpose *Buntai-kanji*). As such the *Buntai* system of the college has been compared to the 'house' system used by public and grammar schools in England at that time. The *Buntai* acted as the 'house' for all competitive activities that Egusa engaged in. The head cadet of each *Buntai* was termed the *Gocho* and the second best cadet the *Gocho-ho*. Thus the *Buntai-kanji* equated to the English housemaster, the *Gocho* to the house captain and the *Goncho-ho* to the house vice-captain. Thus in every sport the *Buntai* competed with one another to win the championship every year for which pennants and cups were awarded to the victors. Some games called for mass participation and in such cases two teams were selected with even-numbered *Buntai* on one side and odd-numbered *Buntai* on the other as competing *Botaoshi*. Over both the *Gakunen-shido-kan* and the *Buntai-kanji*, was a commander, the Cadet-Commander or *Seitotai-kanji*, who kept a close watch on all the various activities undertaken by that year class.

Botaoshi (or Botaushi) was a unique Japanese Navy sport, lost in oblivion today. Colonel Syogo Hattori gave me the following description of it.[32]

'The cadets were assembled in two groups, the red and the white. Each group had a wooden some 20ft long, with a small flag affixed (red or white according to the owner group's team). About ten of the team held onto the lower part of the pole while another ten surrounded it and guarded it. The remaining members of each team were organised into an attack force whose aim was to seize the opposing group's pole and pull down the flag.

'The distance between the two poles was about fifty yards. To commence the game the chief judge of the game signalled "start *Botaoshi*" and the two sets of attackers started off from their position around their own poles and headed towards their opponents' pole. The guarding members intercepted the oncoming assailants and mayhem resulted. The attackers were allowed considerable latitude in their methods. Dashing against their opponents they could beat them, knock them down, kick them, grapple with them; in fact almost anything physical was permitted as long as he used only his own hands, arms, feet and legs. Banned were weapons like stones, bars and similar objects.'

The *Botaoshi* (Pole-Downing game) was one of the special sports of the Naval Academy at Etajima during Egusa's days as a cadet. The scenario symbolised a fight between the tiger and the dragon. In this game, the cadets were divided into odd-number companies and even-numbered ones. Each party was divided into two units, attack and defence. The attack unit had to locate the enemy's weak points and push down the enemy pole. They were free to knock, kick, push and throw their opponents but biting was prohibited.

The game was watched over by the resident naval surgeon and medical officer at the college, with an ambulance parked beside the pitch in case any cadet was seriously injured. The pole, supported by four of the teams' strongest cadets was the centrepiece, with the other cadets making several protective scrimmaging rows in its defence. The opposing team had to lower the pole. The game itself was deceptively simple but in order to win, the players had to adopt complicated tactics and apply them with finesse.

The *Botaoshi* not only required a sacrificial spirit to endure physical injury, but also undaunted spirit to withstand the attackers. It helped develop a resilient character, and was taken very seriously. So much so, that the senior cadets of losing teams often volunteered their teams for further training. For the very junior cadets, it is no great exaggeration to say that participation in the *Botaoshi* was often hell, but it fostered co-operation, teamwork and fighting spirit as well as discipline. The *Botaoshi* was unique to the Imperial Navy with the closest concept in the west being the Royal Navy's field gun competition between various home bases, in which a similar unity of purpose, physical strength and teamwork are essential.
(Miss Misa Matsugi)

Colonel Hattori recalled with a tinge of sadness that, even when he was a cadet at the Defence Academy, *Botaoshi* was still a popular game among the (all-male) cadets. However, soon after he graduated, women were introduced into the Defence Academy for the first time, and all such traditional physical sports were abolished and confined to history.

The range of subjects undertaken by the cadets was enormous, although some were only delivered as fundamentals rather than in depth. The list included:

Aeronautics
Communications
Engineering
Gunnery
Military History
Navigation
Outlines of Naval Organisation
Seamanship
Signalling
Strategy
Tactics
Theory of Naval Education
Torpedo Instruction

These were all delivered by qualified naval staff. Civilians taught the cadets the following range of skills:

Chemistry
Chinese Classics
Economics
Foreign Languages
General Education
Hygiene
Japanese Literature
Law
Leadership
Logic
Mathematics
Philosophy
Physics
Psychology

Military training might seem a strange subject for a young naval cadet, but it must be remembered that the Imperial Japanese Navy had no marine forces as such, and thus they had to understand basic soldiering. This was to become more and more a feature of Japanese naval operations as the situation in China worsened, and was it was therefore considered essential that Egusa and his compatriots had a basic grounding in this, however much they yearned for blue sea or skies! And so Egusa had to drill like any poor 'squaddie' the world over; practice pistol, rifle and machine-gun working at the various ranges on the slopes of Mount Furutaka; undertake bayonet practice (*Jukenjitsu*) and, of course, practise landing troops ashore in the face of a hostile force. Indeed, for the first weeks of his time at Etajima Egusa might have thought he had joined the Army by mistake and drill and yet more drill at the hands of stern and unfeeling Petty Officers.

Should he have considered that bad enough, this was interspersed each autumn with a sojourn ashore at the Military Training Camp of Haramura, close to Hiroshima itself. As well as even more intensive drill and practice exercises in harsh and realistic conditions, the delights of long route marches and night encounters were added. It all produced a very tough young man, should he survive it all. Of course all the many compulsory sports that the cadets undertook already toned up young bodies. As well as the traditional Japanese martial arts, like *Botaoshi, Judo, Kendo* and *Sumo* wrestling, swimming and rowing (pulling), voluntary games like rugby, basketball, American-style baseball, English-style soccer and tennis could all help tone up muscles and eliminate unnecessary fat. You just had to be fit, hence the reason for the strict medical standards before admittance.

Another member of that famous Class 58 of Etajima, who later served on the communications staff of the Combined Fleet, Hidemaru Ichikizaki, was to write in a letter many years later:

'Takashige was full of fun and mischief, but he didn't stand out noticeably and was not an outstanding sports person. Therefore it was not predicted by me that Takashige would become a famous pilot, or achieve such great things during the war.'[33]

Yet another contemporary, Ichiro Shibuya, who also became a naval pilot, was to recall, in a letter to Mrs Kiyoko Egusa:

'Your husband was hostage to nothing, and a man of fathomless calibre. He turned aside remarks as a joke, even if I became very serious. He was like the wind and wrapped in his own natural sturdiness. He was a fine-spirited fellow of disinterestedness *(sic)* and unselfishness. He was as tall as I was, but I remember that he was more than I could cope with in the *Sumou* when we were in the third year class.'

Sumo wrestling was highly rated by the Imperial Japanese Navy as one of the physical training exercises designed to enhance the naval cadets' spirit of attack. Yutaka Izawa, also of the 59th Class, told Uehara that:

'Takashige was a sober cadet in the academy and didn't stand out among his classmates, as I recall. However, his courage was manifest during the war. Courage cannot be awarded marks at the academy.'[34]

The first practical difference Egusa found was that his middle-school uniform was discarded and replaced by the ordinary working garb of a cadet, of white drill coat or blouse, closed down the front with a turned tape-tied collar and a badge on the left breast with the class year and the cadet's family name in Chinese characters, matching trousers, black boots, and naval cap with white cover. In the evening the cadets changed into a blue serge uniform of similar pattern. Next it was the college barber where, like fresh recruits the world over, their hair was close-cropped, shaved usually. This was done deliberately to ensure uniformity among new entrants, and to emphasise he was no longer an individual but part of the greater whole that was the Imperial Japanese Navy. It had the bonus of keeping the scalp clean and free of lice and ticks.

Cadet Egusa with a fellow student in the Etajima town. They are wearing the cadet's blue dress monkey jacket with the five petal golden cherry flower on the collar and the blue peaked cap with the golden anchor emblem.
(Dr Toshimasa Egusa via Mitsuharu Uehara)

The cadets' day was programmed to make the greatest use of each and every hour. The day started with reveille at 0500hrs (with the luxury of being half an hour later in winter). After a very short period allowed for washing, shaving (if necessary) and getting dressed it was out to the parade ground for a series of strenuous physical exercise to really wake them up! Following this they returned to their quarters to make their beds and tidy up before proceeding to the various martial arts halls for a session of kendo or similar. Alternately, it was down to the bay for a bout of rowing. After which a suitable appetite had been worked up for breakfast, which was in the canteen at 0700hrs and woe betide you if you were late as you went hungry.

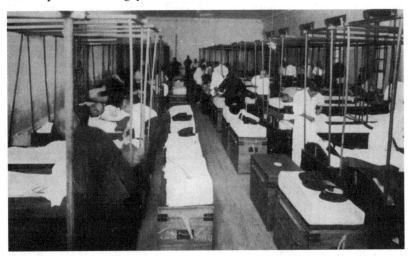

A typical cadets dormitory, with the inmates cadets preparing for bed by donning their white sleeping *kimonos*. Notice the spartan and regimented layout, with each bed protected by a mosquito net on a frame, and the sturdy wooden lockers in which the cadet keeps all his worldly belongings. *(Cecil Bullock)*

Classes started at 0810hrs and lasted until noon. There was a midday meal at 1210hrs with further schooling from 1310hrs to 1400hrs. What was known as the special period lasted from 1410hrs to 1520hrs. This was, in theory, 'free time' for the cadets, but Egusa soon found that this was an illusion. The principle expounded was for the young men to 'develop the power of decision about the use of their own time and to encourage them to increase their general knowledge', but most found time only to clean their kit, rifles and shoes for the next inspection, write a quick letter home or to their best girl, or snatch some sleep.The library might be full, recorded Bullock, but they soon drop off to sleep!'

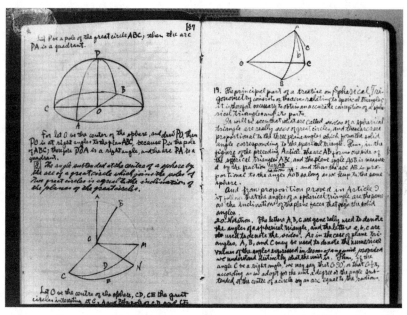

Pages from the pocket book of cadet Murato Kurisu, Egusa's classmate at Etajima. Daily matters are recorded in English, geometry notes, equations, abstracts of history lectures, experimental data and comparison tables about quantities of cider and cakes he and his friends ate and drank in the academy canteen. Because of its importance as a trading language the Japanese Government had made English a compulsory subject in all middle schools. Thus, most naval cadets, on arrival at Etajima, had at least a smattering of knowledge on the subject, although correct pronunciation was felt difficult. The Imperial Navy, of course, used a great many English sayings and words in its day-to-day operations, including even some helm orders up to the 1920s, and therefore placed additional emphasis on knowledge of the tongue. At least three hours a week was devoted to English instruction at the college. *(Dr Toshimasa Egusa via Mitsuharu Uehara)*

And well they might for this was followed by general exercise and drill for an hour from 1530hrs. The exercise varied from day-to-day, be it *Jukenjitsu, kendo,* swimming, running, *judo, sumo* or rifle practice, but it was always strenuous and unremitting. Supper was at 1730hrs. Preparation and revision periods followed from

As an impressive display of naval discipline the annual ten-mile mass swim undertaken by the cadets, from the swimming camp on Miyajima across the north-western neck of Hiroshima Bay and through Etauchi to Etajima College itself, took some beating. The swim was intended to build up stamina and was conducted in total silence, in orderly lines by the whole 600 strong assembly. It took twelve hours, from 0800hrs to 2000hrs.The abilities of the cadets to remain afloat for long periods was deemed as vital and necessary as swimming at speed and over a distance. This exercise tested all three factors to the absolute limit. One cadet recorded: 'some of them fall down when they reach land. You can easily imagine how severe the test is. But, as you see, we are indebted to become warriors. The harder the test, the bolder we become. The life of the cadet is hard but it is also thrilling.' *(Cecil Bullock)*

1830hrs to 2100hrs (2130hrs in winter). The cadets then had a few moments to 'prepare for rounds' from 2150hrs (2145hrs) followed by rounds and lights-out at 2130hrs (2200hrs in winter).

This routine continued from Monday to Friday, and the only variation that Saturday brought to proceedings was that at noon classes were terminated. But there was no rest, the *Seitokan*, studies, canteens and all other rooms and halls all required cleaning fully and swilling down. Practice for *Buntai* competitions followed, either afloat or ashore. The evenings continued with study as usual.

Sunday at least should have brought some respite, and, by comparison with what went on before, it did. Having been confined to the college for six days of the week, the young men naturally eagerly looked forward to the one day when they had more than one hour of free time to themselves. But Sunday (and national holidays also) started like any other day, the only difference to the morning routine being that they were allowed to *chose* which exercise they undertook rather than have it dictated to them. Other forms of excursion included regular mass runs up the slopes of Mount Furutaka.

However, between 0930hrs and 1730hrs their time was their own and they could take leave of the college confines at last. The somewhat seedy and rundown village of Etajima itself was the only 'downtown' to which their island exile lent itself, not a great lure in itself but at least if was different. Some *Buntai* clubs existed there, roughly equivalent to YMCA halls in the west, were they could rest, even sleep, play cards, chess or listen to music. The one cadets' club (*Yokokan*) was within the college itself, however. Walking was allowed, but within strict limits. A short overnight cruise in their *Buntai* cutter under the supervision of a senior cadet was another possibility to get away from it all, however briefly. They could also visit the houses of officers and instructors for a little 'home life' if only of the 'one-step-removed' type.

Etajima cadets were famed for their appetites. It was a tradition that the supervising officer invited some cadets to dine at their homes from time to time, and their wives would usually prepare a meal of *Shiruko* (boiled red beans with sugar, with one or two rice cakes added). *Shiruko* is a very sweet dish and usually one bowl is enough to satiate any adult, but Etajima cadets invariably ate two and some even three, (the giant Shohei Yamada for example, later also to become a famous Val pilot, was recorded as eating four on one occasion and emptying the pot! After leaving the officer's home, he confided to his friends that he wished he could have three more bowls!). Egusa was not in that league but he was a healthy enough young man to eat with the best of them.

The only time longer than this, when they might journey home to spend time with their own families, was a three-week period over Christmas and a month-long break between year-terms in the summer. Otherwise it was a gruelling eleven-hour daily routine that must have seemed unending. But mentally they were also being prepared for the trials that lay ahead of them.

In 1932, after Egusa's time, the then Superintendent of the Naval Academy, Rear Admiral Hajime Matsushita, presented to the establishment 'the five reflections (*Gosei*).' They could fairly be said to sum up the self-critical thoughtfulness that the cadets were indoctrinated in for their future service to their Emperor and nation. They apply equally to spiritual and physical refinement endeavour.

One: Have I compromised my sincerity? (*Hitotsu, shisei ni motoru, nakarishika*)

One: Have I spoken or acted shamefully? (*Hitotsu, genkou ni hazuru, nakarishika*)

One: Have I been lacking in spiritual vigour? (*Hitotsu, kiryoku ni kakuru, nakarishika*)

One: Must I regret the level of my efforts? (*Hitotsu, doryoku ni urami, nakarishika*)

One: Have I lapsed into laziness? (*Hitotsu, bushou ni wataru, nakarishika*)

Every reflection is preceded by *Hitotsu*, 'the figure one', rather than following an orderly sequence as expected in western minds, simply because each point is of *equal* importance to the other four. And each ends with *nakarishika*, asking, 'have I not?'

Thus were the cadets conditioned in mind and body.

The Royal Navy influence was still strong at this period, (all naval cadets had to learn how to eat with knives and forks for example) although, with the rise of ultra-nationalism, it was finally on the wane, and by the end of the decade had almost vanished. However, in the Imperial Japanese Navy of the 1930s, English was

Cadets entering the main red-brick hall at the double. Quickness and order became the fundamental principles of the cadets' lives on entering Etajima. Speed was necessary to react instantly to vital orders in combat, and needed to be reinforced, as it would be impossible to so act in action if one lost presence of mind in battle. The rule at the naval academy was that all preparations were in place and ready for implementation at least five minutes ahead of systematic application.
(*Miss Misa Matsugi*)

widely used. Many English words remained in common usage until the end of World War II, such as pennant, navy, officer, smartness, gunroom and so on. Egusa himself, used English as the basic tongue when studying such a mundane subject as mathematics, and his maths notebooks are written exclusively in that language. This was widespread, and Petty Officers, on becoming Warrant Officers, had to learn English and study history from basic histories like *The Rise and Fall of the Roman Empire*. When moves were made, in the name of loyalty, to abolish such influence, one Etajima Principal, Admiral Inoue stated: 'A naval officer is also a diplomat. There are no Navy officers that cannot speak English in the world.' In the Imperial Navy itself, many were fluent.

Egusa needed every ounce of his dour spirit and resilience during the four-year course, but he emerged from it triumphant. On 18 November 1930, he graduated and was commissioned as a Midshipman (*Shoi-koho sei*) the rank just below ensign.[35]

The Passing Out ceremony was a sombre and dignified one. On the appointed day the Admiral-President and his entire staff, the cadets themselves and members of their families who able to attend to witness the great day, assembled in the Great Hall of the Daikodo. Usually the ceremony was attended by a member of the Royal House, often Prince Hiroyasu Fushimi, Admiral-of-the-Fleet and Chief of the Naval General Staff. On rare occasions the Emperor himself graced the ceremony with his presence. When the Prince entered the hall from the Throne Room, all the audience bowed low to pay homage to a relative of the Divine House. The Prince's *Aide-de-Camp* then read aloud the Royal Decree, which granted commissions in the Imperial Navy to the list of cadets passing out that day. The top three cadets of each year were handed the official diploma by the ADC. Then, as a special Royal Honour, ceremonial daggers were presented to this trio, gifts from the Emperor himself. To the tune of 'See the conquering hero comes' each of the trio marched up onto the stage, again bowed low before the Prince, turned and bowed to the ADC. He then presented the diplomas and honour daggers. Each cadet held his Royal Symbol high with both hands, turned to the centre and bowed again to the Prince, before backing off stage, where, after all three had completed this part of the ceremony, they stand absolutely still, remaining with their daggers held high, until the rest of the class have received their diplomas in turn. Once the presentation was concluded, the Prince, who had remained totally silent throughout the whole procedure, withdrew.

Once the solemn ceremony had concluded and the Prince and his *entourage* had left aboard the cruiser, which had brought him from Kure, it was time for relaxation and expressions of joy. The graduates, now no longer lowly cadets, but midshipmen no less of the Imperial Fleet, ran off to the *Seitokan* to don their brand-new uniforms as befitting their new status. Up to the 1920s cadets had worn a distinctive 'monkey-jacket', almost identical to their Royal Navy counterparts, but by the time Egusa arrived at the college this had been changed for reasons of economy to a normal high-collared tunic with braid-edging, as worn by every Japanese Navy officer of the period, This was described as 'rather drab' by Bullock, who explained that the Japanese gave less attention to the importance of such matters. However, the white summer dress uniform remained the same as before.

There followed the great farewell luncheon, which was usually served in the classroom block, specially decorated with flags and bunting for the event. The Admiral-President gave an official speech bidding the new officers to do their duty to their utmost; other officers made speeches of praise and exhortation. Then a toast was made to the Emperor followed by loud cries of *Banzai* from the assembled throng. The mood of relaxation and abandonment was aided by the fact that at this meal the young men were served ample glasses of *Saké* (rice-wine) for the first time (officially that is).

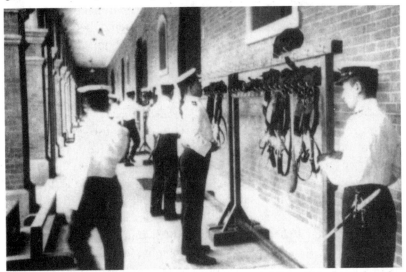

Cadets changing into the dress uniforms with ceremonial dirks. This shows the Historic Corridor, in which the 'God of War' Takeo Hirose, studied.
(Miss Misa Matsugi)

Finally, farewells were made to family and old college friends and the young officers were cheered down the cherry tree avenue to their embarkation point and taken out to the cruiser squadron, which was waiting to take them on their final and greatest journey to date, the long-awaited foreign cruise. As the squadron made its departure from the anchorage, moving slowly out through the channel lined by cheering cadets in their cutters sending them on their way with cries of *Sayonara*, the ships' bands incongruously played the Scottish tune, 'Auld Lang Syne.' For Egusa, the farm boy from the backwoods made good, a whole wide world now opened up before him.[36]

CHAPTER THREE

To Distant Lands

'Warfare is the Tao of deception. When you are capable,
display incapability.' *Sun Tzu – The Art of War.*

Egusa had not yet set his sights on aviation. He had not yet been
bitten by that bug. He concentrated on a conventional naval
career and he had to undergo the normal naval training at sea. His
time aboard the *Yakumo was* well spent. As usual a midshipman was
'the lowest form of life' among the officers, but if one was dutiful,
intelligent and observant, one could learn a great deal and very
quickly. As always, Egusa applied himself diligently to that course,
during the six-month cruise.

The *Yakumo* herself was a unique ship in which to serve. She
was 'special' in more ways than one. For a start she was ancient.
Originally built in 1900 as an armoured cruiser, she was one of the
very few Japanese warships to have been built in a German
shipyard, that of AG Vulkan at Stettin. Laid down in March 1898,
she was launched on 8 July 1899 and completed on 20 June the
following year. On a displacement of 9,735 tons, armed with two
twin 8-inch (203mm)/40 cal Krupp guns,[37] she had been one of the
most modern Japanese warships during the Russo-Japanese War and
had also served during the Great War. But her glory years were now
well behind her and she was totally obsolete.

In her dotage *Yakumo* had been reclassified as a coastal defence
ship, but even this humble assignment had been taken from her
under the terms of the London Naval Treaty signed on 27 October
1930. One clause of this document had decreed that, she, along with
four other similarly aged cousins, '... shall be disposed of in
accordance with Section I or II of Annex II to this Part II.' It went
on to grant them a last reprieve by stating that these vessels, '... shall
be reduced to the condition prescribed in Section V, sub-paragraph
(b) 2 of Annex II to this Part II, and are to be used for training ships,
and their tonnage shall not thereafter be included in the tonnage
subject to limitation.' And so it was.

The matronly old *Yakumo's* best speed had only been a steady
20.5 knots, by the time Egusa joined her she was only good for 16
knots, but that hardly mattered as her only role by then was that of a

training ship. She was part of the Kure Naval District set-up, which was the Imperial Japanese Navy's largest naval base. Kure City faced Etajima across Hiroshima Bay, with the Hashirajima Anchorage, the Japanese equivalent of the Royal Navy's Spithead, near Portsmouth, from which many a famous fleet or squadron has departed. It lies forty kilometres to the south-west. Here the commanding officer of the training squadron, Vice-Admiral Seizo Sakonji (Class of 1900), flying his flag in *Yakumo* (Captain Sato Saburo) and accompanied by her equally aged companion in the training squadron, the *Izumo*[38] (Engineering Captain Tsukahara Mori), awaited their new intake.

The Training Squadron, commanded by Vice Admiral Seizo Sakonji took Egusa and his fellow cadets on a two-part cruise once they had graduated from Etajima. The first part of the cadets' training cruise aboard the old armoured cruisers *Yakumo* and *Izumo*, was termed the Inland Sea cruise and sailed from Etajima on 18 November 1930. The squadron visited the Japanese dependencies of Korea and Manchukuo (formerly Manchuria). The ships called at Chinhai, Inchon, Dalian and Port Arthur, before moving on to China and the ports of Chingdao and Shanghai, before returning to Sasebo on 30 December. The squadron anchored off the coast overlooking Port Arthur, the successful siege of which marked the victorious culmination of the Russo-Japanese war, and the cadets visited the memorial to commemorate the surprise Japanese naval attack that started that war.
(Photo Album of the Fleet Training of Midshipmen, the Class of 1930, Naval Academy of the Imperial Japanese Navy via Richard Watanabe)

With his 112 class commissioned midshipmen, including many who, like himself, were to become famous in the years ahead, Egusa was cheered out by pupils at Etajima as the barges ferried them out to the waiting squadron. Joining them on the training cruise were thirty-six young engineering apprentices, fifteen pay officer apprentices and forty-two medical officer interns. The cruise was split into two sections, the first was 'home waters training' visiting domestic ports around the Inland Sea; the second would be 'overseas training' when they would voyage further afield. Accordingly, the two ships steamed from the bay that evening and set course for the north of Honshu, reaching the port of Maizuru, Kyoto Prefecture, on the central part of the Japan Sea coast, home of the Chigenji temple. Here was established the IJN's Maizuru, while the Naval Supply Officer Academy was at Tsukiji, Tokyo, and the additional midshipmen joined the squadron from both places.

The Class of 1930 Cadets aboard the Training Squadron flagship, the old armoured cruiser *Yakumo*. Takashige Egusa is third from left on the fourth row. Another cadet from this class who became an outstanding wartime officer is Mamoru Seki who dived his Val dive-bomber into the US aircraft-carrier *Hornet* at the Battle of Santa Cruz (third from the right, on the third row). Masatake Okumiya, another dive-bomber specialist, who became an historian of the IJN air operations post-war, and a member of the Japanese Society for History Textbook Reform is seventh from the right on the second row; and Shigeharu Murata, the torpedo bomber ace, eighth from right, on the third row. This talented group, all of whom were to become Lieutenant Commanders on 8 December 1941, also included two future fighter aces, Tadashi Nakajima and Manpei Shimokawa. *(Captain Toshikazu Ohmae and family)*

The training squadron's next leg took them across to the Korean coast, and the port of Chinhai (now Chinhae, Republic of Korea), close to Masan. It was a good natural harbour and reputed to be the most sheltered on the peninsular. It was also typhoon secure and had five deep anchorages. The squadron next steamed around the south-west point of Korea and up the Yellow Sea coast to the port of Inch' on, the major port for the city of Seŏul (Sŏul).

The next port of call for Egusa and his colleagues aboard the *Yakumo* and *Izumo*, was Dalian, (formerly Qingni-wa, Talienwan, Dalny to the Russian occupiers, Darien to the Japanese) in the Manchukuo province of Liaoning (now Liao-tung). The deep bay itself lies on the hilly southern shore of the Lu-ta peninsular, west of Blonde Island. In olden times it was named 'Lion's Mouth'due to its inaccessibility. Manchukuo had been much fought over during the Sino-Japanese and Russo-Japanese Wars and was quite a prize. Although nominally independent, under the rule of the Emperor Kang The (the former Chinese Emperor Pu Yi) since February 1932, Manchukuo (the former Manchuria) was, in practice, a puppet province of Japan, an adjunct to Korea and a bridgehead to the whole of mainland China. But the key port of the area had always been Port Arthur, 50 kilometres to the south, in the Gulf of Pechili, and here the squadron made its way, They came to rest within view of the 'Loyal Spirit Tower', with its great anchor commemorating the Second Fleet's exploits.

So much Japanese blood had been spilt in this area in the two wars, both of which Japan had ultimately won only to be cheated of her legitimate spoils, that the whole region around Port Arthur had the sanctity of a war shrine to any enthusiastic young patriot. The midshipmen were conducted around the whole battlefield, and visited many of the memorials to past heroic deeds and glorious fights. These included 'Two Dragon Mountain' and the obelisk marking the vital 203 metre hill, whose capture had ensured the downfall of the Russian defenders in December 1904. They also viewed the memorial to General Maresuke Nogi's son who fell at the siege, and the six great 6 inch, 45 calibre Armstrong guns (known as the 'Loyal Retainers') mounted there. Also viewed on the tour were the shattered walls and ditches of the great Russian fortress that had been stormed at such enormous cost only three decades earlier and the surrender site at Shui Shuai Ying, where the Russian commander, General Anatolij Michailowitsch Stessel, commandant of the Kwantung Fortified District, surrendered to General Nogi. Here was

The 6-inch, 45-calibre Armstrong guns, known as the 'Loyal Retainers', with which the besieging Japanese army sank the Russian fleet at anchor. *(Photo Album of the Fleet Training of Midshipmen, the class of 1930, Naval Academy of the Imperial Japanese Navy via Richard Watanabe)*

The ruins of the Russian fort at Port Arthur taken by the Japanese at great cost. The cadets visit the Battle Memorial Shrine. *(Photo Album of the Fleet Training of Midshipmen, the class of 1930, Naval Academy of the Imperial Japanese Navy via Richard Watanabe)*

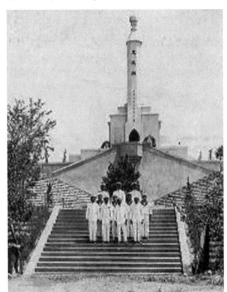

stuff to stir the blood of Egusa and his young companions, still-tangible monuments to Japanese invincibility. It engendered great pride, as it was meant to. Inspirational also were the words of those who fought there, *'Nanji no katana mijkakeraba, ippo susunde'* ('If your sword is too short, take one step forward').

The cadets visited many monuments to the victors and battle sites around Port Arthur, including the battle monument and the famous Hill 203, the capture of which sealed the fate of the Russian garrison. This is also the last resting place of the son of General Nogi who fell in battle during the campaign. The two training ships are anchored off the Fleet Memorial.
(Photo Album of the Fleet Training of Midshipmen, the Class of 1930, Naval Academy of the Imperial Japanese Navy via Richard Watanabe)

The next port of call was Chingdao (Qingdao, Chingtao and now once again known as Tsingtao). Steaming down past Wei-hai-wei, a naval anchorage leased to the British and used by them as a summer base when Hong Kong got too warm, the ships plodded along the coast past the Lao-shan peninsula. Chingtao, anchored off that port, which was the terminus of the southern branch arm of the same Trans-Siberian Railway that led to Port Arthur. Again, almost landlocked Kiai-chow Bay was another perfect harbour. It was also famous in another way, as the home brewery of China's most famous beer. The young midshipmen were not allowed to sample such delights however but were restricted to the usual sightseeing. The final port of call was south again, down the coast of Kiangsu, and across the wide mouths of the great Yangstze Kiang, turning west to reach Woosung and south again to the great International port and finance centre of Shanghai, were they dropped anchor off the Bund lined with European style banks and business centres. Shanghai was a seething and exciting city to visit, especially for a country boy like

Egusa. But it was a city seething with intrigue and tension. While the foreign community prospered and kept themselves apart in the International Settlement, a large Japanese population of traders and their families had established itself in the area and the hinterland. The pot was already simmering when Egusa and his companions toured the vibrant city streets, within a short period it was to boil over into a violent, full-scale conflict.

It was now late December and the six-week cruise was coming to an end. The *Yakumo* and *Izumo* re-embarked their young officers and set sail for home, steering north-east across the East China Sea south of Cheju Do, and arrived at the great naval base of Sasebo, on the north-west tip of Nagasaki Prefecture, on 30 December 1930. Sasebo was the spiritual home of the Imperial Japanese Navy. In 1883 Lieutenant Commander Heihachiro Togo came to what was then nothing but a remote fishing hamlet and recommended its development into Japan's foremost naval base. Twenty years later Admiral Togo led his fleet from that same anchorage to do battle with Imperial Russia's Baltic Fleet at Tsushima. Since then, with the expansion of the Navy continuing, indeed accelerating apace, Sasebo had grown in size and stature. By World War II there would be 60,000 dockyard workers and specialist personnel based here servicing the fleet. At this bustling harbour Egusa and his compatriots disembarked for two weeks leave and a chance to visit both his family and that of his firm friend, Masatake Okumiya.

All too soon this pleasant interlude was over and work intervened once more. Before sailing for his second bout of sea experience aboard the old Tsushima veteran *Yakumo*, the young midshipman had undergone a further preliminary course to lay the groundwork for a future air officer appointment at the first opportunity. This done, Egusa travelled to Yokosuka once more, resplendent in his new uniform with the single gold stripe and bull's eye curl that denoted his officer candidate rank, and rejoined the training squadron at that port. This time a voyage to more distant lands was scheduled. The ships weighed anchor once more on 5 March 1931, first port of call being Keelung, then on to Bako and then on to the British naval base and great trading centre, Hong Kong. Here they posed for a photographic commemoration with the famous peak in the background clearly visible, and not, as today, largely blocked out by gleaming skyscraper towers. They went on to attend an invitation banquet at the new Governor-General's residence.

The second part of the cruise was to Europe. The squadron left Yokosuka on 5 March 1931, and its ports of call were Keelung and Bako. Then it was on to Hong Kong, Singapore, Colombo, Aden and Port Said, all British ports of the Empire. Once through the Suez Canal and into the Mediterranean they ships visited Naples, Toulon, Marseilles, Malta and Alexandria. Then it was down the Red Sea to Djibouti, Colombo once more, then to Batavia and on to Manila and finally Palau. The squadron finally returned to Sasebo on 16th August 1931. Japan allowed the world to see only what she wanted it to see. While these two ancient ships dragged themselves around the world receiving full publicity at every port of call, back home in Japan the shipyards, behind screens to hide them from prying Western western eyes, were working at full capacity building a modern fleet that, ship-for-ship, outclassed every other nation's war vessels by some margin. Here the cadets assemble aboard the flagship *Yakumo* to welcome officers aboard.
(Photo Album of the Fleet Training of Midshipmen, the Class of 1930, Naval Academy of the Imperial Japanese Navy via Richard Watanabe)

The *Yakumo* anchors at the Royal Navy base at the Crown Colony of Hong Kong.
(Photo Album of the Fleet Training of Midshipmen, the Class of 1930,
Naval Academy of the Imperial Japanese Navy via Richard Watanabe)

The *Izumo* anchors at the Royal Navy base at the Crown Colony of Hong Kong.
*(Photo Album of the Fleet Training of Midshipmen, the Class of 1930,
Naval Academy of the Imperial Japanese Navy via Richard Watanabe)*

The squadron anchors off the Bund at Shanghai.
*(Photo Album of the Fleet Training of Midshipmen, the Class of 1930,
Naval Academy of the Imperial Japanese Navy via Richard Watanabe)*

South and west, they arrived at another great British naval
bastion, Singapore, a brand-new naval base still under construction
with legendary (and what later proved illusory) defences to shield
any great fleet the Royal Navy cared to send east. As such,
Singapore was seen both as a warning and an irksome latent threat
and barrier to Japanese expansion south towards the oil and rubber-
rich British and Dutch colonies. The more strident Japanese naval
planners regarded the base more as a challenge than a deterrent
however, for, without a fleet of warships permanently based there,
which the British were less and less able to do as events in Europe
developed, it was, in the words of Admiral Sir David Beatty, merely,
'a sentry box without a sentry.'

The influence and implied power of Great Britain was
everywhere in those distant days. Singapore guarded the Indian
Ocean, which was a British lake. Burma and the Indian Empire, the
east coast of Africa and southern Arabia, all housed British naval
bases and former coaling stations that demonstrated her long reach.
Steering north-west up the Malacca Strait between British Malaya
and Dutch Sumatra, the squadron passed through Ten Degree

Channel between the Andaman and Nicobar Islands. Then it was out into the wide expanse of the Indian Ocean.

Hot, sweltering days followed with nothing but the wide blue sky and the deeper blue sea. One of Egusa's classmates on this journey, Hatsuhiko Watanabe, recalled how Takashige and himself were kept occupied during the following two weeks, making constant astronomical observations by sextant, because there was no land from which to obtain bearings. He also recalled how, at times, while Watanabe was violently seasick, enough to be incapacitated, Takashige resolutely carried on with absolutely no ill-effects whatsoever.

Westward across the blistering reaches of the Indian Ocean the two old cruisers panted, to Colombo, the major port of Ceylon (now Sri Lanka) located on the western side of that great island. It was another teeming colonial city and port, which Egusa was to know again a decade later in very different circumstances. Here the British Governor-General dined aboard the *Yakumo* and the next day the cadets paraded though the city streets and visited the great Buddha and other sites.

The cadets parade through the main streets of Colombo, Ceylon (Sri Lanka). *(Photo Album of the Fleet Training of Midshipmen, the Class of 1930, Naval Academy of the Imperial Japanese Navy via Richard Watanabe)*

Then it was on to Aden, another British naval base in what is
now known as South Yemen, a bleak, baking hell-hole of a place
with little to commend it, other than it guarded the south entrance to
the Red Sea and the approach to the British-owned and operated
Suez Canal in Egypt and gateway to the Mediterranean Sea. The
two cruisers passed through the canal and anchored at Port Said at
the northern end. Here again the British Governor-General
honoured the squadron with his attendance aboard, arriving in
ceremonial barge crewed by Egyptian sailors. The British had a
major fleet base along the coast at Alexandria, but the Japanese
squadron pushed on through the Mediterranean to their next port of
call, the Italian city of Napoli (Naples).

The squadron at sea in the Mediterranean.
(Photo Album of the Fleet Training of Midshipmen, the Class of 1930,
Naval Academy of the Imperial Japanese Navy via Richard Watanabe)

Italy, nominally a monarchy, was ruled by the leader of the Fascist
Party, the vain Benito Mussolini, self-styled *Il Duce*, whose strutting
and aggressive attitude, strict control of the state and towering
ambitions to recreate the old Roman Empire were already leading to
tensions between himself and his French and British neighbours. The
Japanese visitors were refrained by etiquette from commenting on

such matters and were, instead, taken to Pompeii to ponder, as had so many others, the frailty of man. Japan having more than ample volcanic activity of her own, the smoke cone of Vesuvius probably held less power to awe than to many. They were also invited to visit Rome as guests of the Italian Navy Minister, and while there, the new Japanese Ambassador, Shigeru Yoshida invited them to lunch.[39]

However, when it was revealed that the group were to be honoured on their visit to Rome by an inspection by Mussolini himself, some of the young midshipmen could not restrain their feelings. One of Takashige's companions, Murato Kurisu, protested against the inspection and openly declared to his comrades: 'I do not like to the idea of our group being inspected, other than by the Japanese Emperor himself.' Upset, Kurisu began binge drinking on *Sake* (rice liquor) and continued until he began to act violently and had to be restrained by his fellow classmates. For his own sake they tied him down in his hammock until he sobered up. But when, on the following day, the midshipmen donned their formal dress uniforms and on *Il Duce's* appearance, duly 'faced left' to him, Kurisu alone obstinately kept his face straight ahead in protest. Somehow he escaped punishment; perhaps some of his superiors felt similar feelings themselves. It was a good illustration of how loyalty to the Emperor overrode all other considerations.

The midshipmen reboarded their ships for the last leg of this long voyage of discovery, steering up the west coast of Italy, past the isle of Elba and into the Ligurian Sea towards the great French Naval base of Toulon, where they were enthusiastically received. On 17 May, the midshipmen went along the coast to Marseilles to an official welcome before boarding a train bound for the Gare de Lyon and a five-day holiday and sightseeing tour of Paris itself. Like any tourist, Egusa gaped at the Eiffel Tower and Champs Elysee and marvelled at Versailles. It was a memorable time during the late spring in the French capital.

One indulgence that Takashige did allow himself was in his taste for classical European music, so very different from the simple airs of the folk and popular Japanese he had listened to in his native village. Music was one of Egusa's passions from his earliest days, and while in Rome and Paris he was able to purchase vinyl recordings by some of his favourite western composers, Mozart and Chopin, and also a wind-up gramophone to play them on the cruise home. This was the beginning of what was to be a large collection, which he took with

The cadets and their officers on parade at the French port of Marseilles on 17 May, 1931, where they received an official greeting from their French Navy hosts. Following the formal ceremonies, the cadets went by train to the Gare de Lyon, Paris, for a more informal, traditional, five-day sightseeing visit.
(Photo Album of the Fleet Training of Midshipmen, the Class of 1930, Naval Academy of the Imperial Japanese Navy via Richard Watanabe)

him to war. Such records were not sold in Japan at that time. Egusa himself had considerable musical talent, and his wife Kiyoko, was to recall that once, when she was ill and bedbound, Takashige soothed her by playing calming airs on his bamboo flute.

The return leg of their odyssey took them from the premier French naval base in the Mediterranean to the premier British naval base, Malta in the centre of that ocean, which Mussolini was declaring *Mare Nostrum*. The fact that the Mediterranean at this time was nothing like Italy's sea was reflected by the great bulks of the battleships of the Royal Navy's Mediterranean fleet in Valetta harbour. The British flagship, the battleship *Queen Elizabeth*, greeted them with a full gun salute as they moved to anchor off the great city-citadel. Memories of the old wartime alliance were renewed here. During the Great War a flotilla of Japanese destroyers had been based at the island and worked with the Royal Navy on convoy and anti-submarine duties. The Japanese cemetery containing those Japanese sailors killed on these duties were visited and respects paid to their memories

On the first leg of their return journey, the Training Squadron puts into Valetta Harbour, Malta, home base of the Royal Navy's powerful Mediterranean fleet. The British flagship, the battleship HMS *Queen Elizabeth*, fires a welcoming salute to greet them. *(Photo Album of the Fleet Training of Midshipmen, the Class of 1930, Naval Academy of the Imperial Japanese Navy via Richard Watanabe)*

Leaving Malta, the final stop in the Mediterranean was at yet another British naval base, Alexandria in north western Egypt. Once ashore Egusa joined the tours of Cairo, trips down the Nile, and visited the nearby Pyramids, suitably mounted on the 'ships of the desert.' The officers were allowed to don plain clothes and suitable hats to keep out the fierce sun, but Egusa and the other non-commissioned officers had to wear their usual 'whites'and naval caps for the same journey. Again evidence of British power was provided by the presence of the battleship *Resolution* in dry dock, and with immaculate units of the British Mediterranean fleet anchored all around them.

The cadets pay their respects to the Japanese sailors who lost their lives during
World War 1, while serving with the Japanese destroyer flotilla, which operated
from Malta with their British allies on anti-submarine and convoy duties.
(Photo Album of the Fleet Training of Midshipmen, the Class of 1930,
Naval Academy of the Imperial Japanese Navy via Richard Watanabe)

They retraversed the Suez Canal and the Red Sea, but this time,
on passing Perim Island, they turned south instead of north and
anchored on the opposite side of the Gulf of Aden, at the French
colonial outpost of Djibouti in the Gulf of Tadjoura, which was the
capital of French Somaliland. Then they retraced their steps across
the Indian Ocean and again put into Colombo harbour.

Then it was on to another rich and pulsating colonial port,
Batavia in north-west Java. The Dutch had found this city as long
ago as 1619, and it became the headquarters of the Dutch East India
Company and thrived mightily. Now it is known as Djakarta,
Indonesia, but in 1931 it was a trading port and naval base in the
centre of a whole string of Dutch-owned islands, that lay like a
defensive barrier stretching from Sumatra in the west to Timor in the
east, with British New Guinea beyond and above it the myriad
islands of the Dutch Celebes, British Borneo and the Philippines
controlled by America. Rich in vital resources like oil and rubber,
this string of islands to the south of Japan must have seemed

tempting in the extreme for the colonial powers had only small forces with which to defend themselves and these were stretched very thinly over the enormous distances. Eventually that temptation was to prove irresistible to Japanese planners.

The Japanese ships now turned their blunt old bows east and then north, steering through the Makasser Strait into the Celebes Sea and the Sulu Sea to reach the capital of the Philippines itself, Manila. Here, as elsewhere along their long voyage, the Japanese were received with considerable warmth. There were tensions between the United States and Japan, especially over recent events in Manchuria, but, the bulk of the American population and by proxy, those Americans running the Philippines, were isolationist and had little interested in any antagonism. So Egusa and his companions were warmly received by all parts of the city's expatriate American population. Such enthusiasm was not to last of course.

The final stop for the training squadron was the lonely Palau Islands, to the east of Mindanao. This archipelago of more than 200 islands had been claimed, but not settled, by Spain in 1686. From 1783 its closest links had been with Great Britain, but in 1885 Spain reasserted its control, only to sell the islands to Germany in 1899, after the Spanish-American War made them impossible to administer. At the start of the Great War Japan quickly took over the islands and, post-war, was granted the mandate over them by the League of Nations, provided she did not militarise them. At the time of Egusa's visit, this was still largely the case, there was much development and modernisation, electricity, piped water and paved roads were introduced, as were free public schools. Only in the late1930s did defence work there commence in earnest. The *Yakumo* and *Izumo* anchored off Koror, the capital of the islands and the idyllic atoll were explored.

Then it was north again, back to the home islands. It had been a long and eye-opening experience for the young naval officers and much to be digested. But meanwhile there was leave to look forward to after so long away and it was with much joy that the two ships came to anchor finally back at Sasebo on 16 August 1931. As well as instilling into the future naval leaders some considerable knowledge of the many cultures and climes outside their previous experience, such a cruise gave the Imperial Navy knowledge that was to prove invaluable in the decades to follow. They had visited and been entertained by the navies of the great powers, and could judge for themselves how the actuality of what they had seen compared to what they had been told and taught of such cultures and such forces. Moreover, they had seen in their visits to the various colonial naval bases, Hong Kong, Singapore, Batavia, Manila, just how thinly-stretched were the forces they might one day have to face, and how vulnerable all that vast wealth and potential really was.

There was a final bonus, or spin-off. The illusion of Japan's own comparative weakness was exhibited to these self-same rivals. While the shipyards and aircraft factories of Imperial Japan hummed and throbbed with non-stop activity turning out the world's largest battleships, some of the best aircraft-carriers, the most powerful heavy cruisers and fleet destroyers and the world's largest naval air force equipped with modern aircraft in large numbers, what the rest of the world saw of this was nothing. It saw two totally obsolete old hulks dragging themselves snail-like around half the world, and offering no threat whatsoever to their smug complacency. Thus they continued to be deluded until it was too late. The reckoning, coupled with the realisation of their ignorance, was to be devastating.

For the young Japanese officers themselves, reality was not to be so long delayed. On 18 September, within one month of their return home, the Manchurian Railway sabotage incident took place at Liutiaogou, and Japan was plunged into a succession of wars, which were to last for the next fifteen years.

CHAPTER FOUR

The Blossoming of
Japanese Naval Aviation

'He must fight under heaven with the paramount aim of preservation.' *Sun-Tzu – The Art of War.*

The foreign training cruise over, Egusa settled down to work still harder toward his chosen goal. All the IJN midshipmen line officers at that time underwent a series of four short specialist courses, in gunnery; torpedo work; communications and aviation, over a four-month period. They went round the various training schools one-by-one. It was while attending the Torpedo School at Taura-cho town, Yokosuka City that Takashige met his close friend from his middle school days, Toshimasa Imai, who had also volunteered for the Navy after his graduation. Imai had been posted a main battery gunner aboard the training cruiser *Oi* after being further educated at the Kure Training Centre. While Imai had already graduated from the normal torpedo training course in November 1931, he was retained at the school for a further six months as an assistant torpedo seaman, and thus was able to renew his friendship with Takashige. Here also, they met another friend from their middle school days, Midshipman Zenichi Sato. A reunion celebration was clearly called for and the three young men went to a well-known bar close to the torpedo school and started to drink glasses of *Sake* with gusto! As usual, time passed very quickly and suddenly Imai realised that he was due to be AWOL back at base. Unpunctuality was a terrible error in any Navy establishment, but in Japan, it involved loss of self-respect and harsh retribution. Imai recalled how the awful face of his Master Chief Petty Officer flashed across his mind and he realised his fate for breaking the deadline to return to the school. His companions had a later return time and were still OK, but Imai quickly sobered up when he realised the lapse would go on his naval record for all time as a black mark.

Egusa, as ever, remained calm. As Imai was to recall very clearly, Takashige told him: 'OK. I will explain the reasons for your lateness back for you.' The friends helped Imai back to the school and, being met by the fierce CPO at the gate, midshipman Egusa eloquently explained why they had been late and the reason for their celebration. Amazingly, the CPO told Imai his record would not be marked, and that: 'You are very lucky to have such a good friend.' However, the CPO was not completely won over by Egusa's pleading, adding for good measure: 'Never *ever* be late back to barracks again or you are *really* for it!' It was a lesson Imai did not forget, for he later studied assiduously and became a CPO himself later in his career and moved up the ranks to Special Service Lieutenant, despite not having attended Etajima Academy.

Meanwhile, following the four specialist courses, it was time for Takashige to join his first proper warship and take up his proper naval duties. On 24 December 1931, Egusa duly received his orders to join the heavy cruiser *Haguro*, at that time one of the most powerful heavy cruisers in any navy.

The heavy cruiser *Haguro*, the modern warship where Ensign Egusa spent his first year of full naval service, learning his trade as a naval officer at sea. At this time she was engaged on intensive training exercises off Japan and then was used to rush troop reinforcements to Shanghai at the time of the first major incident. This photograph shows her at that period before she was later refitted with improved main armament and other modifications. *(US National Archives, Washington D C)*

In strict contrast to the old training ships shown to their European guests, the *Haguro* was state-of-the-art for the period. Egusa's new ship was a 10,980-ton standard displacement heavy cruiser of the *Myoko* class. She had been built by Mitsubishi at their Nagasaki yard, her keel being laid on 16 March 1925, and was launched on 24 March 1928 and completed on 25 April 1929. *Haguro* had first been commissioned on 16 May 1929 as part of the elite Fourth *Sentai*

(Squadron), as the second ship, where she was to remain until 1933. She, and her three sisters, were the first heavy cruisers built in Japan to conform to the restrictions of the notorious Washington Treaty.

Haguro (named after one of the three sacred mountains of Dewa (*Dewa Sanzan*) was over 631 feet (192m) in length and had a 3.9 inch thick inclined armour belt, and also featured a triple hull and arched longitudinal bulkheads for underwater protection. *Haguro* could carry into battle an formidable armament, with ten 8-in 203 mm), ·50 calibre Type 3 (No.1) main guns in five twin Model D turrets and six 4.7in, ·45 calibre single anti-aircraft guns, twelve 24in torpedo tubes in four mountings and two catapult launched floatplanes, used for scouting. She was good for a high speed of 35.5 knots despite this heavy armament and far outclassed contemporary British and American ships of the same type by a good margin. The *Haguro* reflected the Japanese warship policy of the day, which was to obtain the maximum offensive power within the confines of the treaty (which she, in fact, exceeded). She had a crew of 773 officers and men when young midshipman Egusa joined her strength.

The Manchurian Incident had occurred just two months earlier, and during Egusa's year aboard one of the *Haguro* duties was to convey troop reinforcements to Shanghai where the young officer first saw the fringes of combat at close quarters. Here, from the cruiser's decks, Egusa was able to witness the growing power of the aircraft. Clashes between the Chinese and Japanese took place frequently and made a deep impression upon him.

It had after all only been twenty-seven years since the Wright brothers made their epic flight but much had happened. Twenty years earlier the first aircraft flew in Japan and in 1919 the RAF fliers Captain John Allcock, and Lieutenant Arthur Whitten Brown completed the first successful non-stop aerial crossing of the Atlantic, a feat only duplicated by the American Lindbergh as a solo effort some eight years later. With such strides young men like Egusa were stimulated and their thoughts turned to aviation more and more. In fact from Egusa's 58th Class at Etajima, no less than thirty-two eventually made their way into naval aviation as flying officers, both pilots and navigators.

The Japanese Navy and the homegrown aviation industry were changing also, in response. The Navy's Type 90 carrier-borne fighter aircraft, whose body and engine were both of Japanese construction, took to the air in 1930.

Reflecting on this atmosphere Egusa announced to his family during one period of leave at home: 'I've made up my mind to become an aviator!' There was considerable consternation at home at this decision. 'Stop this idea, immediately', he was told, 'flying is far too dangerous.' Needless to say, this only made Takashige more determined than ever. His stubborn streak took over. 'despite what everyone says, I *will* fly an aircraft' he responded, and nothing could shake his resolve.

Meanwhile, after eighteen months as a midshipman, Takashige's conducted was rewarded by promotion to ensign. This was on 1 April 1932. Meanwhile Egusa's allotted time aboard the *Haguro* had expired and, on 15 December 1932, he was transferred to the ancient second-class cruiser, then rated as a coast defence ship, *Tsushima*. This was considered by the young fire-eater a very retrograde step. Although western modern sources state that she was hulked in 1930, in fact *Tsushima* was still in war service at this time in the despatch fleet for China due to the Shanghai incident. So it was back to the front in China once more for Egusa. However, this duty did not last very long for on 1 September, to his great delight, Egusa was assigned to the Air Student Training Group. He still had to bide his time until *Tsushima* returned to home waters once more, but finally, on 15 March 1933, he joined the Air Student Training Group, the *Kaigun Renshu Kokutai* (Navy's pilot and air crew training unit) as a trainee pilot

The air-training centre was based at Kasumigaura, located in the Ibaraki Prefecture, some sixty miles north-east of Tokyo, and was a copy of RAF Cranwell. It had been purchased at the urging of the pro-air Lieutenant-Commander Yozo Kaneko,[40] under the noses of the Army in 1921. From 1 November the following year it was established as the premier naval aviation training college. Flying skills were imparted but so also were the manners of a gentleman officer. In fact, this was perhaps taken too far. When a certain Captain Isoroku Yamamoto was sent there in 1923 to take flying lessons at the ripe old age of forty, he passed with honours. Three months later Yamamoto was appointed to the Kasumigaura Aviation Corps as Executive Officer and Director of Studies and he immediately brought in a much harsher regime, which he enforced ruthlessly in order to toughen up his young airmen. Long hair was shaved, a rigid dress code brought in, the curriculum intensified and discipline tightened up. When he left to take up his appointment as Washington Naval Attaché in 1925, Yamamoto left behind a very tight ship. Despite this tradition, or maybe because of it, Egusa flourished here. His sturdy farmboy independence had in no way been completely knocked out of him, and his existing virtues of hard work and honest endeavour stood him in good stead when weaker candidates found life unbearable.

The Kasumigaura Air Group, like the other few other original IJN Air Groups at this time, was originally an operational unit which incorporated training as part of its remit, but, in 1930, it became the official basic flight training facility for student pilots. The intake of volunteers from the naval academy, of which Egusa was an enthusiastic representative, had proved inadequate for the vastly expanding air arm and had been supplemented, firstly in 1929 by a NCO training scheme[41] and then, a year later, was further supplemented by direct recruitment from the populace.[42] These soon vastly outnumbered the commissioned volunteers, which led to the latter being regarded as an elite. Having survived Etajima, the very similar disciplines of Kasumigaura held no fears for Egusa and his contemporaries of course and not having to undergo basic naval training, their courses were completed within ten months. While some western historians have criticised their previous experience as 'irrelevant' to air fighting, the new systems also had to indoctrinate the new 'civilian' intake into the ways of the Navy just the same.

It was from the early 1930s that the Imperial Japanese Navy began its great strides forward in naval aviation that was to culminate in the crushing victories of a decade later. The Naval Aircraft Establishment was founded and the *7-Shi* programme was put in hand. This was to create a completely new air fleet, comprising new fighters, carrier-based dive-and torpedo-bombers, and land-based attack planes. Japanese observers had been much impressed by the accuracy and hitting power of the American Helldivers and were determined to utilise this method to achieve a high percentage of hits with a use minimum of outlay. Like the massive shipbuilding programme of the same period, most of the new equipment was kept 'under wraps' from the west and great secrecy was maintained. From this and the earlier programmes, the Nakajima Company produced two experimental carrier dive-bomber types, which went out to the fleet for evaluation. The Nakajima N-35 Tokubaku was powered by a 650-hp Lorraine engine. The Yokosuka Company was also early in the field with a dive-bomber design.

As related, in 1930 the *Yoka-ren* scheme for preliminary pilot candidates was initiated by the Navy to cope with its intended expansion. Although the term *Yoka-Ren* actually related to the position of each pilot in the programme, who had the status of accepted applicants, more often than not it was used as the name of the training programme itself and because of this usage took on that meaning. The programme was started by the Yokosuka Air Group but quickly outgrew that establishment and was transferred to Kasumigaura. Soon even this facility was insufficient and the programme was further extended to the neighbouring Tsuchiura naval air base also. The scheme was particularly attractive to young NCO's as it provided a short cut to flying. They became *Honka Renshusei* (Pilot Candidates). But as a graduate of the Naval College and well on his way to ensign ranking, Egusa bypassed this scheme.

When Egusa arrived at the training centre the organisation was conducted on the following lines, as recalled by Zenji Abe.[43] As part of their early training routine they had spent a week at Kasumigaura. At that time, he recalled:

> 'Generally, we studied in the classroom in the morning and handled a training plane, flying in a two-seater with an instructor, in the afternoon. The initial exercises were checking-out tests of potential pupils by the instructor. We had already undergone equipment and flight-simulator testing. All candidates were also interviewed by a physiologist (Dr Mizuno) and his team. At the end of that week we had to fill in and submit a questionnaire on whether we wished to be an aviator or not.'

Following the required sea-time, those chosen, like Takashige, arrived at Kasumigaura by train from Sasebo. Abe remembered:

> 'There were some wounded classmates from the Shanghai incident among those at Kasumigaura, but these were immediately eliminated in the initial medical examination. Of those that remained there were thirty-four students for land-based planes and about thirty students for seaplanes. The latter received their training and education at the seaplane base located on the southern margin of Lake Kasumigaura. At that date there was no paved runway, though there was a large hangar on the field, which housed the German Zeppelin airship that had flown to Kasumigaura in August 1929.[44]
> 'The curriculum at Kasumigaura was, again, classroom

study in the mornings and flying in the afternoon. We learned the techniques of take-off, level flight, change of course, circular flights, etc, in an elementary training aircraft over a period of three months in the first half of a six-month term. In the second half of the term, we were taught vertical circular flight (*sic*), circular flight, looping, slow-rolling, instrument flying etc.this time using the Type 93 training aircraft. Both the elementary and the Type 93 Middle trainer planes were wooden and fabric construction biplanes.

'We finished the Student Training curriculum in six months. Then we had to fill out a questionnaire about what we hoped to specialise in, air pilot or navigator (reconnaissance) officers. Ten seaplanes would be selected for two-seat or three-seat aircraft pilots and less than ten as navigators. For the land planes, ten men were selected for fighters and ten for three-seater carrier attack planes, as well as reconnaissance officers. The remaining four students of each group were allotted to carrier bomber (dive-bomber) pilots. We were then promoted to sub-Lieutenants in June.

'The four-man group selected for carrier dive-bomber pilots was then assigned to attachment to the Omura Air Group in Kyushu. Here they learnt how to dive-bomb, fire, aerial combat, night flying, etc, at first in the Type 94 carrier dive-bomber (for the first half of the training period) and then in the Type-96 dive-bomber (in the second half period) to qualify as dive-bomber pilots. Again, both types were wooden and fabric biplanes. In August the four qualified dive-bomber pilots were assigned their new posts either aboard an aircraft-carrier or with a land-based unit and left Omura Air Group to take up their new role.'

In Takashige's case, after seven months at the Air Student Training Course, he went on to receive further training in both torpedo-bombing and level bombing at the Tateyama Air Base, which was to stand him in good stead many years later.

Egusa quickly showed great promise as an aviator. Saying little but pondering much, he diligently and studiously absorbed the lessons imparted to him and applied his own logic. Despite his outwardly staid mannerisms, he was a popular young pilot and was always to remain a caring and thoughtful officer. One description of him by a contemporary recalls how: 'He always considered his subordinates very much and became a great leader among his colleagues.' His own skill was obvious to all; his concern for those later entrusted to his leadership equally became a byword. The results were to be made manifest. However, at this time he had to learn his dangerous new trade. Not only was flying from ships itself a relatively new skill but dive-bombing, in particular, was a novel and fresh concept in the Imperial Fleet. Originally used by British pilots of the old Royal Flying Corps in France in 1917-18, the art had fallen into neglect until, nurtured by the US Marine Corps and adopted by the US Navy, it had re-emerged in the early 1930s as a potent force.[45] Not only in the United States but also in Germany, the dive-bomber concept was reborn, and, in her old tradition, Japan eagerly embraced this latest thinking.

It was the head of the Naval Aviation Department, Vice-Admiral Masataka Andō who, from 1929 onwards, had initiated detailed investigations into the dive-bombing technique to ascertain whether it was a desirable addition to the IJN armoury.[46] Like their counterparts in the Royal Navy with the Fairey Flycatcher,[47] the Japanese airmen used existing fleet fighter aircraft for the early experiments. The experiments already conducted by the RAF at the Ordfordness ranges in 1918 using Bristol SE5A and Sopwith Camel fighter aircraft, attacking a small yellow flag planted in the beach shingle[48] were laboriously duplicated ten years later in Japan. The same results were found also; the steeper the angle, the higher the accuracy; that wind drift was difficult to allow for and could only be achieved through experience; that 'eye-shooting' was often as accurate as using a bomb sight.[49] Also the frailty of the aircraft employed called for more specialised aircraft to do the job, built for strength to cope with the stresses caused by high-speed dives and the resultant pull-out.

At this time the fighter was predominant and Japan, whose aircraft industry was still underdeveloped, just did not have any machine suitably stressed for all-out full-blooded dive-bombing as envisaged. Japan had to look around for such a machine. In 1934 the two-seater Vought Colossus was purchased from the United States and they termed them the Type-90 carrier-reconnaissance aircraft, for the true purpose of starting basic dive-bombing training. These aircraft, although not ideal, produced good results in dive-bombing trials. Then the Imperial Navy purchased the single-seater Heinkel biplane from Germany, and modified it into a two-place machine, which was termed the Type 94 Special bomber. The Type 94's were embarked aboard the carrier *Ryujo* in December 1934. Hitherto, it had been the rule that new aircraft were always tested at the Yokosuka Air Station, but, perhaps at Genda's urging, the operational tests of the Type 94 were, unprecedently conducted out at sea, far from prying eyes, aboard *Ryujo*. This was the beginning of the development that was to lead to the Aichi Val and the many achievements of that aircraft in the Pacific War.

As the Type 94 began to commence operational tests with the fleet, so the members of the Etajima 58th class began to serve in the warships of the fleet. As a result, there were more dive-bomber pilots from the 58th year than in other classes. Masatake Okumiya, Mamoru Seki and Akira majored in Hell diving in 1935 and Shigehiko Kawaguchi, Yoshiyuki Terashima, Kiyoshi Kamishikiryo and, of course, Takashige Egusa also did it in the same year. All were members of Class 58 Etajima. Again, according to Okumiya, the pioneer of dive-bombing in Japan, Japans dive-bombers were somewhat nondescript and gave their young pilots many headaches. In combat, also, hell-diving attacks scored a large number of direct hits on their targets, but received much damage in return from enemy anti-aircraft fire.

The precision aspect of dive-bombing had a strong appeal to Egusa. He appreciated the economy of force and the maximising of effort contained in this method of bombing and saw it as the perfect solution for a nation which would always be outnumbered in combat but which might mitigate this drawback with skill and expertise. Egusa specialised early in dive-bombing. On 15 November 1933, he passed his flying tests with honours and was promoted to Sub-Lieutenant and, a fortnight later, he was assigned to his first regular unit, the Tateyama Air Squadron in the Chiba Prefecture. Within a short time, on 29 April 1934, Takashige joined the aircraft-carrier *Hosho* operating in the China Sea.

During two years of flight-deck operations, using the new dive-bombers, Egusa's skill became readily acknowledged. Unfortunately, the aircraft themselves were not a success. But much trial and experimental work was conducted which led to the establishment of tactics and procedures, which were to endure with little modification.

It quickly grew clear that a more reliable design was needed to allow the dive-bomber to achieve its true potential. A number of aircraft-carriers were now in commission and, increasingly, the

The world's first custom-built aircraft carrier, the little *Hosho*. Egusa made his first deck flights and landings on her decks. *(Authors collection)*

aviation side of the Navy regarded itself as the true fighting power of the fleet. This view was not shared by the majority of the admirals but a few were far-sighted enough to back this thinking, among them Yamamoto himself. The first such machine, developed under the 6-shi programme, was built by the Nakajima company. Powered by an A1 engine and designed to carry a single 250kg bomb under the fuselage, this aircraft made her debut flight in 1932 but soon came to grief and was written off in a crash. The following year, under the 7-shi programme a second aircraft followed but was not a success.

Again, Japan turned to foreign designers to help her find the answers to her needs and the Aichi company imported a Heinkel He66 single-seater dive-bomber from Germany for evaluation. Under the terms of the new 8-*Shi* programme, in 1934 Aichi's design team under Tokuhishiro Gomei modified this aircraft, making it into a two-seater with a stronger undercarriage and a Nakajima radial engine. As the Aichi D1A1 Type 94 'special bomber', this sturdy aircraft gave the Japanese Navy a power base on which to advance the art further. A third design from Nakajima, the D2N, and another experimental type from Kuu-Shou, the D2Y were produced but were not then further proceeded with and the Aichi formed the mainspring of the dive-bomber expansion.

The Aichi D1A1 carrier bomber, Japan's first custom-built dive-bomber. They served in the early China campaigns, and were developed further in the light of combat experience to become very successful aircraft. They were still in service, albeit as second-line units, at the outbreak of the Pacific War in 1941 and were code-named *Peggy* by the Allies. *(Authors collection)*

The D1A (or *Susie* as the Allies later codenamed her) proved highly successful in combat. She was a single-engined biplane, stressed for carrier landings and dive-bombing and was extremely tough. She was built with a metal basic frame, with composite metal and fabric covering. She could haul a single 250kg (550lb) bomb, mounted under her central fuselage, plus two single 30kg (66lb) wing-mounted bombs. For defensive armament she had two fixed, forward-firing 7.7mm Type 92 machine-guns mounted in the radial engine cowling, with a single flexible-mounted weapon of the same type in the after cockpit. The pilot and the radio-operator, who doubled as the tail-gunner, sat in tandem in the open cockpit.

Various engine improvements were tried as the D1A was developed further in the light of experience. Initially, the modified Heinkel He66 and the first 118 DA1's used the Nakajima Kotobuki 2 Kai 1 and a nine-cylinder air-cooled radial was installed. This engine was rated at 580hp for take-off and 460hp at 1,500-metre altitude and drove a two-bladed propeller. The last 44 D1A1's however were powered by the Nakajima Kotobuki 3, also a nine-cylinder air-cooled radial, which was rated at 640hp for take-off and 715hp at 2,8000 metres, which drove the same propeller. A final development of the *Susie* saw the adoption of the Nakajima Hikari 1 nine-cylinder air-cooled radial, which was rated at 730hp for take-off and 670hp at 3,500 metres, and this variant became the D1A2.

An Aichi Val carrier bomber in flight. This is the later version, the D1A2 that appeared in 1942. Egusa trained the pilots of units converted to the new dive-bomber from the old biplanes. *(Yoichi Tanaka)*

Some structural modifications accompanied the engine changes. The wingspan of the D1A2 increased from 11.37m to 11.40m (37ft 4¹/2 inches); overall length was reduced from the D1A's 9.40 m down to 9.30m (30ft 6in) and the overall height of the D1A2 was similarly reduced from 3.45m to 3.41 m (11ft 2¹/4ins). The wing area increased, from 34.1 square metres to 70 square metres (373.52sq ft). These changes affected the aircraft's weight also, the D1A empty weighed in at 1,400kg, which increased to 1,516kg (3,342lb) in the D1A2, although fully-laden the difference was not so marked, only increasing from 2,400kg to 2,500kg and a maximum of 2,610kg (5,754lb). Wing loading increased from 70.5kg/m² to 72.0kg/m² in the D1A2. This gave much more favourable power loading differences of 4.3kg/hp in the D1A down to 3.8kg/hp in the D1A2.

Performance was enhanced accordingly with top speed increasing from 152 knots at 2,050 metres from the D1A to 167 knots at 3,200 metres in the D1A2. Climb rate to 3,000 metres improved from 9 minutes 30 seconds to 7 minutes 51 seconds. The service ceiling was reduced in the D1A2, from 7,000 metres down to 6,890 metres and range was similarly curtailed, from 578 nautical miles (930km) down to 500 nautical miles, never a good change for a carrier aircraft.

In all, the Aichi Tokei Denki KK plant at Nagoya produced a total of 206 D1A1's in the years 1934 to 1937, and 428 D1A2's between 1936 and 1940 before production ceased. Egusa flew both variants and became highly proficient in the art of extracting the maximum from them, whether with the 12th *Kokutai* ashore or from the deck of the *Ryujo*, and, at a time when her main rivals at sea, Great Britain and the United States were only producing dive-bombers in penny-packets, Japan's relatively large programme and continuous combat testing gave her an increasing edge in skill and experience.

The Aichi D3A1 carrier bomber being readied prepared for a combat sortie at the combat land base at Han-k'ou (Hankow) during the 1940 campaign in China. After Egusa's team had flight-tested and carrier-tested the new dive-bomber they entered battle with the Combined 12th *Kentai*. Egusa proved to be the master of this little aircraft and trained and honed the units under his command to an extremely high-pitch of efficiency and accuracy by the eve of the Pacific War. *(Authors collection)*

Great secrecy surrounded the IJN's development of the dive-bomber, as with so many projects. The term dive-bomber itself was forbidden; instead the talk was of *Tokushu bakugekki* (special bombing aircraft.) or later *Kanjō bakugekki* (carrier bomber aircraft).[50]

Together with the subsequent D1A2, Type 96 carrier bomber produced in 1936, a total of 590 aircraft were built, numbers far in excess of any equivalent dive-bomber anywhere else at this time, showing just how highly the Imperial Navy rated this method of attack. Egusa was to be in the forefront of its testing and application at sea.

Further advancement was swift as the Navy expanded. On 16 November 1936 Sub-Lieutenant Egusa was given his first command, a company in the Saheki Air Squadron, based in north-eastern Kyūshū, which had been established just over a year before. Saheki (*Saeki*) Naval Airfield, in the Oita Prefecture, had been opened on 15 February 1934, and was situated close to the shallow bay of the same name close by the entrance to the Bungo Straits. Just over a year later (on 1 December 1937) Egusa was promoted to Lieutenant. Intensive testing in peacetime exercise involved the bombing of fast-moving targets and this quickly proved the effectiveness of dive-bombing over altitude attacks. The obsolete battleship *Settsu* was converted to such a target ship, being radio-controlled much like the Royal Navy's *Centurion* and the United States Navy's *Utah*, and similar results were obtained. But soon Egusa was to become involved in a real shooting war in which the theories were put into practice.

The festering sore that was Sino-Japanese relations was further deteriorating and leading, almost inevitably, to all-out conflict. The threat of another war between Japan and China, with its long and complex background, tended to dominate all that Egusa and his fellow naval officers did and thought during their formative years. To understand how this situation had developed we must go back to the immediate aftermath of the First World War.

CHAPTER FIVE

The War in China

'Now, if someone is victorious in battle and succeeds in attack but does not exploit the achievements, it is disastrous.'
Sun Tzu – The Art of War.

The gains that Japan had made at the expense of China during the Great War had quickly been eroded once the western allies no longer had any need of her help in the post-war situation. Indeed, they now tended to regard her, not without some justification, as the main threat. In the aftermath of Washington, the two powers now pressured Japan into withdrawing the bulk of the twenty-one demands. Even Tsingtao was to be returned to Chinese rule, adding yet further resentment of Great Britain and the United States to the pyre of the wartime alliance. As an indication of this, the formal Anglo-Japanese Treaty was allowed to fall into abeyance and replaced by a new and quite fatuous four-power replacement, which did nothing but save face.

Although nullified, the fact that such outrageous claims had been imposed upon China by Japan at all led to a deepening of the hatred and mutual mistrust between the two nations that only laid the groundwork for further conflict. While Chinese anger translated itself into a rejection of all things Japanese, the latter continued to smart under what they saw as their legitimate rights in both China and Manchuria being continually eroded and attacked. With such mutual antipathy so prevalent it is not surprising that the spark to inflame the hatred between the two nations was not long in coming. This was the so-called 'Manchurian incident.'

On the night of 18 September 1931, a section of track belonging to the Japan Manchurian Railway Company at Liutiaogou, west of Beidaying at Mukden (now Shenyang) was blown up. The Japanese authorities accused the army of Zhang Oue-laing of the attack on the rail link, and of attacks on the Japanese garrison. Retaliation quickly followed. The Japanese Kwangtung Army, reinforced by troops from across the Yalu River in Korea, moved into the area, seizing the vital airfield at Fengtian and taking Beidaying the next day. Within five days the Japanese forces had occupied virtually the whole of Jirin and Liaoning Provinces and were advancing on Jinzhou. Although suspected at the time, it was not until later that it was revealed that conspirators and activists in league with Japanese Army and Secret Service plotters had carried out the attack as a pretext for the occupation of the whole of Manchuria to pre-empt moves by the Chinese Kuomintang party to extend control in the region.[51]

In fact these conspirators and the Army were acting almost independently of their own Government, and many in the Japanese cabinet opposed the operation. Despite promising to withdraw back to guarding the railway, the complete take-over of Manchuria was quickly achieved and by February 1932, a puppet state named Manchukuo was set up under the nominal rule of Pu Yi, last of the Manchu Dynasty who was installed as Regent at Changchun, which was renamed Xinjing (New Capital). Although recognised only by Germany and Italy, Manchukuo continued to serve as a vassal state and military-run base for Japan until 1945.

Meanwhile, back in Japan on 9 January, a disaffected Korean nationalist made an abortive attempt to assassinate Emperor Hirohito. When certain Chinese newspapers made sneering references to the incident, Japanese honour was impinged and apologies were demanded which were not forthcoming. Intemperate outrages against five Japanese monks in Hongkou, Shanghai, brought about counteraction and the Japanese destroyed some Chinese factories and shops and several Chinese policemen were killed.[52] The Senior Japanese Naval Officer at Shanghai, Rear Admiral Shiozawa Kiochi, sent ashore a force of Special Naval Landing Forces (*Rikusentai or Naval Brigade*),[53] from his squadron to reinforce the garrison. Unfortunately for this force, which was lightly armed and on its first-ever combat mission, they ran straight into elements of the Cantonese 19th Route Army who gave them a very bloody nose. Fire support was demanded from the Japanese warships in the river and much damage was inflicted on the city. Regular Army units had to be brought in to rescue the SNLF units and naval aircraft from the carrier *Kaga* were also brought in to assist. Hard fighting dragged on for several weeks before being brought to an end through the good offices of the British Admiral Sir Howard Kelly which led to the signing of a ceasefire with the Songhu Agreement.

Once again Sino-Japanese relations spiralled downward, and Japan again earned herself the censure of most of the world community, but the League of Nations did nothing except launch an

Investigation Commission under VAGR Bulwer-Lytton, Second Earl of Lytton, which affected matters not one iota! With most of world opinion against her, however, Japan used this as an excuse to withdraw from the obligations of the League on 23 February, and sent troops into Jehol, Inner Mongolia on 4 March. By the end of 1932, Japan had also withdrawn totally from the obligations of the Washington Naval Treaty and set about stern and earnest rearmament without restraint.[54]

Already the old ties seemed distant. As we have seen Great Britain and, in particular, the Royal Navy, had always been the Imperial Japanese Navy's friend and mentor. No longer and, as the resentment grew, the special relationship weakened and quickly turned to outright hostility. Looking ahead, by 1936 a Japanese naval officer, Lieutenant-Commander Tota Ishimaru (29th Class) was able to write these prophetic words in a book which outwardly declared the feelings of many, 'the friend of yesterday has become the foe of today.'[55]

The same author forecast the scenario once war broke out. Weakened by the surrender to America at the Washington Conference; the two-power standard abandoned; tied down by fear of Germany in the North Sea; fear of Italy in the Mediterranean and with Soviet machinations stirring unrest in the Indian Empire, the Dominions indifferent, Japan had nothing to fear from British intervention in his eyes. A repeat of the Russian fiasco was to be expected. He envisaged the occupation of Borneo, raids on Australia and a final fleet action in the Sunda Straits leading to the decimation of the British fleet. He went on to conclude that whatever the outcome of such a war, the only beneficiary would be America. He predicted, in fact, what indeed came to pass within a decade of his work, 'in a word, the collapse of the British Empire.'[56]

Although one rather shallow reviewer described this message as 'trivial and bizarre',[57] in fact in one respect Ishimaru was perfectly correct in predicting that only America would gain from such a conflict. It was not just the rabidly anti-British Hearst Press that continually ranted against British Imperialism in the United States at this time. Ignoring their own occupation of Hawaii, Midway, Wake, the Philippines etc, politicians in Washington viewed every British move with suspicion. Franklin D Roosevelt saw the spectre of the 'land grabbing tendencies of the British'[58] everywhere also. Even when bridges were attempting to be built between the two western powers, the 'big navy' and virulently anti-British lobby in Washington DC, typified by Admiral Ernie King and his ilk, stonewalled and worked against it continually, and continued to do so throughout the Pacific War as British wartime Admirals Sir Andrew B. Cunningham and Sir James Somerville later found to their dismay.[59]

While such firebrands as Ishimaru in Japan were expressing their views on the inevitability of war with England, other matters were stirring the pot and leading to further turmoil and unrest. As well as the world-shaking events triggered by events in China, Egusa and his young compatriots were influenced by events closer to home. Here, the growing number of outrages directed against the Government and rulers by the more violent and extreme elements among the armed forces were the cause of grave concern. In March 1931 the so-called 'March Incident' had revealed plotting on a large scale by disaffected elements, even though the outrage itself was aborted. In October of the same year, yet another thwarted attempt came to nothing, this was the 'blood pledge corps' incident originated by civilian elements of the populace. Turmoil was everywhere behind the scenes in the Empire. On 15 May 1932, the Navy became embroiled for the first time and the seventy-seven year old Prime Minister, Inukai Tsuyoshi, was assassinated. Although the ten young naval officer perpetrators were quickly brought to justice, they turned the proceedings into a political bandwagon to air highly ultra-nationalistic views, which won the approval of many of the population. There was even talk of a sub-plot as Sub-Lieutenant Ito revealed that they planned to assassinate the Ambassador and Consul 'of a certain power',[60] Admiral Takeshi Takarabe and 'all the judicial authorities concerned in the Naval Disarmament Conference.'

Their inspirational leader was a product of Etajima, Lieutenant Commander Hitoshi Fuji. He had fervently embraced the 'great Asia' principle whose desire was to evict the white races from all their eastern possessions. He won over Sub-Lieutenants Kiyo Koga and Isao Murakami, and eight others joined them. All were convinced, in the words of their court martial indictment, that 'party politicians, financial cliques and the privileged class are all rotten and degenerate with no sense of duty to the state, and that through their misconduct of affairs, things in all fields, political, diplomatic, economic, military, and thought reached a deadlock.' Their patriotism was never questioned and they received light sentences and easy jobs in Manchuria. However, older and wiser heads in the Navy were gravely disturbed. The living embodiment of the Navy,

Admiral Togo himself, then in his dotage, and always a taciturn man above politics, was moved to comment:

'All officers in the Imperial Navy must be prudent in speech and action.'

At Etajima itself, the President assembled the whole academy in private and addressed them on similar lines, concluding that, whatever their motives, 'shooting down an old man in cold blood was not a samurai-like act.'

Nor was this the end of the scheming. Two more conspiracies came to light, the 'heaven sent soldiers unit' incident of July 1933 involved military plotting which was brought to light before it could be initiated, and in November the following year an assassination and *coup* planned by Army cadets was discovered. Events continued to follow a sinister trend, and in August 1935 a young Army hothead murdered General Nagata Tetsuzan. But events reached a bloody climax on 26 February 1936. Civilians and young army field grade officers took over a large section of central Tokyo around the Imperial Palace. During the confusion several prominent courtiers were murdered, including Lord Privy Seal and former Prime Minister Saito and Finance Minister Korekiyo Takahashi. Grand Chamberlain Admiral Baron Kantaro Suzuki was wounded but Prime Minister Keisuke Okada escaped with his life. The Emperor issued a proclamation declaring the assassins to be 'rebels.' Troops loyal to the Royal House and heavy artillery were brought up against them and the coup failed. The majority of the young officers were ruthlessly executed without any public trial for them to use as a propaganda platform.

Nationalistic ambition was therefore again turned outward and on 25 November 1936, Japan joined with Nazi Germany as signatories of the Anti-Comintern Pact to fight against Moscow-inspired Communists and other left wing plotting worldwide. Then came the fateful events in the summer of the following year at the Marco Polo Bridge.

With the Japanese advance into Chahar Province at the end of 1932, and the subsequent defeat of the Chinese 29th Army under General Song Zheyuan, and the annexation of Rehe the following year, allegedly to give added security to Manzhougho, the city of Peking was outflanked to both the west and the north. These conquests were given legality by the Ho-Umezu Agreement signed on 9 June 1935. The same year the Japanese established the East Ji Anti-Communist Autonomous Administration. By the summer of 1937 a Japanese force was encamped to the east of the city at Tongzhou; to the north-west at Nanakou and to the south, and the western end of the Lugouqiao (Reed-cutter) bridge (known to the Japanese as the Roko Bridge, and to westerners as the Marco Polo Bridge). This famous and ancient bridge was located at Fengtai a southern suburb of Peking and was a choke point of the Peking-Wuhan Railway, controlling the only entry to the Kuomintang-held part of the city from the south. If the bridge fell to the Japanese the city would be totally cut off from outside help. Consequently the 37th, 132nd, 143rd Divisions of the Chinese 29th Army held the other end of the bridge and vital areas of Hebei Province, with the 219th Regiment of the 110th Bridge, 38th Division, charged with holding the bridge itself.

With tension at flash point, at dawn on 7 July, the Chief of Special Mission Organ of the [Japanese] Army[61] at Peking (Peiping now Beijing), Colonel Takuro Matsui, sent a telegraph message to the Wanping garrison, stating that one of their soldiers had gone missing and was suspected to be in the town. He demanded the right to enter the town to search for him, but Colonel Ji Xingwen of the 219th curtly refused, and was backed in his stand by General Song. Taisa replied that unless permission was given the town would be fired on and, at midnight, made good his threat with an artillery bombardment, followed by an assault with infantry and tanks at first light. The bridge was temporarily taken, then, with reinforcements, the Chinese retook it and there was a pause in the proceedings. While both the Japanese Government and diplomats, and the Chinese themselves, appeared anxious to restrict the spread of this isolated incident, at local level there was much confusion of purpose, with neither side prepared to 'lose face.'

The Chinese commanders on the spot were at variance in how to deal with the situation, but finally Song overruled opposition to negotiations and sent General Zhang Zhi-zhong of the 38th Division, to meet Colonel Kingoro Hashimoto, the Japanese C-in-C, to try to resolve the issue peacefully. Zhang mistrusted the Japanese totally even though Hashimoto assured him he was seeking a peaceable outcome.[62] Meanwhile fresh Japanese forces were spotted *en route* from Manchuria and Song likewise called in reinforcements. At the end of July, by which time both sides had greatly increased their numbers of troops in the face-off, Hashimoto informed Zhang that he would not attack the city provided the Chinese carried out three requirements: to eliminate all anti-Japanese organisations and activities in the city; to accept responsibility for the 7 July incident and that General Song, and nobody else, should make a formal apology. Zhang conceded the first two points but said he could not answer for his commander on the third. He then left the talks to return to the city and the Japanese attack recommenced in greater force. By 10 August the bridge and Wanping were taken, with Nanwan falling next day and two Chinese Divisions, the 37th and 132nd, smashed in the fighting, the survivors falling back on the city. The 29th Army pulled back after Song handed over to a subordinate and left Peking virtually defenceless. The Japanese Army marched in on 18 August and moved on to take Tianjin three days later leaving the whole northern Chinese plain open to occupation.

What part did the Navy play in this military operation? It remained the case that whereas the Navy advocated the obtaining of self-sufficiency for Japan by expansion to the south toward the oil and rubber rich colonies of Great Britain (Borneo, Malaya, Singapore, Burma) and the Netherlands East Indies (Sumatra, Java etc) the Army also advocated the coal and mineral rich areas of China abutting upon Manchuria as the logical area for further advance and consolidation. The two services continued to press their opposing policies, a weak Japanese Government was often ignored, and the inevitable clashes escalated. Japanese expansion ran into the Nationalist Revolutionary Army led by Chiang Kai-shek, which was gradually succeeding in uniting the dispersed parts of China, while at the same time combating the Soviet-inspired Communist threat.

Following the initial flare-up at the Marco Polo Bridge, Japanese preparations were made for a quick campaign and, while the Army prepared itself to advance on Peking, they requested air support. Because they were the most readily available air units, the Imperial Navy's Second Combined Air Flotilla, commanded by Rear Admiral Teizo Mitsunami, based initially at Ohmura and later at Shanghai, was called upon to perform this duty. This force included the 12th Air Corps under Captain Osamu Imamura, with twelve of the Nakajima Type 94 dive-bombers on its strength. By December, the fleet had moved 1 and 2 Carrier Divisions to the China coast to support the Army further as the situation developed into a full-scale war. Aboard the carrier *Ruyjo* were fifteen Nakajima Type-95 dive-

bombers while aboard *Kaga* of 2 Division were twelve further
Nakajima Type 95s. *Hosho* initially had no dive-bombers embarked,
just a *Daitai* of ancient Nakajima A2N fighter aircraft under
Lieutenant Kiyoto Hanamoto. Both carriers sailed from Sasebo base
on 12 August and cruised off the Ma-an-shan Islands from 16
August flying support missions for the troops ashore.

To recap, on 11 July 1937 the Navy had established the 12th
Kokutai from the Saeki (Sacki) *Kokutai*. Egusa was appointed
Commander (*hikūtaichū*) of the dive-bomber *daitai* of this force,
with fourteen Type 94 Aichi D1A1's under his direct orders. Along
with a dozen Nakajima A4N1 fighter aircraft and twelve Type 92
Yokosuka B3Y1 attack bombers, this unit was assigned to the 2nd
Rengo Kokutai (Combined Air Group). Egusa's unit left Saeki and
moved over to Manchuria on 7 August, being initially based at
Shusuishi (Chou-Shu-Tze, ZhouShuiZi or Chowshihtze) airfield at
Dairen (Dalian, Luda) for the following three weeks.

Egusa's first combat squadron. D1A1's of the 12th *Kokutai* deployed in China.
(Dr Toshimasa Egusa via Mitsuharu Uehara)

Meanwhile hostilities had broken out to the south once more,
with the 'second Shanghai incident' of 13 August, leading to an
extension of the fighting there yet again. Initially the Naval General
Staff had signed the Army-Navy Agreements on North China
Operations and North China Air Operations on 11 July, with the
Army General Staff. The following day the Navy also approved an
informal policy for subsequent operations against China. Although

the Governmental line of restricting the fighting was given lip service, the spread of the confrontation was considered highly likely and the 30,000 Japanese residents, their property and rights would be impossible to defend without further action.

Once the Army had decided on the despatch of reinforcements from the home islands the Navy made their own plans in readiness for an escalation. The first stage was the cautious evacuation of some 30,000 Japanese, Formosan and Korean residents from the upper Yangtze beyond Hankow. A special fleet was to be sent out to China once organised to give the necessary protection to this; a 'first stage' mobilisation plan was to be implemented and two battalions of *Rikusentai* were to be readied at Port Arthur for Tsingtao. The main air base on Taihoku was to be reinforced by personnel and supplies, which would sail from Fukue aboard the transports *Kitakami* and *Sata*. Top Secret Telegram No 551 which was sent out on 28 July to the C-in-C Third Fleet, Naval Attaché in China and officers resident in Nanking and Hankow, stated flatly that it was anticipated that, '... the present conflict will develop into an all-out war between Japan and China.' On the same date Prince Hiroyasu, Chief of the Naval General Staff, sent Telegram No 1 regarding naval operations, including the following:

'Special orders will be issued for the movement of the 1st and 2nd Combined Air Groups to advance their bases to Formosa, Quelpart Island and Chou-Shui-Tze and for the advance of the 21st and 22nd Air Groups to China.'[63]

This, and related moves, were probably prompted by secret information received by the Chief of Staff, Third Fleet, to the effect that, '... in Shanghai and its vicinity Chinese forces have completed their preparations for immediate action and are planning to take concerted action in every area at any moment. All naval forces are requested to keep strict guard and maintain special prudence until our preparations are completed.'[64]

Also on the 29th the Japanese Naval Attaché at Nanking was instructed to inform the Chinese authorities there[65] that while the Japanese wished to keep the lid on the various incidents and prevent them escalating, anti-Japanese activity and incitement, including proof of a concentration of further Chinese troops in central and south China, required control. If the Chinese failed to do so then the Japanese Third Fleet '... would be forced to take armed action.'

While the Chinese replied that they understood the delicacy of the situation and promised to act, such threats could only ratchet up the tension yet further. And so it proved. News from the north spoke of a great Chinese victory over the Japanese Army which, although false, much emboldened the local populace, and incidents increased. Many of the Japanese residents at Tongzhou in the east of Peking were slaughtered by Chinese rioters on 29 July.[66]

The eastern Peking (Beijing) suburb of Tongzhou formed a buffer-zone between the Japanese Army and the Chinese. It was protected by the East Ji Anti-Communist Autonomous Administration, (also termed the *Kito (Jidong)* government) which had established themselves there. There was a small (about 380 people) Japanese (and Korean, at that time Japanese nationals) presence in the area and a small Japanese Army force was on hand for security. This force was reduced due to pressure elsewhere and the Chinese took this opportunity to vent their hatred on 29 July.

Organised and co-ordinated attacks took place on the remaining Japanese garrison and then the Chinese militia (the so-called 'Tongzhou Guard Troop'), urged on by Li Tsung-jen, a Communist, turned their anger against innocent civilians in the most brutal fashion, sparing nobody. Almost 260 Japanese civilians were butchered by the rampaging mob, which, not content with rape and murder, dismembered the corpses.

Eventually the Japanese troops returned to restore order, but too late for the majority of the compatriots. One soldier of the Japanese relief force, Fumio Sakurai, with No 2 Regiment, later described the horrifying scenes that met their eye on return.

'As we went out of the east gate of the defence area, we saw corpses of Japanese residents, both men and women, laid every few metres. In one restaurant, every victim was beheaded, with both of their hands cut off, and the female victims, if they were more than fourteen or fifteen years of age, all raped... As we entered *Asahiken*, a Japanese restaurant, we saw seven to eight women all stripped off, raped and shot dead; some with a broom pushed into their private parts, others with sand packed into their mouths, and others with their abdomens cut open vertically.'[67]

Photographs taken at the time, especially the series of eighteen by a Swiss photographer, confirmed every sickening detail.[68] The details of this frenzy, when they reached Japan, aroused enormous revulsion and thus, when a fortnight later, on 12 August, 12,000 Chinese troops surrounded 20,000 Japanese civilians in Shanghai, who only had about 1,000 Japanese naval landing troops to protect them, there was widespread alarm.

Eventually, the Chinese administration recognised responsibility and paid reparation, but far too late to influence the ramifications of their day of terror and madness. This is the other side of the coin to the Nanking massacre allegations, and while it does not excuse such a form of revenge, should not be totally ignored.

The Chinese build-up intensified, with the Chinese Air Force deploying sixty of their most modern aircraft, imported American Northrop and Martin bombers, to Kuei-Ten, Hung-Chiao, Hsiao-Kan and other airfields north of the Lung-Hai railway, while increased numbers of reconnaissance flights were made over Japanese naval vessels in the Shanghai and Saddle Island area.

It only required a final spark to ignite the tinder-box and that was duly triggered on 9 August. At 1830hrs that evening the commander of the Western Detachment of the *Rikusentai*, Lieutenant Isao Oyama, along with his driver, Apprentice Seaman Yozo Saito, were ambushed by a Chinese mob purporting to be from the Chinese Peace Preservation Corps, while in their official car near to Hung-Chiao airfield, western Shanghai. The crowd were worked up into a frenzy by left-wing agitators, who falsely accused them of being spies, and the mob killed both men out of hand. Despite further efforts to persuade the Chinese authorities to bring the murderers to book, nothing was done and both sides prepared for the worst. Two days later, at 1030hrs on 11 August, Chinese forces already established in the Shanghai Commercial Press Building began firing machine-guns into the Japanese troops at the Heng-Pang bridge without provocation and this was followed up that same evening by artillery and aircraft attacks against Japanese positions in the Patsu-Ch'iao area, hitting the *Rikusentai* Headquarters, the Consulate Building and warships. The Japanese thus attacked, still only 5,000-strong and hugely outnumbered and outgunned, defending themselves with the inevitable result. Back home the Japanese Government authorised the despatch of regular Army units into the Yellow and Yangtze River areas of Central China. By 15 August the Navy had established the War Preparations Research Committee, which held its first meeting on 23 August 1937. This body took into consideration the effect on the Navy of a prolonged war in China, and the possibility of the eventual intervention on the Chinese side of a third power. These led to firm plans to accelerate new warship construction and modernisation; complete full war preparations; requisition merchant shipping for the needs of the Navy; and most importantly for Egusa and his contemporaries, remodel existing aircraft-carriers and accelerate the manufacture and supply of naval aircraft.

Meanwhile, the first Japanese Army units landed in Shanghai on 23 August, while a further 12,000 Japanese civilians were hastily evacuated from Fuchow, Amoy, Swatow, and Canton in south China to Tsingtao by the ships of the 5th Destroyer Squadron under Rear Admiral Masakichi Okuma.[69] By the middle of August some 50,000 Chinese troops were besieging the 4,000-strong Japanese naval brigade. On 14 August, a dozen Chinese aircraft bombed the Headquarters of the Naval Brigade in Shanghai, attacked the cruiser *Izumo* in the Huangpu River and another Japanese cruiser off Wusong. A Japanese naval air group of medium-sized bombers flew over the Eastern China Sea in the early morning of 15 August to bomb enemy forces at Nanchang.

Further Japanese reinforcements, two divisions of regular troops, landed to the north-east of Shanghai, and, again, the Navy was asked to provide close air support.

In central and southern China, fighting was intense and the dive-bombers were in the thick of it. Japan seized Peking (Beijing) on 8 August. The Chinese took the case to the League of Nations on 12 September as the fighting intensified, and, on 6 October, the United States Government loudly accused Japan of being the aggressor and of violating the Kellogg Peace Pact. During the last week of October, the Japanese Army was strong enough to launch an offensive. This was soon successful everywhere. A Mongolian Federal Autonomous Government was set up on 28 October and on 5 November further Japanese forces landed at Hangchow Bay, and had also reached Shanghai on 9 November and Nanking, the capital, by 13 December.

The Navy assembled all the dive-bomber and fighter units then based at its various home naval air stations, other than those of the Yokosuka Air group, and combined them into the 12th and 13th (Special) Air Groups, under the overall umbrella of the Second Combined Air Group for the duration of the emergency. Their task was to co-operate with both army and naval forces in preserving the peace and trying to contain the outbreak of fighting, and, once this had deteriorated into action, to support the troops' advances. The Japanese Army, in their advances were supported by Navy dive-bombing. Initially all did not go well and some severe losses were suffered but gradually the upper hand was obtained and the missions achieved some notable success.

Egusa and his compatriots had not been trained in the role of supporting land warfare – hitherto all their efforts had been concentrated on attacking shipping – and at this stage mainly conducted convoy escort duties, However, at the front, the inherent accuracy of the dive-bomber proved itself invaluable in this new role. Improvisation saved the day and the young airmen and their supporting ground-crews proved adaptable to a degree matched only by the Luftwaffe in the early stages of the Second World War.

Under Egusa 12 Air Unit was equipped with a dozen Type 94 carrier bombers on 15 July, while 13 Group had eighteen Type 96s. The 12th began preparing for the shift from Saeki Air Base in Kyushu to the Asian continent. Egusa's dive-bombers arrived at Chou Shui Tzu (between Talien and Lushun/Port Arthur on the southern tip of the Liaotung peninsula) on 12 July via Korea. The 12th made the transition without mishap, all eighteen dive-bombers and accompanying fighter squadron putting down safely at the 'Air Gateway to Manchuria' as Chou Shui Tzu was grandly proclaimed.

The reality was somewhat more prosaic, the airfield being a small (400m x 800m) dirt field of bare yellow earth with no actual runway. The facilities were, to say the least, basic, even primitive, and this was especially relevant given the climatic conditions they found on arrival. Egusa and his companions landed in temperatures in excess of 35°C, and worse, the humidity was more than 70 percent. There was no wind to ease the oppressive heat, nor to aid take-offs and landings. Even at night these conditions remained much the same, the aircrew sat and sweated. One eyewitness said that they just drank hot beer, which tasted foul and failed to quench their thirsts and slept as if they were dead men. For six days the whole unit stagnated and although there was some flying, there were no combat incidents and, thankfully given the difficulty in concentrating the mind, no accidents either.

It was not until the end of the first week, on the seventh day of their idleness and frustration, that the order was finally received for all the dive-bombers to arm up with 30kg bombs fitted with instantaneous fuses. Naturally, this led to considerable speculation as to their probably long-awaited target for their first mission. All were keyed up and expectant, never having flown in full war combat conditions before, and were eager to prove themselves in the face of the enemy. The general consensus among Egusa s young pilots was that they were to attack an enemy airfield and that the small bombs would be deadly against parked Chinese aircraft.

The reality proved a terrible let down. Sub-Lieutenant Sadamu Takahashi, the senior flight commander, had been briefed that enemy guerrilla bands had released dozens of sea mines into the tidal water of the upper Liao river, and these had been carried down into Popohai (now Liaotun) Bay presenting a large threat to Japanese shipping bringing in reinforcements and supplies and their naval escorts. Their precise location was, of course, unknown and thus the threat itself was disrupting the whole bay area.

The dive-bombers were assigned the task of locating and then bombing and destroying these mines. This was thought to be a safer and simpler operation than attempting to minesweep the whole bay with ships, but, even so, finding such a small target as a mine floating beneath the surface of the muddy yellow water of the bay was obviously not going to be easy. Egusa himself got down to carrying out his instructions and began to plan a three-plane sortie for his flight scheduled for that same afternoon. But others of the squadron were not so dedicated or certain of the mission. The aircrew began muttering to each other thus:

> 'We are dive-bomber crews. It is not our mission to waste our skill on attacking floating mines.
> 'Even if we find them, we cannot focus on floating mines through a dive-bombing sight. There is no way we can successfully attack them. Cannot the destroyers or minesweepers do the job better?'[70]

This went on for a time, and even in their eyes it could be seen that there was little or no enthusiasm for the task they had been given. Egusa noted their discontent and, in his way, decided to tackle it head-on. He was not leader of the unit, but, as the commander of the squadron that had trained these men he felt it was his responsibility to straighten them out on just where their duty lay. He ordered all hands to gather just before he took off on his own patrol and, according to an eyewitness, addressed them thus:

'I consider this to be a very important duty, even though it is mundane. I will therefore continue this operation for as long as it is ordered. I, myself, will fly the first search, today. Those who remain behind, enjoy games of volleyball!'[71]

The scorn he felt for those who felt that a warrior could pick and choose his missions was made very clear. Takahashi took off with his three-plane flight and carried out a diligent and systematic grid-search search, but in vain. His was the only unit that flew the first day. Egusa still felt strongly about what had occurred that same evening. He told his three aircrews on their return:

'Some people think that men who can't win the "Golden Kite"[72] are not soldiers at all when war breaks out. But these are really "pretend" soldiers who want to go the battlefront for some great exploit for the glory of it. The prime purpose why we are here is to suppress the activities of the enemy air forces in Peking and Shantung provinces. This is correct and right, but I don't want be involved in the second point, which is the struggle between the Army and the Navy as to who is superior. The fighting at the front sounds good for the ears of the people, but I don't like it. I don't desire that such a contest for shallow glory dominates everything. I don't know the full reasons for the war with China, but, *if* it is to be fought, then I want it to be fought calmly and with a lot of care and thought.'[73]

The conditions continued in the same way, and the mine-spotting patrols continued to be flown, but with absolutely no result whatsoever and no mines were ever found, let alone dive-bombed. Even the resolute resolve of Egusa was tried to breaking point. Toward the end of August the dive-bombers were ordered to patrol the narrowest area between the Liaotung and Shantung peninsulas. For a time it appeared that the Japanese were likely to overextend themselves and lose the main issue due to the drive and obsession to make a rapid exploitation. Takahashi recalled that Egusa was very dissatisfied with this shallow approach and wondering himself just why the dive-bombers had been sent to that remote area. Egusa said to Takahashi:

'The distance between Chou Shui Tzu and Peking is six hundred miles. The action radius of the Type 96 bomber is less than half that distance. We cannot even reach Chingtao!'[74]

In other words he considered their mission a waste of skilled aviators. Further conversations revealed that the deep-thinking Egusa was very critical of the way in which these operations had been mounted, as well as of the whole Sino-Japanese conflict. In the end the same thinking finally occurred to Tokyo, and the 12th Air Group was recalled to the Omura Air Base in Kyushu on 31 August.

This proved to be part of the regrouping of forces and soon Egusa and his unit were on the move again, but this time closer to the real fighting. With eighteen fighter aircraft and six reserve planes, and with the same numbers of dive-bombers, the 12th, refreshed and reformed, was moved to Kungda (GongDa) Airfield (which was the former Kungda College ground), which was situated close to the Concession area of Shanghai on 5 September. They were joined there by the 13th Air Group of similar strength on 9 September. Two days later, additional Japanese forces, some three further regular army divisions, one heavy armour brigade and three independent battalions were rushed to the area north of Shanghai.

At the Kungda airfield (the former Kungda College ground), Shanghai, September 1937. From left to right: Lieutenant Mochibumi Sakamoto; Lieutenant Mochibumi Nango; Lieutenant Hajime Tanaka; Lieutenant Takashige Egusa; Lieutenant Shoichi Ogawa and Sub-Lieutenant Sadamu Takahashi. *(Dr Toshimasa Egusa)*

By this time China had mobilised forces some 600,000 strong for the defence of Shanghai and had concentrated their air forces at Nanking. The Japanese Navy knew the efficiency of the Chinese Air Force at that time, because of what they had experienced of their worth during the 1932 fighting. On that occasion three Japanese Type 3 fighters commanded by Lieutenant Mohachiro Tokoro operating from the carrier *Ryujo* had been patrolling over Shanghai on 5 February when they were surprised and attacked by three Chinese fighters in what was the first aerial combat.

The lessons from that earlier period were emphasised by Lieutenant Tokoro to both Takahashi and Egusa, that, as far as both aerial warfare skill and tactics were concerned, the Japanese and Chinese were equals.

The pressure on Egusa and his young pilots was intense and operations were conducted at full stretch. During the earlier advance on Shanghai in August, the 1 Carrier Air Division had been ordered to mount all-out assaults on Chinese positions on 15 August, but typhoon-like conditions kept them grounded. Next day, taking advantage of the Japanese aircraft's absence, the Chinese Army launched a counteroffensive and, for a time, the situation was critical. Both *Hosho* and *Ryujo* were operating from the vicinity of Ma-an Island and began launching their aircraft early that morning despite heavy seas. Despite difficulties in taking off fully laden from the pitching flight-decks, all the carrier aircraft got airborne and bombed Chinese airfields at Chia-Hsing (now called Jiaxing) in Chekiang Province (now Zhejiang), Hung-Chiao (Rainbow Bridge), Chiang-Wan and Ta-Chang-Chen. Their accuracy was first-rate and great success was achieved, ten enemy aircraft and a large hangar were destroyed at the latter base for example, and the nearby railway was also wrecked. Two opposing Chinese fighters were also destroyed in aerial combat. This set the pattern for future navy dive-bomber support from both carrier and land bases.

The 12th and 13th Air Groups were at that time under the command of the Third Fleet, operating off China, The overall commander of the combined attack force was Captain Teizo Mitsunami, Commander of the Second Combined Air Group.

Throughout that month, the dive-bombers of Egusa and his unit had been constantly in demand. On 10 September three carrier-based dive-bombers attacked Chinese field-artillery positions on the Pootung side of the river. Next day fifteen bombed large enemy

Egusa relaxing at a land base in China. *(Dr Toshimasa Egusa via Mitsuharu Uehara).*

concentrations on the Hangchow road. Four dive-bombers carried out an armed reconnaissance of Haimen, Tung-Chou, Soochow, Kahsing and Chiang Chiao on 12 September and the same day saw another twelve hit large enemy units at Ta-Chang-Chen and Liuchiahsing.

Aichi D1A1's carrier bombers (dive-bombers) over China. *(Authors collection)*

Bomb-loads at this stage were primitive. When 1 Attack Unit flew into battle on 22 September, each of the twelve Type 92 carried-based bombers was armed with six standard 60kg bombs only. They were able to place these where they were required, on the target.

On 19 September, Egusa led his bomber *daitai* on its first combat mission, in support of the Army during the intense fighting between Ta-Chang-Chen and Nansiang (NangJing). His dive-bombers were part of a force of seventeen under the overall command of Lieutenant Commander Tetsujiro Wada. They had an escort of twelve A5Ms commanded by Lieutenant Shichitaro Yamashita of the 13th *Kokutai*, with three further fighter aircraft flown from the carrier *Kaga* and led by Lieutenant Chikamasa Igarashi. They were also sixteen reconnaissance seaplanes involved in this combined mission.

The dive-bombers were intercepted by a force of twenty-three Chinese fighters, five Boeing 281's, two CR.32's and sixteen Curtiss Hawks. Three of the Japanese dive-bombers were lost before the defending Japanese Navy escort intervened and dealt with these firmly, shooting down eleven of the Chinese interceptors for the loss of only one Japanese fighter. The surviving D1A1's, including Egusa's *daitai*, were then able to go about their business without further hindrance, but a valuable lesson had been learnt. Between October and November the fighter *daitai* of the 12th had its aging Nakajima A4N1's replaced with the superior Mitsubishi Type 96, A5M fighter, which improved the odds once more.

On 3 October, the first bombing of Nanking by Japanese carrier dive-bombers was planned. The operational instructions were that the eighteen bombers of the 12th Air Group would approach Nanking from the east, cross the city and precision bomb enemy anti-aircraft battery positions at Hsiakuan, in the west corner of the city. The air staff officer of the Second Combined Air Group explained the detail of the sortie thus:

'The main purpose of this operation is not the attack on the military targets (the anti-aircraft gun batteries, machine-gun sites and meteorological observatory), but merely to appear to carry out such an attack in order to lure in enemy fighter aircraft, for us to shoot them down. The dive-bombers are only required to be decoys and thus it will be OK even if your actual bombing is not precise. Set your minds easy, because the enemy's anti-aircraft guns have an effective ceiling of less than 3,000m.'

It was emphasised that the object of the operation by seventy-six aircraft, both fighters and bombers, was to gain command of the air. The impression of the dive-bomber aircrew was that the briefing officer had told them something that he found very difficult to say. He knew that these proud young men would not be happy to be relegated to mere decoys. On the other hand Takahashi thought that his aircrews would be elated to make such an attack if they were told to. He questioned Egusa on the matter. As ever Egusa had thought the matter through beyond just the actual attack. He answered:

> 'It is not easy to gain control of the sky, or to invade enemy space, as long as the enemy still have any fighting spirit. It is certainly impossible to obtain complete air control over a patch of sky with just one attack. The name of "Air-Control Squadron" (fighters) is an honourable title, but meaningless in fact. It is a glory name assigned to satisfy the minds of men who lead the van of the force. Don't resent it, because there have been such inspirational names since the days of Kenshin and Shingen.'[75]

Takahashi agreed with Egusa's analysis, mainly because Lieutenant Mochibumi Nango who was standing close by, fully agreed with Egusa. Nango was already famous as a great fighter ace, and his backing carried considerable weight. He was later to be idolised in the Japanese press as a 'hero of the skies' after he was later killed in action on the China front.

The 12th Air Group's dive-bombers duly took off on this mission from Kunda airfield, Shanghai and headed for Nanking. In overall command of the whole force was the Commanding General of Bombing Force, and also Commander of the First Company, Lieutenant Mochibumi Sakamoto. The Commander of the Second Company was Lieutenant Egusa, and the Commander of the Third Flight of that company was Sub-Lieutenant Sadamu Takahashi. The dive-bombers left Kungda field at 0800hrs on 3 October and routed themselves along the line of the Chang river to Nanking at an altitude of 3,000m. As they made their approach over Purple Mountain they were shocked to their stomachs to be greeted with thick black smoke bursts and fire from massed anti-aircraft batteries located nearby.

It was a matter of faith among Japanese naval officers that the accuracy and hitting rate of the Chinese anti-aircraft fire would be almost zero. At this time the accuracy and rate of hits achieved by the anti-aircraft guns mounted even in the most modern Japanese warships, which used the latest fire-control methods and ranging, with expert gunners, was also almost zero and the Chinese gunners were expected to be far worse than these. This common supposition turned out to be totally wrong. According to Takahashi, the Chinese used a German triangular targeting and ranging system. They had established three widely separate measuring posts at various locations around Nanking and used their observations and calculations to put up a unified barrage from about 100 anti-aircraft guns, of great strength and accuracy. Many of these AA guns had an altitude reach of 5,000m, whereas the Type 94's dive-bombers practical operational ceiling was only 4,000m. In addition the Chinese had seemingly endless numbers of lighter machine-guns, all of which were automatically controlled. It was as sophisticated a barrage system as existed anywhere.

In his memoirs Takahashi ruefully recalled:

'It was foolish of us to show up in the sky over Nanking without being fully aware that such a formidable enemy awaited us. The enemy's first barrage aimed at us was set at 3,000m and was laid down at five second firing intervals, with thirty shells a minute. It was too late that we uttered our cries of surprise because we had all entered the jaws of death. Our surprise at our reception on arrival was almost as tangible as real damage to us.'[76]

Not that actually damage was lacking, the dive-bomber of the Commander, Lieutenant Mochibumi Sakamoto, took a direct hit in the fourth barrage and fell in flames like a shooting star. Despite the loss of their leader, the first company continued straight on their appointed course, threading their way through the barrage exactly as planned, now led by Sub-Lieutenant Shoichi Ogawa. This latter was so worked up to inflict the maximum damage that he later put down on an enemy airfield at Nanchang in order to set fire to enemy planes parked there.

The current dive-bombing practice in the Japanese Navy was for each section to form up in single file at the optimum agreed diving point and commence the dive in line astern toward the target. In other words, each dive-bomber, in strict succession, started their dive from exactly the same point, one after the other. It resulted in each dive-bomber passing through a fixed spot, allowing the enemy to concentrate their cone of fire on this point for the maximum effect. This method of dive-bombing was nicknamed by the Japanese pilots with some sarcasm, as 'swimming exercise on the mats.' Thus after the leader, the fifth aircraft was also shot down at the same position as the Sakamoto and was lost.

However, the commander of the second company, Lieutenant Egusa, was smart and sharp. His aircraft had been positioned tenth in line behind Sakamoto and he had time to assess the situation. Egusa turned 90 degrees left as soon as he saw the second dive-bomber hit, and the enemy's barrage moved to follow him, bursting to his right-hand side, and ahead. Takashige saw the damage taken by the leading section and decided to change his method of attack dive. Takahashi and other members of the second section followed Egusa's lead, which saved them from the fate of the leading group. Within a short time the Chinese barrage fire began to adjust and follow them round and Takahashi closed with Egusa's aircraft at top speed, spurred on by another barrage that exploded close astern. He made frantic hand signals to his flight members to increase their own speeds likewise, but they didn't fully understand the meaning of his hand gestures.

How very much longer it seemed to Takahashi than the five minutes it took to fly across the city of Nanking, even at full speed in an effort to escape from the blazing hell of exploding shells. To their great relief the further anti-aircraft firing failed to inflict further losses. Once the barrage fire fell away astern, Egusa turned his unit back around to complete his assigned mission, which was to attack the enemy anti-aircraft positions emplaced in front of the Chinese National Party Head Office at Hsiakuan. Egusa was determined to exact a fitting revenge for the two lost aircrew. Once over the target he led into the dive at 60 degrees. The enemy 13mm machine-guns now joined in the barrage in a desperate attempt to deter them, with an eyewitness describing their fire as red ice-candy chains lancing up at them, but in vain. All the dive-bombers released on target. Sub-Lieutenant Takahashi pulled out of his dive at an altitude of 600m and escaped out over the Chang river, where Egusa was flying zigzag formation awaiting his unit to reassemble on him. Thankfully Egusa counted every aircraft and found none had been lost. They put down their narrow escape from near-certain death to Takashige's quick reaction and the taking of proper steps to meet the unexpected situation they found themselves in.

On landing back at Kunda field the aircrew disembarked from their machines and stood in a row before Second Combined Air Group HQ. They found out that the fighters led by Lieutenant Nango had shot down seven of the enemy fighters as a result of the attack.

They could see that the Commander and other ranking officers were beside themselves with this good result, but they heard not a single word of condolence from either the Commander or his four staff officers, for the deaths of four dive-bomber aircrew sacrificed to make this victory possible for the fighters.

Egusa glared at the Air Staff Officer who had originally briefed them, standing silent before the Commander and made his report to him, curt and brief, as if not trusting himself to say more. He spoke in a loud, raging tone, that almost made the tents of the HQ tremble, but all that Egusa said was:

'The enemy's anti-aircraft guns reached the altitude of 3,000m.'[77]

He then turned on his heel and walked back to the tents of the dive-bomber squadron without a single glance back at his superiors. Takahasi followed his lead again, and felt that the four dive-bomber men killed in the action might at least be able to rest in peace because of Egusa's words.

Maybe also because of Egusa's words, lessons were learnt from this first attack and a different attack plan was drawn up for the next operation, which took place on 10 October. The dive-bombers made a surprise attack from the direction of the Chang river to Hsiakuan adopting a staggered 'slant row' formation, and passed over the city of Nanking at a very low altitude giving the enemy defences no time to compute their course and speed. Although the direct hit rate of their bombing dropped a little by not using full dive-bombing, they incurred absolutely no losses in this second raid.

It was on this raid that Egusa again made an outstanding contribution. The unreliability of the Type 96's engine was well known, and had been since 1935. On this occasion Egusa's mount started emitting black smoke from the engine exhaust immediately after he had delivered his bombs directly on top of the Hsiakuan gun battery. To put out the fire Takashige steered his aircraft almost to the surface of the water and then rapidly climbed again. He repeated this dangerous manoeuvre three more times before making a safe landing back at Kungda. Despite this, accidents by crashing into the ground out of control, caused by this poor engine, continued to take a toll and did not cease after war had broken out. Some pilots became resigned to an early death from such a mishap if not from enemy action and clearly surrendered themselves to their fate.

The twenty-year-old Egusa's approach was very different to these 'already lost' pilots. He studied technical manuals and the engine instruction books, often reading them in his tent past midnight in order to learn how to prepare and overcome such accidents, although this was not a pilot's job. Thus he knew what to do when the inevitable happened and lived to tell the tale when others might not have come back.

During October the Japanese naval aircraft working out of Kunda had a total of fifteen 'carrier bombers' (dive-bombers) on its combined strength. They bombed and strafed the retreating Chinese troops during the ensuing rout. The Japanese dive-bombers were flying almost daily missions in support of Japanese marines hard-pressed at Te-Chih. And so it continued.

The 12th carried out their third sortie against Nanking on 12 October. This time they made their initial approach in a single line over the Chang river and then made a combined sharp left turn together, and headed in once more against the anti-aircraft batteries at Hsiakuan. On this occasion the third aircraft of the second flight in the first company was seen to break formation and make a turn to the north back toward the Chang river in order to escape the enemy barrage. Takahashi saw that aircraft leaving the formation in front of him, but he lost sight of it. That same aircraft seemed to miss the return formation of the dive-bombers after the attack also and did not rejoin until it landed at Kunda.

Other keen eyes had not missed the deflection. As commander of the squadron, Egusa cautioned the pilot of that aircraft very privately. It was not a severe reprimand for the young pilot, but it was a sharp caution from his leader that he could not make his own rules, for his own sake and for the good of the unit. However, that same pilot performed the same actions on the fourth sortie, which took place toward the end of the month.

This second insubordination Egusa dealt with summarily. The pilot had been granted a second chance, and had failed to take it. After the dive-bombers had landed back at Kunda field, Egusa strode over to the offending pilot and there and then before everyone, stripped the wing markings from the man's uniform and flung them to the ground. He then strode away without uttering a word to the youth and finished writing out his battle report to the Commander of the Second Combined Air Group.

Takahashi had repeatedly told this pilot, before each of the sorties, that he was not to leave his position in the battle formation, but the pilot was a boy of just eighteen, wilful and obstinate. He seemed to enter combat without any thought of his orders. But Egusa's action got through to him. Takahashi recalled how he had called this boy over to a corner of the airfield after sunset that day. The pilot was sobbing, striking his head with his hand and crying at the humiliation Takashige had handed out to him. Takahashi wished to be kind to the young pilot but could not, because there were ground crew in hearing distance who could listen to what was being said. They were openly contemptuous of the boy, calling him a coward. 'I have never hated the dirtiness of a group of people, who cover their selfishness by speaking ill of others, deeper than I did at that time,' Takahashi recalled many years later.[78]

There was a sequel to these events. About a week later this same young pilot came to Takahashi in the evening to persuade the latter to allow him to join the next attack sortie, planned for the following day. The pilot seemed in good spirits and his face now held colour whereas in the week before his agony of spirit had drained all such from his youthful face. Gazing into the boy's eyes Takahashi seemed to find vigour fearless to anything and a determination to make good. Takahashi, therefore, took the pilot to Egusa who likewise gazed into the pilot's eyes for a long time, without a word being spoken. It was assumed that Egusa had granted permission for the sortie for Egusa's own eyes were moist with tears at the young man's decision.

Next day the pilot joined the formation, but flew without his radio operator. He took part in the dive-bombing approach but made no effort to pull out of his dive and deliberately crashed his dive-bomber straight into an enemy anti-aircraft battery located at the Nanking Central Arsenal. Whether he had survived this mission or not, pilots who fled in the face of the enemy were automatically sentenced by the Japanese Navy to be shot by firing squad after a brief court martial. There was no way any mitigation would have been given to him for cowardice in the face of the enemy and he knew it. Egusa would not have spoken of the incident, but all had seen it, not once, but twice. He never spoke of it but those around him felt that he approved of the manner of the pilot's death and atonement.

Egusa's reputation grew, even the enemy acknowledged his prowess, though not always for the right reasons. It was common for the Chinese to distribute propaganda leaflets of particular Japanese they wanted to find and execute showing their photos and offering a reward for their capture. Prize money for the arrest of Egusa was the

Lieutenant Egusa at home in Ashida-machi, Fukuyama City, Hiroshima Prefecture, during a period of leave from the China front. From left to right: His eldest brother Kazumi; his mother Kita; Takashige; and his cousin Sakae.
(Dr Toshimasa Egusa via Mitsuharu Uehara).

highest for any aviator because the Chinese considered him to be the top leader, due to the size and quality of his moustache![79]

In total, the 12th Squadron made eleven dive-bombing sorties against strictly military targets in Nanking before the city fell to the Japanese. Referring to these sorties, Takahashi told the historian Mitsuharu Uehara:

> 'We certainly did not attack Chinese private houses because we had a sense of the same family with the Chinese. There was just no sense in doing that. Confronting the enemy's anti-aircraft fire, our carrier dive-bomber squadron did our best to hit the Chinese Government's war machine. We did not do such attacks on civilians as we would have been criticised by international law.'[80]

The Japanese Government issued a communiqué at the end of September 1937, which stated categorically:

> 'Bombing targets are limited to military targets only and bombings are executed accurately with the utmost care.'

By and large any neutral analysis of the precision dive-bombing of the

Navy's 12th and 13th *Kokutai* confirm this to be a true and authenticated fact. However, in the subsequent general condemnation of the Japanese occupation of Nanking, with its allegations of mass murder and rape, along with the fact that Japan withdrew from the League of Nations, world opinion came down firmly against her, whether the allegations were partly true or mainly black propaganda.[81]

At this time the Chinese Army abandoned the defence of Nanking, many thousands of them throwing away their uniforms and merging with the civilian population, and fell back upon Chungching. Egusa also left mainland China. On 1 December 1937, Egusa, freshly promoted to Lieutenant was reassigned to command the Air Company of the aircraft-carrier *Ryujo*, which was reassigned as a training carrier. Here Takashige devoted himself to the training his student aircrew in take-off and landings at sea, interspersed with military duties, mainly flying air patrols and searches off the Chinese coast to maintain the blockade and remained aboard her when she returned to Japan.

Meanwhile, with the fall of Nanking in December, both the 12th and 13th *Kokutais,* lacking the sound thought and careful control of Egusa, moved base to nearby Daikojo and then flew combat missions against Nanchang and Hankow with great success. There were also some mistakes of judgement however, which Egusa might have well prevented had he still be present. The most famous of which involving the dive-bomber forces, was the attacking and sinking of the United States gunboat *Panay* on 12 December 1937. The dive-bombers of the 2nd Combined Air Group under Rear Admiral Teizo Mitsunami were assisting the Japanese Army in their continued advance. The *Panay* was a 474-ton river gunboat built at Shanghai for the US Navy's Asiatic Fleet in 1928, and armed with two 3-in guns and eight.30 calibre machine guns. She was commanded by Lieutenant Commander James J. Hughes. A rump group of four US Embassy staff had remained in Nanking until the last moment before the city fell to the Japanese Army and *Panay* was ordered to embark these, along with four US nationals and five foreign personnel on 11 December. *Panay* sailed, escorting three American-owned Socony Vacuum Oil Company river tankers, the *Mei Ping*, *Mei Hsia* and *Mei An*.[82] They headed up-river in the wake of a similar British convoy, and the local Japanese Navy commander was duly notified of their movements to avoid incidents. A Japanese landing barge stopped the group and was notified of their intentions, whereupon they were allowed to proceed.

However, according to American historian Samuel Eliot Morison,[83] there were many pro-war *Kodo* factions in the Japanese Army, and one of these, a certain Colonel Hashimoto, who had been involved in the assassination attempts on the Government earlier, authorised the deliberate shelling of the *Panay* and her convoy as they passed his artillery positions, but fortunately no hits were scored. Hashimoto's objective was said to be to provoke the United States into a declaration of war, thus eliminating all weak and corrupt civilian influence from the Japanese Government as part of the so-termed 'Showa Restoration Plot.' No mention of this incident is contained in the Court of Enquiry, however. Apparently it was not Hashimoto but another army unit that actually ordered the Navy air force to destroy any and all shipping on the Yangtze river above Nanking which they stated were Chinese vessels evacuating key Nationalist Army personnel. This was a deliberate falsehood and the Navy, knowing of the American and British convoys, queried the order, only to be told to carry it out.

After anchoring off Hoshien, some twenty-seven miles north of the capital, the next morning to hoist US flags and paint others on their sides and decks, the *Panay* group was found by Japanese Navy aircraft at 1327 and the air attacks started. *Panay* was near-missed forward by an initial strike by three high-altitude aircraft and then attacked by six dive-bombers and nine strafing fighter aircraft. The dive-bombers 'attacked from ahead, diving singly and appearing to concentrate on the USS *Panay*. A total of about twenty bombs were dropped, many striking close aboard and creating by fragments and concussions great damage to the ship and personnel. These attacks lasted about twenty minutes during which time at least two of the planes attacked also with machine-guns.' Furthermore these dive-bombers were, 'unmistakingly *(sic)* identified by their markings as being Japanese.'[84] *Panay* was abandoned by her crew and her passengers and boarded by the Japanese, but she sank at 1554. Two of her crew were killed and forty-eight passengers and crew injured in the attacks. Japanese army landing craft closed the sinking ships and machine-gunned survivors struggling in the water. One of the tankers, *Mei An*, was also sunk and her captain, Carl H Carlson and many of her crew also killed. The other two tankers got clear, only to be sunk in further air attacks further upstream, despite attempts by Japanese army forces nearby trying to stop the assault by waving Japanese flags and suffering casualties in the attempt.

The same day as the USS *Panay* incident, Japanese Navy dive-bombers attacked two British gunboats, HMS *Cricket* and HMS *Ladybird*, which were anchored upstream of the Chinese capital. Fortunately the two Royal Navy vessels were recognised during the attack, and the assault was called off before any hits had been scored. The British ships returned downstream to rescue their American colleagues but found only the two abandoned and sinking wrecks and *Panay's* launch.

The US Ambassador lodged an immediate protest and, eventually the Japanese Government accepted responsibility for what they claimed was an 'unintentional' attack. They paid an indemnity to America on 22 April 1938,[85] much to the relief of a pacifist and isolationist American people, and war was avoided. This, despite the fact that a United States Naval Court of Enquiry held at Shanghai, heard ample evidence that the attack was deliberate and cold-blooded.[86]

However, Commander Okumiya, who was a pilot in the dive-bomber squadron that sank the *Panay*, claimed that the attack was initiated not by Colonel Hashimoto, but by Army Intelligence. It is strange that the Japanese Naval Attaché, who knew the truth, had no input on this naval operation. Okumiya also claims that these naval fliers failed to recognise the USS *Panay* but mistook her and her convoy for Chinese merchant ships, which again, does not say very much for warship recognition in the Japanese Navy.[87]

Meanwhile, after a short refit in Japan, *Ryujo* resumed operational flying in mid-March 1938, when she joined the 2nd Carrier Division with *Sōryū*. But even these routine duties brought episodes of high drama that, yet again, demonstrated Egusa's dogged determination to stick by a decision once he had made a considered judgement, in the face of strong opposition.

Sub-Lieutenant Sadamu Takahashi, who had fought with Egusa in the battle line in China, had also been assigned to *Ryujo* and so they continued to serve together. At the start of September 1938, *Ryujo* was working in the area of Tinian, Saipan and Rota islands in the Marianas. The purpose of this cruise was to continue aircrew training in the conditions of intense heat and condition the new aircrew.

On the morning of 7 September, Takahashi took off from *Ryujo's* flight deck with a wingman, in a position some 100 miles south-west of Rota Island at 0700hrs. This was part of a navigation and communication training flight of some six hours duration by the two

Type-96 dive-bombers. Unfortunately, on the return leg, the two dive-bombers were swallowed up by a rapidly-developing typhoon, which was building up fast some fifty miles out from the carrier.

They stuck to their course but, on arrival at the point where their mother ship should have been awaiting for them, there was only empty sea. The *Ryujo* herself had been caught up in the storm. There was terrible air turbulence, which tossed the little biplanes around like kites, and heavy driving rain, with frequent squalls and strong gusts of wind. It was a nightmare scenario for an expert pilot, let alone novices. Had the two aircraft not been sturdily built dive-bombers, and so designed to sustain 12G stress, they would have broken up in mid-air. As it was their fate seemed certain until, with great relief, Sub-Lieutenant Takahashi caught a glimpse of the blacker shadow of the *Ryujo* against the darkness and through the murk, and was joined by his wingman.

Finding the carrier was one thing, Takahashi later recalled, getting aboard was something else. They could see the carrier thrusting her bows into violent waves. She was rolling continually more than 30 degrees and scooping up the waves over her flight deck. Great cataracts of water were washing over the flight deck and cascading down her sides. Surely it was impossible to land back aboard her in such appalling conditions?

The commanding officer of the *Ryujo* at this time was Captain Kanae Kosaka. He called Egusa to the bridge and told him: 'Let the two Type 96 bombers make forced landings on Rota Island, it is the only way to save them.' At this time Rota Island was Japanese mandated territory and the aircraft would be secure. Egusa disagreed, and said so: 'Oh, no. Let them land back aboard the *Ryujo*! It will be OK provided Takahashi does it.'

Captain Kosaka was appalled. 'The ship's stabiliser will be broken in such a sea!'

'I don't care about that, Sir!' responded Egusa.

'Let him make a forced landing at Rota', the Captain insisted and again Egusa refused to agree for reasons of his own which he had already worked out in his head, 'Oh, no, NO. Let him land on the flight deck!' Takashige refused to concede to his captain's point of view.[88]

Circling over the mother-ship Takahashi wondered why he had received no indication of permission to land. After some twenty agonising minutes he at last saw the *Ryujo* begin to turn to windward as her stabiliser started to take effect. Egusa had dug his heels in and won the argument, Captain Kosaka risked wrecking the ship's stabiliser. Soon the heavier rolling of the carrier eased and then stopped. There were still spindrifts of waves washing over the wheels of the dive-bombers as they bounced down on *Ryujo's* deck which were extremely dangerous, but Takahashi used his skill and expertise to steady his skidding aircraft, keeping her straight until the tail hook caught the wire arrestor cable and brought her to a halt on the wet deck. There were no injuries. His companion aircraft followed him and he also touched down and was safely secured.

Later it was revealed that both aircraft had just enough fuel remaining for less that one hour's flying time. Egusa had worked it out, there was just no way to save the two aircraft other than risk the deck landing, for Rota Island was at least 100 miles distant, and the Type-96 could not have covered that distance in those conditions in the time left to them.

Takashige had again stuck to his guns, but had put his neck on the line once more. Commander Susumu Takaoka, two years Egusa's junior at Etajima, and also aboard *Ryujo* during this incident, told Mitsuharu Uehara that not only would his superiors have had his hide but that:

> 'Captain Egusa would have censored himself had the two bombers failed to land safely back on board. Captain Egusa was a man who drew a sharp line between something possible and something impossible, and held out for what was possible.'[89]

Reaching Rota would have been impossible and two aircraft would have been lost with both sets of aircrew; landing back aboard the *Ryujo* was possible, even if extremely risky and so Egusa held out for that and was justified. Care for his men had always been one of Egusa's claims on the aviators who served with him, and such incidents quickly went round the fleet, reinforcing that trust in his judgement, a trust that was soon to extend to the highest levels of the Navy. If there was a dive-bomber problem to be fixed, Egusa was the man to do it. But *only* after careful consideration.

The carriers eventually returned home to refurbish their air groups in 1938, before returning to the war. In October 1938 Egusa joined the Kuangtung Operation as Commander of the Dive Bomber *Daitai*, again aboard the *Ryujo*. Along with the carrier *Sōryū*, the two ships forming the 2nd Carrier Division, the *Ryujo* operated in the

South China Sea for the next twenty days, supporting the new Army operations ashore.

On 12 October a strong force had landed unopposed at Bias Bay (Ta-Ya Bay) just to the east of Hong Kong, and quickly advanced toward Canton (currently known as Kwangchow). The operation was deigned to open a second front against Chiang Kai-shek's armies who were already stretched in trying to defend the Wuhan-Hankow (Wuchang) area, then already under threat from Japan's 'Yangtze upstream operation.' The South China Navy Force (5th Fleet) gave support to Lieutenant-General Mikio Furusho's 21st Army ashore. The Japanese met little opposition in the air either and had control of the skies for most of the time. By 21 October Canton itself had fallen, and the vital fortress of Humen on the Chu river fell on the 23rd. Two days later Samshui to the west was taken. To the north, two days later, Japanese troops marched into both Hankow and Wuhan, forcing the Chinese Government into another hasty departure, this time to Choneqing. By November the ease of the operation led to the recall of the carriers back to Japan once more.

Life was not all fighting and aerial battles for Egusa at this period, however, as this lull would show. In the brief periods of leave back home in Japan he was invited to the home of Okamura, and introduced to, courted and won the heart of Kiyoko Okamura. Although the nation was advanced in technology, much about Japan remained traditional and their courtship was in the highly formal and stylised manner, which, in the west, would have been considered 'Victorian' in the extreme. It was the practice then for influential parties to bring together suitable young couples with a view to marriage but it was the sister of another Navy pilot that had caught Egusa's eye. Motoharu Okamura was to become as famous a pilot to fighters as Takashige Egusa was to dive-bombers, and in the last years of the Second World War, he was appointed commander of the 'divine thunder' Corps of kamikaze pilots. However, that lay far ahead and undreamt of.

During the successful Kuangda campaign, Lieutenant-Commander Okamura, then the flight leader of the 12th Air Group's fighter squadron, was much taken by Egusa's personality while they were flying and fighting together over central China. Even at this date Okamura had won high renown as a pilot and as a trainer and developer of new air fighting tactics in the Navy. Together with Yoshito Kobayashi and Minoru Genda, Okamura united to form an acrobatics team called the 'air circus.' This group did stunt flying with the Type 90 carrier fighters when the naval arsenal had been established at Yokosuka in 1932. He was said to have iron nerves and could recognise similar qualities and skills in Egusa in combat conditions. So impressed was Okamura by Egusa that he determined that there could be no finer potential bridegroom than Egusa for his beautiful younger sister Kiyoko, although there were many naval air officers of higher rank who aspired to that honour.

CHAPTER SIX

Courtship and Marriage

'Two Butterflies leave a dream and fly into the May Sky.'
Takashige Egusa

Lieutenant-Commander Motoharu Okamura, commander of the fighter unit of the 12th Squadron in China, while serving with Lieutenant Egusa, quickly decided in his own mind that he embodied all the most admirable attributes, in life, leadership and combat, and in both thought and deed. Indeed, so impressed was Motoharu by Egusa's whole attitude that he came to the conclusion that there really could be no other naval air officer suitable as a potential husband for his young sister Kiyoko.[90]

The beautiful girl who won Egusa's heart. Miss Kiyoko Okamura in 1938. She was the sister of the famous naval fighter pilot Captain Motoharu Okamura, who was serving on the central China front with Takashige at this time. He had invited Takashige to his home during a period of leave because he felt him to be the man worthy of his sister. It is said that Takashige carried this photo of her always when he was assigned to land duty.
(Dr Toshimasa Egusa via Mitsuharu Uehara)

Kiyoko herself was a highly intelligent and spirited girl, who had graduated from Tsuda College in Tokyo, but had since selflessly devoted her time and talent to caring for and tutoring her mother in the family home in the city, without thinking of her own career or marriage prospects. She was a beautiful girl with many potential suitors but Motoharu thought none matched the young Lieutenant of dive-bombers who fought so well alongside him and disposed himself so diligently when between missions.

The Combined Fleet entered Beppu Bay, Kyushu, in December 1938, with the 12th Group re-embarked aboard its carrier, and this gave Motoharu his opportunity. He invited Takashige to visit him at his home in Beppu City, the occasion superficially being to celebrate Okamura being appointed Flight Leader of the Oita Air Group. Accepting the hand of friendship, Egusa did not know his friend had an ulterior motive.

Meanwhile Kiyoko was instructed by her brother to make sure she waited at her brother's home for the same reason! The other navy guest invited to the meeting was Lieutenant Kazuo Nishioka, a fellow classmate of Egusa's at Etajima, who was also kept in the dark about the true reason for the get-together. Jokingly, Takashige said: 'It will be very good for me if the other guest is the Flight Leader's sister!' as he had been shown photographs of Kiyoko and had been smitten. But when he learned that (officially) the other guest was to be Nishioka, he was perplexed, although he knew that Nishioka came from the same province of Kochi Prefecture, Shikoku, as Okamura.

When they all assembled at the house, Kiyoko was introduced to the two young officers by her brother, but was so excited she became confused as to which one was Egusa and was unable to recognise him. Then she heard one officer speaking in the Kochi dialect and knew it must be Lieutenant Nishioka. She recalled how she held her breath as she then realised that the other young man, with the fine moustache, must be Egusa of whom she had heard so much from her brother. As usual, the outwardly taciturn Takashige, was silently drinking his *sake*, and just nodding at the conversations of the other two men, while watching her. Kiyoko, still uncertain and shy of Egusa, cut short her stay in Beppu after this initial meeting and returned home to her mother, her head a whirl.

Next day, Takashige's mother, made the journey from Fukuyama to Beppu to meet the girl who might be the wife of her son, but arrived after Kiyoko had left to return to Tokyo, so did not see her. Takashige, as was his way, made no explanation of her absence to his mother, but instead, found lodgings for her at a nearby inn in Beppu. His first meeting with Kiyoko decided Takashige's fate, for as always with him, there was no hesitation, and the dictates of his own heart took over. To his friends at that time, for the first time, he seemed disorientated and not himself, a feeling which all those who have known first love can sympathise. He took his mother up in his aircraft during her stay there, but, far from handling it gently for her initiation, threw the machine around at low altitude. Kita was much taken aback by her son's strange behaviour. Egusa appeared to be in a considerably wild state, when normally he always stayed cool and calm. It is said that even the chambermaid at the inn was surprised by Takashige's agitation 'blue face' when he first escorted his mother there. It seemed it was unable, for once, to conceal his emotions.

Attracted though the couple were to each other the correct formalities had to be undergone.

By February 1939, after much fussing between the families, eventually the marriage of Kiyoko to Takashige was formally arranged. Tadashi Nakajima, another Etajima classmate of Egusa, was appointed as *nakoudo* (matchmaker) and accordingly visited Lieutenant-Commander Okamura's house in Beppu for the formal exchange of betrothal presents, following the traditional rite known as *Yui-no*. These presents, by ancient precedent, consisted of two fresh sea bream, three bottles of *sake* and two sets of silk. The sea-bream were much-honoured gifts, always used to mark auspicious occasions. The bride-to-be was given an *Obi*, as her main gift, which represented female virtue, whilst the bridegroom-to-be's fidelity was expressed by a *hakama* skirt.

It is recorded that Nakajima's verbal message at the exchange of *yui-no* was 'original' 'Egusa is simple and honest, but please accept these presents', was how he phased it, which, while being the actual truth, was a rather awkward way of putting it to say the least. In truth, Nakajima felt rather overawed by the occasion and the stern presence of a very senior naval officer, for Okamura, who accepted the gifts formally, sat silent and straight before him. Nakajima very much later confessed to Kiyoko that, while he had willingly accepted the duty of conveying the *yui-no* as a favour to his friend, that was not how he had meant the announcement to come out!

Lieutenant Tadashi Nakajima, Egusa's good friend, who acted as messenger between Egusa and his bride-to-be Kiyoko. *(Dr Toshimasa Egusa via Mitsuharu Uehara)*

Nakajima returned to say that the gifts had been accepted, which marked the couple's formal engagement, and they received the heartfelt congratulations from families and friends alike.[91]

Once the engagement had been thus announced and accepted by the brother of the bride, Egusa's visits to Okamura's house became frequent as he paid court to Kiyoko and the couple came to know each other better. When Okamura's first wife died, he took a woman as his second wife. Okamura's other children soon became firm friends. Both Takehiko (the son) and Yoko (the elder daughter) became close and both referred to the sister's suitor as their 'uncle moustache.' But this was in stark contrast to their stepmother, about who both appeared very luke-warm and they made little effort to get close to her. It was said that Egusa used to bathe with Takehiko, '... to wash the dirt off Takehiko's hands' when he visited the new Mrs Okamura which, if the phase is recalled correctly, gives some indication of how things stood! However, Egusa loved them both regardless of this.

The date of the marriage between Takashige and Kiyoko was fixed for the end of October in Tokyo, which was the soonest that Takashige could get sufficient leave time away from his ship and his squadron. In the meantime, Kiyoko spent time alternately back and forth between her mother's house in Tokyo and her brother's house in Beppu, Kyushu. The young couple's first date, time alone together for once, was a trip by train from Beppu to Tomitaka,[92] some sixty kilometres south of Beppu, which was the Naval Air Training base where Egusa was working as a dive-bomber instructor, taking batches of new converts and teaching them the skills in the old reliable *Suisei* biplane. Egusa came to call for her at her brother's house in Beppu, and said, 'I'd like to borrow Kiyoko-san!' (San being a general honour title in Japan corresponding with Miss, Mr and Mrs in

A sketch of Egusa, seen drawing a frog in an animal pictorial book in his personal cabin
aboard the aircraft carrier *Ryujo* off China. This portrait was by Lieutenant Tadashi
Nakajima, commander of the fighter squadron aboard the same ship and a good friend
and companion of Takashige. *(Dr Toshimasa Egusa via Mitsuharu Uehara)*

English), which later became his standard joke greeting for their
assignations. The young couple then journeyed to Tomitaka by rail.
Unfortunately, Kiyoko was far from fully well at this time, although
that did not stop her going of course. She had lost weight and had
mild tonsillitis at that time. The weather was moderate, neither too
hot nor too cold for their journey, but the train had to pass through
several long tunnels *en route* and, however hard they tried to shut up
the windows at those times, the smoke from the engine found its way
into the compartment and further inflamed her throat. Although
Kiyoko did her best to not inhale the smoke by covering her nose and
mouth with her handkerchief and the loose sleeves of her *kimono*, by
the time they reached the inn at their destination that evening, she
was in considerable pain and had a fever.

Although Egusa wanted to stay with her, he could not, for he had
to take a dusk training flight that very same evening. Poor Kiyoko was
thus left to her own devices in a strange inn with no companion and
feeling very bad. It was far from an auspicious start to their courtship.

On their second date, the next month, May, they planned to climb Mount Aso. This mountain is part of one of the most famous holiday resort areas in Kyushu and is located some seventy kilometres north-west of Tomitaka (the present-day city of Hyuga). The climbing of the mountain was a suggestion from Takashige, who suggested they do this the next time his ship entered Beppu Bay with the fleet, because he felt there would be no time for them to enjoy another such trip by themselves in the increasing bleak war conditions. Kiyoko recalled he seemed preoccupied with the thought that their precious time in each other's company was a treasure which they should make the most of, as time was fast running out and the international situation darkened each day. Alas, Egusa was to be proven only too correct in this prediction.

Takashige's plan aroused considerable opposition from those around Kiyoko, who felt that it was not proper for them to make the trip as a couple when they were still only engaged and had not yet had their wedding. Kiyoko recalled that she herself hesitated about what to do for a time. Egusa told Kiyoko: 'the wedding is to swear the marriage between you and me in front of God and man. It will, therefore, make no difference if we sexually unite before the ceremony. Let us cancel the trip if you feel even a little uneasy. If not, then trust me, and let us make these several vacation days full of really pleasurable and beautiful memories for our lifetimes.'

Kiyoko immediately made up her mind to go, on hearing this statement. She later recalled that she instantly believed that here was an admirable and sincere man, to whom she was ready to entrust her life. She was to state of this moment:

> 'He may have appeared very stoical to people at that time, but he was, I could feel, a real man of freedom far removed from stoicism. Generally speaking, men have more-or-less self-centred characters. However, Takashige was admirable free of such a trait, and always showed consideration and sympathy for everyone. He just did not show self-seeking ostentation toward others.'

Accordingly, her mind made up and the decision made, Kiyoko waited at her brother's house in Beppu, welcomed Egusa there and together they set out for the slopes of Mount Aso in high spirits on a fine May day. They covered the first part of the ascent, from the foot of the mountain as far up as the eighth staging post romantically by way of a horse-drawn carriage with a bell, then descended and completed the journey to the summit on foot. She was awe-struck on looking down into the vast crater, but already gentians were flowering in the shade of the mountain on the way to the summit, tingeing them in spring with the colours of autumn. Even more than forty years on from that day, Kiyoko clearly remembered in her mind's eye the neat gentian flowers, seemingly blooming just for them.

The young couple stayed at the inn at the eighth staging post that night. There were hardly any other visitors staying there at that time and Kiyoko enjoyed her bathing. In fact, there was only one other visitor, Takashige in the men's bath, so that they could enjoy bathing adjacent to each other for a long time and exchanging conversation across the separating board wall between them. As a result of this extended bath, added to the natural fatigue of the long journey, Kiyoko's frail health broke down again. Her fever rose from 39 degrees that evening, to 40 degrees by the following morning and her tonsillitis worsened dramatically. Her throat filled with a white pus and she was in such pain and agony that she was unable to even drink water. Ice bags failed to abate the fever and a doctor was called from the foot of the mountain to attend her. He arrived in haste by horse and found Kiyoko on the borders of consciousness and half asleep most of the time. In her delirium she kept telling herself she must not let go, but return, for their vacation was only to last for three precious days. She was later told she kept repeating over and over, 'let us come back.'

Kiyoko was also told by the maidservant that Takashige continually changed the instantly-melting ice-bags on her forehead, and that his eyes were moist with tears at her condition. After a long period, Kiyoko's fever started to abate a little and she was through the worst, although not yet safe. She slept peacefully for a time and later recalled how she dreamt of two butterflies playing in the May fields. She smiled because they were so pretty and vivid. When she awoke, Takashige questioned her. 'What is the matter with you, why do you smile?' She recorded that she told him how she had dreamt of the two butterflies playing happily. Egusa took a sheet of paper and began to write.

In seconds he held up a *Haiku*[93] and read it out to her:

'*Cho futatsu yume o nukedashi, satsuki zora.*'[94]

Eventually her high fever subsided, thanks in part to the medicines she received and the warm care Egusa lavished upon her, and she was able to recover sufficiently to drink fruit juice to ease her throat. She was invigorated. They had come to Mount Aso to get pleasant memories for later, but the fever lasted the whole period. Despite this, Kiyoko only remembered this journey with affection as they symbolised the bloom of their devotion to each other. Over the whole three-day period Kiyoko partook only of water and fruit juice, nonetheless, with the resilience of youth, she was able to stand and make her way down the mountain safely, when their time limit came at the end of the vacation.

During the whole subsequent period of their courtship, Kiyoko recalled that her frail health, with bouts of fevers and whooping cough (another killer in those days), continued to be a source of anxiety to Takashige, but that, regardless of it all, he took it all in his stride and accepted her as she was, always expressing concern and care. Following this traumatic trip, she undertook many further such trips with Egusa, whenever his carrier was in port, but with complete peace of mind and tranquillity. Kiyoko gave Takashige her photo and he carried it in his personal bag everywhere whenever his unit moved to other land bases in Japan. He also wrote long and beautifully scripted letters to her at every opportunity.

By the middle of May, following the Mount Aso journey, Kiyoko had sufficiently recovered to make the long journey, along with her own mother, to meet Takashige's mother and family in the village of Arima, near Fukuyama City. On arrival Takashige's eldest brother, Kazumi, thanked her for her devotion. Egusa's father Kyuemon had died on 8 December 1938, and Takashige had returned home to attend the funeral service. His eldest brother, as was the tradition in Japan as well as the west, had inherited the family home and lands. He combined tending the family fields with his job teaching in the local primary school, while his wife assumed the household duties.

Kazumi greeted her. 'It is very kind of you to have made up your mind to marry a man who is alive today, but may lose his life tomorrow,' a reference both to Egusa's dangerous lifestyle and the looming imminence of war in the Pacific. Because these words were totally unexpected, they stuck in Kiyoko's mind forever.

They all seated themselves and Takashige's mother Kita began by asking Kiyoko and her mother, with a smile: 'May I ask your name and address?'

Again, both the visitors were surprised by the questions as both ought to have been already known by his family from Egusa himself, but Kiyoko's mother answered formally and calmly in keeping with the occasion, both their names and their place of birth, Tosa.[95] Kazumi's wife, however, seemed to understand perfectly the surprised feelings of Kiyoko and her mother, and explained the reasoning behind it to them in this way:

> 'Takashige-san sent us a letter of just three lines, stating "I've decided to marry this time!" His letter was just like a letter of divorce[96] and there was nothing else written either before or after that brief sentence. As a result of it, we were all asking ourselves, "Who is the bride, and where was she born?"'

Kita replied in a like and frank manner, also with a laugh. 'I have always thought that there would *never* be any doubt about the bride once Takashige decided to marry!'

The wedding ceremony took place at the *Kaikosha Kudan* (Army Officers Club) near to the Yasukuni Shrine, Tokyo, on 20 October 1939. Takashige married Kiyoko through the good offices of Rear Admiral and Mrs Takijiro Onishi, in accordance with the full *Shinto* betrothal rite. Rear Admiral Onishi was one of the greatest of naval aviators. The reason why a naval wedding took place at the *Kaikosha*, and not the *Suikosha* (Naval Officers Club) was because the latter had already been reserved by another couple that day.

Egusa had shaved off his moustache, of which he was particularly proud[97], especially for the occasion at his future wife's request. His friends took that as the final proof of his love for his bride-to-be.

Before their wedding, Kiyoko made Egusa trim down his grand moustache!. Here the friends and future brothers-in-law, Takashige Egusa and Motahru Okamura, commander of the 12th Air Group's fighter unit, are seen together at their operational base in central China. As a Captain, Okamura was to commit suicide at the end of the war, as he could not face Japan's humiliation and defeat. *(Dr Toshimasa Egusa via Mitsuharu Uehara).*

The simple ceremony lasted for about fifteen minutes. A Shinto-style ceremony was, of course, full of tradition. The wedding ceremony itself featured only the immediate families, the *nakoudo* and the *Shinto* priest. The bride wore a white kimono for purity, with an elaborate headdress while the groom wore his best dress uniform. The bridesmaids all carried fans instead of flowers, as in Japan a fan is the symbol of happiness, its expansion symbolising a larger and grander future.

The couple exchanged vows before the *Shinto* priest. These solemn toasts were from three different sized *sake* glasses and were exchanged nine times between the bride and groom during the ceremony. Then, the families joined to celebrate the union of the two houses. Everyone attended the wedding banquet in another great room of the club. Here all the decorations featured the lucky colours, red and white, throughout. All parties joined to celebrate the wedding. The master of ceremonies introduced the attendants. The Admiral began to express his congratulatory address including the introduction of the bride and groom as well as their families. The master of ceremonies nominated a toastmaster when Admiral Onishi's speech finished. All the attendants toasted the newly-married couple, following the toastmaster's lead.

Most guests gave money as gifts, which is always welcome by any young couple setting up home. As the evening wore on another tradition was enacted.The invitation to the guests to perform, songs, drama, poetry or sketches were all deemed suitable once the *sake* had flown a little.

The honeymoon was a trip to Hakone for four days. Hakone was part of the Fuji-Hakone-Izu National Park, located about 100 kilometres from the centre of Tokyo. It was, and still largely is, famed for its scenic splendour and natural beauty. Like Yellowstone in the States, it features hot springs, many outdoor sporting activities and facilities, as well as Mount Fuji nearby. It remains one of Tokyo's greatest holiday break areas. The young couple were captivated, but, as always, the halcyon days slipped by all too quickly.[98]

On their return, Takashige and Kiyoko set up home in a new house in Kamakura, close to Yokosuka, because Egusa had been reassigned as a dive-bomber instructor from Tomitaka to the Yokosuka Air Group on the very day of his wedding. It was to be a period of intense activity for the young aviator, who was charged with preparing the Imperial Japanese Navy's dive-bomber crews for war with the might of the American Navy.

When the marriage of Takashige Egusa and Kiyoko Okamura, took place it was
both a happy and a traditionally formal occasion. The arrangements were held
through the good offices of Rear Admiral and Mrs Takijiro Onishi at the *Kaikosha*
(the war veterans' fraternal society) in Kudan, central Tokyo, on 20th October 1939.
(Dr Toshimasa Egusa via Mitsuharu Uehara)

Lieutenant Egusa as a dive-bomber instructor (front, centre) posing with four of his students in front of a Type 96 dive-bomber ashore at the Tomitaka air base (exact date of photo unknown). *(Dr Toshimasa Egusa)*

CHAPTER SEVEN

Prelude to the Pacific War

'One who does not know the enemy but knows himself will sometimes be victorious, sometimes meet with defeat.'
Sun Tzu – The Art of War.

The newly-weds were not to know many years of undisturbed happiness but their marriage was given an excellent start for ten days later Egusa was assigned as Company Commander and Instructor at the Yokosuka Air Station.

This was at the main dockyard of the Imperial Navy, situated some twenty miles from Yokohama City itself. Although operational units were periodically based at the Naval Air Station, its main function then was for the training and evaluation of men and machines. The Yokosuka Naval Air Station (Oppama) was built on Natsu Island, which was connected to the mainly via a causeway. A long (1475ft) and broad (196ft) asphalt runway, running roughly north-east to south-west, was surrounded by grass. The whole site totalled 126 acres. The seaplane base from which the whole complex had originated, was located on the mainland, and was complete with both land and sea plane facilities, with fuel and underground repair workshops, and twenty-one hangars, seven of which were used for landplanes. To the south of the seaplane base was the Aeronautical Research Centre and the Yokosuka Naval Air Factory. It was the hub of activity as the last months of peace slipped by and Egusa became embroiled in intensive dive-bomber training.

As the months slipped by this training went into high gear. It was not hard to see the reasons for this. Already in Europe, Poland had fallen to Nazi Germany, largely through the effectiveness on the battlefield of the dive-bomber.

Kiyoko and Takashige had their marriage duly blessed when their son, Hiroyuki, was born on 19 July 1940. On the international scene, the situation steadily worsened.

On the 16th of that same month, came the collapse of the Yonai Cabinet, largely brought about by the behind-the-scenes plotting by an Army cabal.[99] A new ruling group, the Second Konoye Cabinet, took its place. That this group was heavily under the sway of the

146

militarists was confirmed when the Army's Section of the Imperial General Headquarters and the Government drew up a policy document, 'principles to cope with the changing world situation', and this document was taken aboard as Government policy.[100] With the sanction of the Minister of the Navy, Admiral Zengo Yoshida, who later suffered a mental breakdown through stress, the bonds linking Japan to the other 'have-not' states, Germany and Italy, began to be strengthened significantly. Yoshida was replaced by Admiral Koshiro Oikawa on 5 September, but meanwhile the German wooing of Japan had been advanced by a conference between the Japanese Foreign Minister, Matsuoka and Major-General Eugen Ott, the German ambassador.[101] On 3 August, the Nazi's Foreign Minster, Joachim von Ribbentrop, had sent a Special Envoy, one Heinrich Stahmer, to speed things up.[102] Within eighteen days Stahmer successfully worked out the Tripartite Pact.[103]

More than diplomatic wooing, the overwhelming German military successes in Europe between 1939 and 1940 suitably impressed the bulk of the Japanese population, who felt that here was a potential ally far more in keeping with their own martial history than the weak-kneed and pacifist democracies that had collapsed so humiliatingly within a few weeks. Even though a large part of the Naval High Command was basically opposed to a formal alliance with Germany and Italy (mainly due to the need to maintain good relations with Great Britain and the United States, at least until the Navy was fully prepared for conflict), and the previous Foreign Minister Arita had been against it, ultimately this euphoria swept them along in its tide.[104]

During September 1940, the heads of the Navy Ministry and Naval General Staff held a series of meeting to discuss the proposed pact with Germany, during which even the most steadfast doubters were won over. The Foreign Minister, Yosuke Matsuoka, cleverly turned the Navy's own arguments against them. While agreeing on the need to avoid war with the United States at this time, Matsuoka argued that the signing of a tripartite alliance with the victorious axis powers would give hawkish American politicians pause for thought. It would strengthen the strong isolationist element and pro-Nazi advocates, like Charles Lindberg, and compel the USA to act more circumspectly towards a Japan with such powerful partners. The Navy hierarchy also gave due consideration to the need to maintain a firm front and not to widen the already considerable gulf between

Navy and Army policy, for the good of Japan. The populace was largely in favour and would not have looked with much approval on any Navy attempt to thwart their wishes and which might ultimately reflect on Navy rearmament.'[105] The Navy fell into line,[106] also consoled by the fact that Japan was not committed to enter any war on the side of the axis, even if the United States intervened on Britain's behalf at some future point. Only a few voices in the IJN continued to express contrary viewpoints, mainly those like the C-in-C, Combined Fleet, Yamamoto, who had seen the industrial potential of America at first-hand. He would obey of course, but considered that the Navy's leaders who had reached this conclusion suffered from a 'far too political' line of thought.

However, the die was cast. When a meeting was held on 26 September 1940, by the Investigation Committee of the Privy Council, it was stated that: 'War between Japan and the United States is considered inevitable.' Even the Navy Minister, Admiral Koshiro Oikawa, seemed sanguine about the result. He said: 'There is a good chance of victory if speedy decisive action is taken against the United States at this time. At present, various armament plans for the future are being formulated.'[107] The go-ahead for the Tripartite Alliance Pact received unanimous approval and was signed in Berlin the following day. Japan became a member of the axis.

If war against the United States was inevitable, then it would be a naval war. Great Britain was fighting for her very existence against the other two axis partners, therefore the major opponent for Japan to consider would be the United States Navy. Inevitably also, air-sea warfare would form a major part of this, even if most leaders on both sides considered battleship-v-battleship would form the ultimate showdown. Initially the fleet's aircraft would feature in any encounter. The omens for Egusa, Japan's leading exponent of this form of warfare, were obvious. Relations with the United States were strained almost to breaking point by the war in China and the later imposition by the west of various embargoes on vital goods,[108] only set the seal on the inevitable, pushing Japan into a stark choice of surrender or fight. There could only be one answer from any world power to such an *impasse*, especially one with such a long proud martial tradition as Nippon.

Meanwhile Japan was given a year's breathing space to prepare for the final battle and Egusa was to use that time imparting his extensive knowledge to the Navy's new dive-bombing recruits. The old biplanes of the China War were now steadily being replaced by a new dive-bomber, a sleek monoplane, but with a fixed, spatted undercarriage similar in style in many ways to the famous German Stuka that was even then devastating western Europe. The new Japanese dive-bomber was the Aichi D3A and had been developed as a result of war experience and from another Heinkel design, the He 70, which had also been imported and studied in depth. Powered by a Nakajima Hikari I radial engine, this sturdy little aircraft made its maiden flight in December 1937 and has been steadily developed and improved ever since. It featured the slatted dive brakes under the wings, and the engine was later changed for the larger 840-hp Mitsubishi Kinsei 3. During competitions held in 1939 the Aichi bomber came out top over the Nakajima D3N1 and was placed in full-scale production as the Type 99 carrier-based bomber. Further increases in engine size and other modifications resulted in a first-rate dive-bomber and all front-line squadrons had been re-equipped with it by the eve of the Pacific War. Deck trials were conducted during 1940 aboard the carriers *Akagi* and *Kaga* and evaluation tests were conducted by Egusa at Yokosuka. Already the new aircraft had seen extensive combat in China. Working from the newly-occupied airfield at Hankow toward the end of 1938, the Val (as it was later codenamed by the Allies) began to fly dive-bomber sorties in close support of the Army.

Although other foreign types were imported for examination in 1938, principally the German Junkers Ju 87, the Heinkel DX-He1 and the American Douglas DX D1 along with examination of captured Northrop models in China, it was the home-grown dive-bombers that continued to feature for future carrier-borne development at least. The Aichi's successor was destined to be the Nakajima (*Kuu-Gi-Shou*) D3A *Suisei* (Comet), a sleek and fast dive-bomber with fully retractable undercarriage initiated under the 17-*shi* programme in November 1941. She could tote a 500kg bomb at more than 100 miles an hour faster than the Val, but delays in development meant that she did not see meaningful combat deployment as a dive-bomber until 1943, although two or three experimental models were aboard Japanese carriers at Midway, but stripped down for use in the reconnaissance role. So it was the Val that carried the dive-bomber burden of the IJN for the first two years of conflict.

At this date the 12th was still operating the Type 96 biplane dive-bomber working out of An-ching and Chiu-ching airfields, but these were their last combat operations before being replaced by the new Aichi D3A1. By 13 September 1940 the 12th Air Corps had the Val working out of Han-Kou airfield and started flying missions against Chinese Army positions around the city of Chungking deep in the heart of south-west China. Two sorties were flown, which involved the Vals in making refuelling stopovers *en route*. Even with this method, Chinese targets at Kunming remained out of range of the dive-bombers until skilful diplomatic pressure on the Vichy-French collaborist Government in French Indo-China, allowed the use of French military airfields at Gia Lam, Lao Kay and Phu Lang Thuong.[109] The Aichi's of the 14th Air Corps were thus able to shift their bases from 23 September onwards. The first dive-bombing sorties were flown on 7 October, with Vals hitting Chinese airfields around Kunming, destroying facilities and aircraft on the ground. Operations gradually extended to other previously inviolate targets, like the Chinese air base at Siangyun, which was dive-bombed on 12 December.[110] Meanwhile back at Yokosuka, Takashige had been notified that he would hold an additional post as commander of the dive-bomber squadron aboard the aircraft carrier *Sōryū* as from 25 August 1941.

Thus the Aichi D3A1 Val had proved itself totally and this little dive-bomber had become Egusa's regular mount. In his hands and in the hands of his elite band of young experts, this aircraft, dismissed by the Allies as obsolete by 1941, was to create a fearful trail of havoc when war finally arrived.

All this intense preparation was deliberately concealed from the outside world, a policy that succeeded beyond the wildest dreams of the Japanese. In this they were considerably aided and abetted by the west's own in-built prejudices and attitudes, as Antony Best has made clear. 'It will be argued that, from the time of the Great War onwards, British policy in East Asia was characterised by a profound ambivalence about Japan and especially about its potential threat to British interests. On the one hand it was portrayed as a nation bent on regional domination, but on the other was seen as a backward power that lacked the resources necessary to achieve its goals.'[111]

The American public was equally lulled into a totally false sense of superiority. In their plans, the Japanese were aided by the incredible stupidity and ignorance of self-professed experts in the media, who, in 1941, no less than today, were woefully deficient in knowledge but large on self-promotion. One typical example of this

The Aichi D3A1 carrier bomber, the Imperial Navy's first monoplane carrier bomber (dive-bomber). The fixed undercarriage, similar to the German Junkers Ju 87 *Stuka*, was a deliberate feature from the designer Gomei, which gave added strength and stability in the dive and did not impede on the aircraft's manoeuvrability. Indeed the *Val*, as it was later code-named by the Allies, was occasionally pressed into service as a make-shift fighter in combat. Egusa first used this dive-bomber in China, and it was highly successful during the early years of the Pacific War. It was later developed as the D3A2, before being superseded by the much faster single-engined Yokosuka *Susei* or *Comet*. (*Smithsonian Institute, Washington D C*)

self-delusion masquerading as informed information was an article written in the US magazine *Flying and Popular Aviation* in January 1941, by one Leonard Engel. Some of the more bizarre statements were that the *Sōryū* could only carry about thirty planes, when in fact her aircraft complement was more than seventy aircraft.[112] He also made the bald statement that just before the outbreak of war in Europe Japan's naval air service had about 100 fighters, 150 torpedo bombers and 75 heavy bombers in commission. These numbers were so inaccurate as to be farcical, and he did not mention dive-bombers even though these had been in combat over China for several years. He similarly sneered at the quality of the aircraft, claiming they were 'not in the big league in quality or performance', yet a few months later American pilots in Brewster Buffalos and P-40 Warhawks were flying near-suicide missions against Japanese Navy Zero's. He was equally dismissive of the flying abilities of Japanese pilots.

Journalists, have always been woefully ignorant of military matters, (and continue to be so right up to the present today) but even the professional military intelligence services continued with such wishful thinking, even on the very eve of war with Japan. One British observer, the Assistant Naval Attaché, Commander George Ross, reported on the Japanese 24-inch Type 93, pure oxygen-driven torpedo, fitted with a 1,080lb warhead,[113] during a visit to the IJN torpedo school. His report was dismissed as nonsense by the Naval Intelligence Division (NID) of the Admiralty, as a torpedo of such size, 'could never be fitted on the deck of a destroyer.'[114] Not on any *British* destroyer, true enough, but since the late 1920s, Japan had been building destroyers of almost 2,000 tons displacement, which carried two sets of such weapons, and reloads, in addition to six dual-purpose 5in turreted weapons which the Royal Navy was unable to match until 1944. The British Air Intelligence Directorate (AID) Weekly Intelligence Summary for October 1940 reported 'a very poor impression of the performance of the Japanese aircraft'[115] following the visit of a Thai delegation to Japan, and this included the Type 99 (Val) dive-bomber as well as the Type-O (Zero) fighter. They were soon to be disillusioned from such wishful thinking.

In fact, during dive-bombing exercises held during the Combined Fleet Exercises of that year, the target ship *Settsu*, moving at a speed of fourteen knots, was attacked by dive-bombers from the fleet, who attacked at heights that varied from 1,000 to 2,000 feet (350-700 metres). Of 123 bombs dropped, sixty-six were direct hits, a hit rate of 53.7 percent and unequalled in the USA or Great Britain. Egusa was determined to achieve even higher rates of accuracy. During intensive dive-bomber training at the Kasanohara airfield, close to Kanoya, southern Kyushu, he sought, and obtained, special permission to press his attacks down to below 1500 feet (450 metres) before bomb release, to be sure of obtaining direct hits on his primary targets, the American aircraft carriers.[116]

Zenji Abe, who was present, described to me how Egusa had strived for accuracy above all else.

'With the increased tension between the USA and Japan from the middle of 1941, our dive-bomber training became much more severe. We went out to practice two or three times each

day. Our CO, Lieutenant-Commander Egusa, was not satisfied
with the results we were achieving, good though they were. He
ordered a reduction in the height that we released our bombs,
down to 600m. The results were again much better, but still not
good enough for Egusa. He again ordered us to reduce the
bomb-release height, down to 400m. Day by day we had diving-
bombing training at our base ashore. We used 1kg practice
bombs at this time, but, in practice, there was no noticeable
difference in effect when we switched to 500kg bombs for the
real combat operations, the Val handled exactly the same way.'
'Egusa, as our leader, estimated the wind velocity and we
followed his lead. The pilots concentrated on the dive, our
eyes glued to the telescopic sight, the observers watched the
altimeter and called out the heights, 800, 700, 600 and so on.
When our observers sang out 400m we released our missiles
and then pulled out of our 55-degree optimum dives. If the
leader's bomb missed the target, over or under, the next one
following corrected and compensated automatically. At this
time we concentrated on a fixed target and only attacked the
old *Settsu* once or twice. Within seconds it seemed we were
within 20-30m of the surface of the sea but nobody ever went
in. Night bombing was also practised for a short while, but
this proved unsatisfactory and was abandoned by the
beginning of September 1941.'[117]

By the autumn of 1941, the die was cast. The Japanese Navy had
staked all on surprise and the skill of her warriors.[118] The best pilots
were taken from the schools and training squadrons and given
command of front-line units. Detailed plans were drawn up for an
attack on the United States Pacific Fleet based at Pearl Harbor in
Hawaii. That September saw intensive practice being undertaken
against mock-up targets in the secret harbour of Kagoshima Bay in a
remote part of Japan. Egusa was naturally the first to be so selected
when the time was ripe and on 25 August 1941, he was assigned as
Flight Leader aboard the new aircraft carrier *Sōryū*. He was entrusted
with the most important mission of all – the destruction of the
United States aircraft-carriers – and was given the cream of the
Imperial navy's dive-bomber crews. Eighty Aichi D3As were to be
placed under his direct command from the six big carriers of the
Nagumo Task Force. It was an awesome responsibility but

characteristically Egusa met it head-on. Practice dive after practice dive was undertaken until his young crews were honed to perfect attunement and were eager and ready to show off their skills.

Japanese Navy dive-bombers were at this stage achieving between 30 percent and 34 percent direct hits in practice dives, as against the average of 25 percent being attained by the German Stuka forces; and against the maximum of 3 percent achieved by any nations' level bombers. Against fast-moving warship targets, a different approach was required. Under the *aegis* of prominent dive-bomber instructor, Lieutenant Sadamu Takahashi, (61st Class), in 1940-41 the IJN formulated a precise doctrine (*Nikuhaku-hitchū*) for dive-bomber attacks.[119]

The standard formation was twenty-seven aircraft in three divisions, the Command division, First division and Second division. Each division consisted of nine aircraft each, with the lead command division ahead, and the other two to port and starboard astern, in fairly loose formation, with their fighter cover above them.

This established an optimum approach was made at heights that could vary from 6000 to 6500 metres. The final approach was made at around 10,000 feet (3000m) but varied according to weather conditions. Attacks were to be made from dead ahead or astern of the target (ideally an enemy carrier, but the same principles applied to any warship), providing there was a low wind speed. This reduced the amount of defensive fire the target ship could put up against the approaching formation. When some twenty-five miles from the target, the Vals would slip to *en echelon* for the initial shallow (*circa* ten degrees) approach dive to be put into effect at top speed. This reduced the distance as quickly as possible and did not give the enemy very much opportunity for controlled, predicted defensive barrage fire. When numbers permitted, the standard practice was for 'converging' attacks from several points to split and confuse the anti-aircraft fire. Should wind speed over the target vessel exceed thirty knots, then advantage was to be taken of this and the extra impetus thus provided would help lessen wind-drift errors in the deliverance of the ordnance.

Over the target the final attack dive (at approximately 65 degrees) would be adopted by the leader and followed in succession by the rest of his unit, taking advantage of an up-sun position if possible. Dive-brakes were fully extended and an aim-off point slightly ahead of the target vessels course would be aimed for, aided by machine-gun fire from the forward guns. Bomb release height was first set at around 2,000 feet (600 metres); upon which the brakes were retracted fully and the stick pulled hard back, and at low altitude the aircraft would jink away and then make rendezvous with their leader, forming up on him as quickly as possible for mutual defensive fire should they be attacked by defending fighters.

However, Egusa's drive and enthusiasm overrode this doctrine almost immediately. Whereas the 1941 Combined Fleet Exercises saw an improvement in hit rate by the dive bombers of 55 percent over the 53.7 percent of 1939, actual combat results in the Indian Ocean using Egusa's methods, pushed this up to 82 percent with the sinking of the *Hermes,* and 88 percent with the sinking of *Cornwall* and *Dorsetshire*, an incredible achievement.[120]

One pilot later recalled the intensity of that training in the build-up to war. Zenji Abe was assigned to the *Akagi* as commander of a group of nine dive-bombers in April 1941. He recalled:

'We were not initially informed of the purpose of our training, but it went on day and night without rest. My group of Aichi Type 99 dive-bombers typically attacked at 50 degree to 60 degree dive angle and we usually released our bombs at an altitude of 400 metres (1,312ft). During this training period, our target was a naval vessel[121] which attempted to escape from us as much as us attempting to hit it with eight practice bombs.

'Accidents were common and some aircraft dived into the sea because their pilots were unable to withstand the G stresses in the face of exhaustion brought on by the severe training schedule. The training procedures of the Japanese Naval Academy and in special advanced training courses for pilots were so rigorous that we faced death every day.

'Not knowing what mission we were training for, I trained my men with strict attention to the achievement of precision in dive-bombing. These practice missions continued over and over, on some occasions for five hours or more.

'By October, the proficiency of all elements in training had reached the required level of excellence. One day that month, all officers at and above the grade of company commander were assembled at the Karasebaru airfield in southern Kyushu. Commander Minoru Genda, the operational staff officer, came into the conference room and without formality withdrew the curtain covering the front wall of the room. I remember a chill running down my spine when the model of the island of Oahu and Pearl Harbor were suddenly revealed.'

Sōryū, (ID Code JQVA) under the command of Captain Ryusaku Yanagimito, had been assigned to the First Air Fleet, CarDiv 2 on 10 April.

Leave to all concerned was given in November and Egusa had a last opportunity to visit his wife. He could not share with her the great secret of his forthcoming mission, nor warn her of the grave danger he was in, but they could enjoy their time together, although this was tinged with sadness. Proud as he was to be so chosen to strike the initial blow for Japan, Egusa had a secret burden when he finally left his family to rejoin his Air Group. Unbeknown to his comrades their commander was concealing worries over and above those concerning the attack. His beloved Kiyoko was expecting their second child and it was proving a difficult pregnancy. Also, their son, Hiroyuki, was fighting for his very life with a serious illness. Egusa could not be at their side at this grave juncture, and rarely can any commander have gone to war with so many burdens on his shoulders.

Meanwhile at the highest levels Egusa's fate, with millions of others, was being decided upon. The Liaison Conference between the Japanese Government and Imperial General Headquarters was held on 1 November 1941. Here the Navy Minister, Admiral Shigetaro Shimada, again reiterated the prospects of a war with America and Great Britain:

> 'In the event of war, the Naval High Command believes that the Navy stands a very good chance of victory in both the early stage operations and the interception operations against the enemy fleet, with the present power ratio. However, should the war continue into its third year and become long term, according to comprehensive research by the various Navy departments, shortages of war materials and the inadequacy of Japan's industrial potential will then begin to have their effect on the Navy's strength. Under the latter conditions, it would be difficult for us to have any measure of confidence that we could bring the war to a victorious conclusion.'[122]

On the other hand if Japan was to fight, then *now* was the time. Admiral Osami Nagano, Chief of the Naval General Staff, explained this viewpoint three days later: 'If we allow the present state of affairs to continue indefinitely, our Empire will not only ultimately lose its war potential but will be placed strategically at a great disadvantage.' But he went on to add the Navy's usual prediction and proviso: 'Should Japan's negotiations with the United States fail and war begin between Japan and the United States, Great Britain and the Netherlands, I believe that, on the basis of the present strength of the operating forces in the Pacific, we have a good chance of defeating the enemy both in the first phase operations and in the interception operations against the enemy fleet, provided hostilities begin in early December.' But he urged his distinguished audience to be prepared for a long war both spiritually and materially.[123]

Nagano's Army counterpart, General Hajime Sugiyama, Chief of the Army General Staff, had few such doubts. Speaking at the Imperial Conference the following day, he stated without reservation:

> 'From the operational standpoint, each day of delay in the commencement of military operations will place us at a great disadvantage so that finally it will become impossible to conduct operations.'

He listed the reasons for this as inability to match the United States in an armaments race, especially in the field of aircraft production; increased defence preparedness in the Philippines; co-ordination and reinforcement of American, British and Dutch forces; the fear of a two-front war in the spring with northern Pacific and Siberia added to their tasks.'[124]

In the face of such arguments, the Imperial Conference held back no longer, and the Joint Army-Navy Supreme Military Council agreed unanimously that Japan should go to war. In truth, preparations were already well in hand.[125]

On 2 November a signal from the Navy Minister to Yokosuka Naval District ordered Air Depots 2 and 11 supply live bombs to *Sōryū* and the other carriers, 'to ascertain their capabilities.'[126] A further signal of 5 November, informed them that in order to give the carriers the necessary range, in addition to refuelling from the specially equipped tankers of the fuelling force, the strike force would be required to carry a deck cargo of oil drums. This caused some alarm and the Chief, Bureau Military Affairs Section signalled to Chief of Staff, 1st Air Fleet that these additional cargo of full oil drums would affect the strength of the hull and the ship's performance. In order to mitigate this *Sōryū* was to embark under 400 tons, evenly spread over the length of the ship.[127]

Before the officers took their departure from Kyushu for Etorofu Island, the final assembly point, Vice Admiral Chuichi Nagumo, the commander-in-chief of Task Force Nagumo, threw a party for them at a restaurant in Kagoshima. He toasted each officer and shook hands with each and every one of them. Abe recalled: 'It seemed to me that I saw the sparkle of a tear in his eye, and I suppose he was under the strain of the same emotions felt by the Forty-Seven Rodin.' This was a traditional tale of forty-seven masterless Samurai who embarked on a mission to avenge the death of their Lord. They succeeded in their task, but because this was incompatible with the Samurai Code of Honour, all committed ritual suicide (*Sapucaia*) on their return.

The order for all units to maintain wartime radio silence on short-wave commencing 0000hrs November 11 was issued on 10 November. On the same day Admiral Isoroku Yamamoto and General Count Hisaichi Terauchi, C-in-Cs of the Combined Fleet and Southern Army respectively, set their seals on the 'central agreement' which laid out in detail the objectives and stages of the coming conflict with the Americans, British and Dutch. Stage one called for the occupation of British Malaya and Borneo; Dutch controlled Celebes, Sumatra and Timor and Australian mandated Rabaul; and American controlled Philippines, Wake, and Guam as well as Makin Island. Stage two would see the occupation of Dutch Java and the invasion of British Burma from the south via Siam while Stage three would eject the British totally from what remained of Burma. The whole vast area would then be pacified and the Greater East Asia Co-Prosperity Sphere established in the place of the white colonial empires thus overcome. In effect, this was Japanese hegemony and security of oil and rubber supplies. Thus consolidated, an outlying defensive chain would form the basis for a second operation stage, which included the occupation or destruction as speedily as possible, in the south of New Guinea, New Britain, the Solomons, Fiji and Samoa; to the east, Midway Island, and to the north the Aleutians. The Empire would be ringed by defences from the expected retaliation from America and Australia would be cut off from all source of supply, either from east (the USA) or west (Great Britain).[128] It was a bold plan, but one that would be implemented, with almost contemptuous ease, almost fully.[129]

Each of the six assigned carriers, escorted by their single destroyer 'plane guard' (used as escort and to rescue ditched aircrew in the event of accidents) left their home ports on 17 November

1941, and made their way to the rendezvous point at Hitokappu Bay in the fogbound and remote Kurile Islands, far from the sight of prying eyes. Meanwhile, as part of the deception to fool American Intelligence aircraft from the training schools scattered across Kyushu, carried on transmitting routine radio traffic to maintain the illusion that the carriers were still at their bases.

A few days were spent as the force assembled, in meetings and detailed planning conferences aboard each ship. In addition to the six carriers, *Akagi*, *Kaga*, *Sōryū*, *Hiryū*, *Shokaku* and *Zuikaku*, heavy support was provided by the fast battleships *Hiei* and *Kirishima*, and heavy cruisers *Tone* and *Chikuma* under Rear Admiral Gunichi Mikawa; and a strong force of destroyers led by Rear Admiral Sentaro Omori aboard the light cruiser *Abukuma*. There was also a refuelling force of eight oil tankers with destroyer escort under the commanding officer of the *Kyokuto Maru*, Captain Masanao Ohfuji. The latter group sailed in advance to take up position for refuelling the force en route to the target. Finally, at 0600hrs on 26 November, the Task Force sailed, steering an evasive route that kept them well clear of the normal shipping lanes to preserve their secrecy. The final decision to attack had still not been made at this period, but all prepared themselves for the ultimate sacrifice.

CHAPTER EIGHT

The Desperate Gamble: Pearl Harbor

'A victory that is long in coming will blunt their weapons and dampen their ardour.' *Sun Tzu – The Art of War.*

Egusa was now a Lieutenant-Commander, his promotion having been confirmed on 15 October on his appointment to the Task Force. Following the then current Japanese practice, the tail of his Aichi dive-bomber (or Val as the Allies were soon to codename it), No BI-231, was painted in a special red-flame colour scheme that differed starkly from the usual overall grey-green (*Hairyokushoku*, also known as 'Ameiro'or 'Grey Poupon') that the Aichi dive-bomber carried on her upper surfaces at this period. This was used as a rallying point for units to close up formation prior to and, more importantly, immediately after an attack. As such, Egusa's personal mount was known in the fleet as 'the red horse.'[130] She also carried three yellow stripes, with the coding BI-231 between the first and second stripe.

Egusa's mount also carried the standard white drift indicator stripes on the upper part of the horizontal tail surfaces. These were painted at a 5-degree angle spacing from abaft the rear cockpit and enabled his navigator/rear-gunner to correct navigational error on long flights. At intervals, an aluminium powder dye-marker would be dropped from the leading aircraft to float on the ocean's surface. A set distance travelled or time would enable the drift of the formation's flight-path to be measured accurately and any corrections to the true bearing required, due to local wind speed/direction, would be made. Some sources state that these were used as 'aim-of' markers for the rear-gunner to prevent the shooting off of his own tail in action, but this is not so, as they would have been useless in this role in a fast-moving air combat scenario. Instead the Imperial Japanese Navy used a mechanical stop to prevent the gun training dead astern for this reason, as indeed, did all other nations dive-bombers.

All the Val's had their wing racks for light bombs removed for this operation, (but not the rack-fixing studs of course) as range was important and all just carried the single grey 250kg bomb. The (D/F) Direction Finding loop housing was removed for the same reason.

The dive-bombers were very slow and their defensive armament was limited. Thus, they relied largely on the protection of their covering fighters, but in combat, once the bombers were committed to the attack dive, they were very much on their own. The danger point was after bomb-release. For a split-second at the bottom of the dive, the pilots tended to 'black-out' and each aircraft broke away at low level and high speed as best they could from the wall of flak that met them. Enemy fighters usually chose this moment to attack and so it was essential that the dive-bombers rendezvoused quickly and formed up in tight sections for mutual self-defence. Painting the leader's tail a distinctive colour made recognition and formation easier for the rest, and this followed the then current practice among German dive-bomber units who painted their wing leader's tail yellow. However, it also marked out to the enemy the leaders of the dive-bomber formations, a pride of place target which they accepted as an honour.

To understand something of the attitude of Egusa and his compatriots as the *Kidō Butai* (Task Force) sailed on its mission, one must recall that, although they were highly skilled technicians and twentieth-century warriors, their thoughts and way of life were viewed through the Shinto religion. Shinto means 'The way of the Gods' and its message and practice permeated further than most western religions into everyday life and custom. In its original form, it evolved from primitive nature-worship and from that became associated with the Gods and Spirits and the symbols of these deities in nature. Thus, mountains and rivers were holy, the Emperor was claimed to have direct divine ancestry, and everything had a mystic purpose.

Shinto, 'The Way of the Gods', was separated from Buddhism in 1875 and had become a form of state religion by 1900 after a thousand years of assimilation through neglect. The average Japanese citizen was perfectly free to follow Shinto, Buddhism or Christianity if he so wished, but a reverence and respect for one's ancestors was universal.[131] However, whatever religious path might be chosen, the ingrained and almost universal acceptance of that time was the acceptance that the 124th Emperor, Hirohito, was a direct descendant of the very first Emperor, Jimmu, himself grandson of the Sun-Goddess Amaterasu, and was therefore 'divine and sacred.'

Self-sacrifice in the service of the Emperor, even to the supreme sacrifice of one's own life, was therefore the norm and although for a period this religion had been absorbed and superseded by Buddhism, when it was re-established in the mid-nineteenth century, state Shinto incorporated these old values. Legends from the 'time of wars' laid down that Japan could never be defeated with such divine blessing protecting the race, and that to die in battle ensured the greatest worship open to any warrior. This almost lyrical way of life was reflected in the naming of Japanese warships and aircraft. For example, the carrier *Sōryū* in which the Egusa Air Group was embarked, translates as 'deep blue dragon', her sister ship *Hiryū* as 'high flying dragon.' The great battleship *Yamato* with her nine 18in guns was named after the sacred country of Japan, and the lithe destroyers frisking about the great ship's flanks had evocative names of winds, clouds and similar poetic ideas, such as 'shore breeze', and 'summer mist.'

Just as pertinent was the edict handed out to the soldiers and sailors of the empire on 4 January 1882, by the then Emperor. It laid out clearly and succinctly what was expected of them by their Divine Ruler, and was as pertinent in 1941 as it had been fifty years earlier.

'We are your Commander-in-Chief. Therefore we regard you as our limbs, and you, on your part, will look upon us as your head, and thus our mutual relations will ever be closer. Soldiers, it rests entirely upon your faithful discharge of your duties whether by, guarding our country, we can requite the grace of heaven and the benevolence of our forefathers. If, unfortunately, our country's glory fades, you must participate in our sorrow. But if military glory brightens our country's name, we will share our joy with you. Befall of you faithful in discharging your duty, and unite with us in one mind for the protection of our country. Thus shall our nation forever enjoy the blessing of peace, and thus shall our national glory become the glory of the world.'

There followed a detailed list of five instructions to govern the conduct of the 'limbs.' The chief duty of the fighting man was loyalty to the sovereign; he must be courteous in his demeanour; courage was essential and regarded as the highest of all virtues; he must be faithful and conscientious; habits must be simple and frugal. It ended with the exhortation, 'Soldiers, in accordance with our commands, discharge your duty to your country under the guidance of these rules, and not only shall we be satisfied, but the whole of Japan will rejoice'.[132]

Thus motivated and prepared, the men of the Imperial Japanese Navy went to war.

It had never been the intention of Japan to mount what the Americans later claimed as a 'sneak attack.' Negotiations still proceeded, but the Japanese were realists and the oil embargo gave them little room to move or chose.[133] It was either surrender or fight and nobody who knew the Japanese, as the American President Roosevelt did, would expect them to do the former without a struggle. Bad weather fortunately hid the ships during the early stages of their long roundabout journey towards Hawaii. Last-minute preparations were made and oiling took place at a pre-arranged rendezvous. On 2 December 1941, the die was cast and Admiral Nagumo received the signal: 'This despatch is top secret. This order is effective at 1730hrs on 2 December. Climb Niitakayama 1208, repeat 1208.'[134] The die was now cast. *'Niitaka Yama nobore'* (Climb Mount Niitaka), was the final 'go' signal for the operation. This meant that the Japanese Government had decided to go to war and that a declaration would be made on 8 December (Tokyo time).

Egusa's main preoccupation was whether or not the American carriers would be present. These were the opponents most naval pilots wished to eliminate first. By contrast, their senior officers were concentrating almost totally on the eight battleships, which formed the core of the United States Pacific Fleet. The dive-bombers could not sink these monsters by themselves, but they could pulverise their upper decks and anti-aircraft (AA) positions to enable the torpedo-bombs to approach unmolested and finish the job. For attacks on battleships, however, heavy, armour-piercing bombs were required. Such weapons were more suited to high-level attack and therefore these targets were originally to be bypassed by the first wave of dive-bombers. They, with their smaller bombs and their precision, were to take on the US carriers, with their wooden, not armoured, decks. Should these targets fail to be present, then the dive-bombers were allocated as targets the various Army and Navy airfields around the base, with their lined up rows of gleaming silver aircraft parked out in the open offering tempting alternative targets. All depended on the final reconnaissance verdicts. They had initially hoped to catch four or five of the six American flat-tops but, alas, by the eve of the launch, they knew (via an intelligence report timed at 0050hrs) that in fact, not a single US carrier was present at Pearl Harbor. In truth, three American carriers were operating in the Atlantic, one was on the US West Coast and the other two, Hawaii-based, were at sea, one ferrying Marine dive-bombers to Midway Island, the other exercising.

That same evening the crews of the warships were called up on deck and given the dramatic news. In a grand gesture the 'Z' battle flag of Admiral Togo was hoisted, which had last flown at his flagship *Mikasa* at the Battle of Tsushima forty years earlier. That battle had been an overwhelming victory by the Japanese Navy over the navy of Imperial Russia and had marked her coming of age among nations. In addition, a stirring signal originated then by the same Admiral at that battle was received from Admiral Yamamoto aboard *Nagato*[135] back in Japan, which read like Nelson's signal before Trafalgar. 'The destiny of the Empire depends on this battle. Every man must do his duty.' Nobody knew better than Egusa that this was the case. The lifts began to bring the planes up on to the pitching decks to be made ready for the scheduled take-offs at 0600hrs on 7 December. The launching point was some 275 miles due north of Pearl Harbor. By 0615hrs all 183 aircraft of the first wave of two planned waves, were in the air.

The carriers of the Nagumo Task Force on the way to attack Pearl Harbor, Hawaii, December 1941. A still from a Japanese movie newsreel.
(Authors collection)

There were forty torpedo-bombers, forty-nine high-level bombers and forty-three fighter aircraft in this wave, as well as fifty-one Aichi Val dive-bombers, of the 15th and 16th Attack Units, led by Lieutenant Commander Takahashi and Lieutenant Sakamoto respectively, each one armed with a single 250lb General Purpose (GP or ground-attack) bomb. The targets assigned to these aircraft were US military aircraft on the ground at Ford Island, Hickham Field, Wheeler Field, Barber's Point and Kaneohe airfields. These were drawn from the total of 126 dive-bombers embarked in the Task Force, which, in all, comprised Vals of the Air Groups from the carriers, the older battle-cruiser and battleship conversions, *Akagi* (18) and *Kaga* (18), the more recently completed half-sisters *Hiryū* (18) *Sōryū* (18) and the new pair, *Shokaku* (27) and *Zuikaku* (27), each crewed by the cream of the corps.[136]

It should be noted here that the Japanese *Kokubokan hikokitai* (Carrier Air Groups) trained and operated in combined carrier pairings. This was the normal practice. With No 2 *Koku Sentai*, the *Sōryū* had No1 *Hiko Daitai* and her aircraft were coded BI with three numerals and painted with a single blue band on their fuselages for recognition and formation aiding. Hence *Hiryū* (with aircraft Coded BII-and three numerals, with twin blue bands on their fuselage) and *Sōryū* first and second launches combined Vals from both carriers under a combined leadership. This was different to how the United States, and in their much smaller way, the British strikes were formed.

The new aircraft carrier *Sōryū*. The first of the modern breed of Japanese carriers was smaller than the earlier battleship and battle-cruiser conversions, but featured many modern improvements and could still carry a sizeable Air Group, including twenty-seven Aichi D1A1 carrier bombers into battle at high speed. *Sōryū* is seen here from the destroyer *Oboro*, in Sukumo Bay, Shikoku in May 1939. (*Kaijinsha, Tokyo*)

Much as Egusa wished to lead the first aircraft against the enemy, he knew that the men of the second wave would have the hardest time of it. They would not have the element of surprise on their side, but would be attacking a fully alerted and vengeful opponent. Egusa knew his duty. Lieutenant-Commander Takahashi led the first wave, and Egusa himself chose to lead the second wave. He allocated to Takahashi, in the absence of the American carriers, the task of eliminating the air bases of Hickam Field and Ford Island. The former was believed to hold the long-range Boeing B-17 Flying Fortress bombers, which might reach out against the Nagumo Task Force; the latter was thought to be a fighter strip (but, in truth, was only a seaplane base). The second wave consisted of 167 aircraft, fifty-four level bombers, 36 fighters and, the main force, Egusa leading his eighty-one (some sources state seventy-eight) dive-bombers on 'targets of opportunity.' This, in the main, meant what remained of the battleship line, most of the American fighter aircraft having already been destroyed on the ground by the first assault. The few interceptors that did get airborne were mainly dealt with by the deadly Zero fighters of his escort.

The eighty-one Vals, each carrying a single No 25 Land Target 250kg bomb, were sub-divided into four Special Attack Units:

13 Special Attack Unit	Lt-Cdr Takashige Egusa	18 aircraft
14 Special Attack Unit	Lt. Michio Kobayashi	18 aircraft
11 Special Attack Unit	Lt-Cdr Takehiko Chihaya	18 aircraft
12 Special Attack Unit	Lt Suburo Makino	27 aircraft.

Abe recalls the atmosphere after the first wave had left in the darkness of the pre-dawn.[137]

'The carriers became anthills of activity; planes were raised by the elevators from the hangar decks and readied for the launch of the second wave, which was to follow the first an hour later. From *Akagi* the second wave consisted of nine Zeros led by Lieutenant Saburo Shindo and the eighteen Val dive-bombers, of which I led the second company.'

The Japanese carriers had fully enclosed hangar decks with the aircraft-crammed spaces entirely surrounded by mechanical workshops, protected bomb storage, maintenance units and crew spaces. Thus, the Japanese carriers more resembled the latest Royal Navy citadel layout,[138] than the open United States Navy construction.

There was no provision to allow natural direct ventilation inward from the ship's hull, they were sealed units and relied on forced through drafts. Subsequently they were dangerous places in which to work and operate with any accidental detonations of explosives or fuel spillage held in the metal box of the hangar itself and unable to vent freely. This danger also precluded the common Allied practice of warming up aircraft engines below decks.

Stowage in the hangar itself was in a pre-ordained 1.5 metre grid pattern, painted on the hangar deck. Each dive-bomber was held firmly in place, with chocks under the wheels and by the usual wire cable tie-downs to fixed points at the aircraft's tail and folded wings, and this applied also when the aircraft were spotted on the flight deck for any period. In Japanese practice the aircraft were mainly serviced, fuelled and armed below decks, raised on the lifts and, once on the flight deck, their radial engines run up to full military power, necessary for launching.

Although Japanese carriers had aircraft refuelling points positioned around the perimeter of their flight decks, these were infrequently used for normal operations, due to the Japanese continuous stowage (*Renzoku Shuyo*)[139] method of continually rotating aircraft down to the hangar decks to keep them clear for operations. Exceptionally the dive-bombers *could* be armed on the flight deck,[140] concurrent with their initial engine warm-ups, which cut their normal 'lag' period of forty minutes or more between being brought up from their centrally located hangars, to actual launch.[141] Once pushed off the lifts and manhandled into position, the aircraft's wings would be unfolded, chocks placed beneath the wheels, and often ties replaced. Then their skittish Mitsubishi *Kinsei* (Golden Star), fourteen-cylinder, twin-row, air-cooled radial engines would be started up and then left to run to their optimum operational temperature, this being checked on every Val by the Assistant Air Officer (*Sho-hikochô*). The aircrew waited on the sidelines while this was done. They received their last-minute combat and flight briefings around the carrier's island superstructure, to which blackboards were affixed for the purpose, and *only then* boarded their aircraft.

As Abe recorded:

'My men stood in formation on the deck, their eyes bright and eager and their mouths firm. I knew that their training had been so rigorous that, even under unexpected circumstances they would do all they had to be done. My only order to them was "go!"'

The 171 aircraft of the second strike took just under an hour to assemble and ready,[142] and then took off at about thirty-second intervals, those aircraft with the greatest range leaving first, those with the least endurance the last off the deck. Once airborne, the various units formed up on their strike leaders at the pre-determined altitudes before heading off to the target. The eighty-one Aichi D3A1 Vals in the second wave, were all under the command of Lieutenant Commander Egusa, who also led the *Sōryū's* dive-bombers. Egusa led the first of the *Sōryū* Val groups personally and this group was made up of dive-bombers from *Hiryū* and *Sōryū*. The second Val group of the second wave consisted of dive-bombers from *Akagi* and *Kaga* and was led by Lieutenant Takehiko Chihaya from the former ship:

> 'The *Akagi* turned into the wind and we took off, clearing the bow one by one just as the first wave had done. We circled to port and assembled our formations as we gained altitude in the lightning sky. Our second wave was commanded by Lieutenant Commander Shigekazu Shimazaki, and was made up of thirty-six fighters and eighty-one bombers under Lieutenant Commander Takashige Egusa. I was the leader of the rearmost company of the dive bomber formation.'

Egusa was in the air from *Sōryū* at 0715hrs, with Miki Ishii as his trusty tail gunner and observer, and the mass formation quickly headed toward the target. The flight towards the distant island was a long one, two hours pounding steadily onward, each man alone with his thoughts.

Abe recorded:

> 'The weather was not ideal. We encountered a wind from the northeast blowing at more than 10km/hr (6mph), and the sea was rough. As we climbed through 1,500 and 3,000 metres (4921 to 9483 feet) altitude there were dense clouds, but from my position in the formation I felt quite safe with my view of the mass of the aircraft before me. My plane, which had waited through too many hours in practice for this day, spread his wings staunchly, with his engine singing quite merrily. Finally, with my altimeter showing 3,200 metres (10,500ft) we broke out of the clouds which looked like scattered cotton below us.

'Our mission was to attack aircraft carriers, but according to our latest intelligence there were none in Pearl Harbor. If we could not find the carriers, my particular targets were to be the cruisers.

'I don't know how long I meditated but was suddenly aroused by the voice of my observer, Warrant Officer Saito, from the back seat telling me that he had heard of Commander Mitsuo Fuchida's radio signal ordering the first wave to attack. It was 0319hrs Tokyo time and 0740hrs Honolulu time. I turned to watch the eight planes in my section following me steadily as if I were their father.'

Shortly afterwards, they received confirmation that the first wave's attack had been successful.[143] Now the Americans would be fully alerted and ready for them.

Long before Pearl Harbor hove into view the columns of fire and smoke from the burning ships and installations gave Egusa's dive-bombers a perfect landfall and the knowledge that the first wave of the attack had been pushed home hard. In fact, so intense was the smoke over the target that it caused a serious hazard in picking out suitable targets. They were also met by considerable anti-aircraft fire from both ships and shore. Abe counted some 200 black bursts that gradually closed in on the formation. Some twenty aircraft received damage from these bursts, but no plane was lost at this stage and they droned on, leaving Kahuku Point to starboard and overflying Kaneohe airfield, exactly as rehearsed so many times. Abe recalled that: 'all the action seemed just like an exercise. Everything was right, it seemed, and as my nervousness faded I became calm and steady.'

The Vals flew in at 4,000 metres (13,124ft) just below the cloud base as Egusa took his dive-bombers in a wide swing around the mountains to the east of the harbour to attack from the direction least expected. This gave Lieutenant Saburo Shindo's fighter escort time to make strafing sweeps against Hickham Field, Kaneohe and Ford Island to pave the way. This calm circling over the flak-filled battlefield was typical of Egusa. He wanted to make absolutely certain that his prized targets, the American carriers, were not present. So, he took his time. His next step was finding the next most useful target for his bombs.[144]

Then he led in, deliberately selecting, as best he could, those warships, which seemed to have suffered the least heavy damage. As

Leading the dive-bombers of the second wave, Egusa found the defences fully alerted after the initial attack. Notwithstanding, he deliberately circled the target area to make absolutely certain the American carriers, his main target, were not present. This photograph was taken by Petty Officer Miki Ishii, the rear-seat navigator of Egusa's Val, during that circuit. The battleships of the US Pacific Fleet can be seen covered with flames and smoke from the first attack on the right-hand side of Ford Island, with other warships clear to the left. During this reconnaissance Egusa observed the battleship *Nevada*, unscathed and making her famous dash for open water, and determined to target her to stop her escape. *(Kunio Kosemoto)*

the dive-bomber group flew over Honolulu, they increased speed and adopted their attack formations. Two battleships appeared to have escaped the carnage that had overtaken their sisters, the *Pennsylvania* and the *Nevada*. The latter had backed out from the blazing battleship anchorage and was trying to reach open water in order to gain manoeuvring space in which to fight back. Egusa was determined to stop her and, if possible, sink her in the fairway, which would bottle up the rest of the fleet. He waggled his wings to lead his section against this ship and carried out a precision dive-bombing attack on her.

Egusa's dive-bomber attacks the US battleship *Nevada* as she attempts to escape the carnage of the battleship anchorage. *(Painting by Iichiro Sekiguchi in Authors author's collection, by artist's permission.)*

As they dived, anti-aircraft fire became even more intense, and, in contrast to earlier, more accurate. Even so, the red-tailed D3A1 bore a charmed life as Egusa's section nosed down from 3,000 metres building up to 200 knots (230mph) as they did so. One by one, the Vals deposited their single bombs firmly into the still undamaged *Nevada* as she moved steadily down the channel in her break for freedom.

One of Egusa's pilots, Kunio Kosemoto, gave this description of the attack on the moving battleship, as his rear seat man called out the rapidly decreasing height of the Val:

"'1500!" yelled PO2 Takano. At around this height, machine-gun fire from all nearby enemy AA guns, as well as those of the target ship, swam into my eyesight like red candles. "Altitude 1000". The AA fire was now more intense and my sight was full of the battleship and the candles. I could even hear the close ones fly past my aircraft. "800". I aimed at the bridge. The battleship loomed huge. "600" Get ready. "450!" Bomb away! I yanked the ejection cable with my left hand. The No 25 bomb (250kg) was released noiselessly. At the same time, I pulled back on the stick with all my strength in the middle of black smoke and AA fire. I banked slightly to my left and continued on down. I almost blacked out from the G force. As I recovered my sight, I heard PO2 Takano scream. "A direct hit! *Banzai!*"'[145]

The US battleship *Nevada* under attack by the Val dive-bombers of Egusa's second wave strike. She took seven direct hits and was forced to beach. After months of intensive training to sink the American aircraft-carriers, Egusa's airman were thwarted when they were absent on the day. They soon turned their attention to other targets, the under-way *Nevada*, the dry-docked battleship *Pennsylvania* and destroyers *Cassin*, *Downes* and *Shaw* were all attacked.
(*US National Archives, Washington DC*)

Watching from ashore as Egusa's Vals attacked the *Nevada* and hit her again and again, was Lieutenant Commander Howard L Young, USN, the USS *Enterprise's* Air Group Commander, who had only just flown back ashore from his carrier. He described Takashige's dive-bombing as, 'practically perfect.'[146]

Meanwhile yet more Vals went for the battleship *Pennsylvania* in dry-dock along with the destroyers *Cassin* and *Downes*. The latter pair were heavily hit and wrecked, as was the destroyer *Shaw*, hit in the floating dock, and her magazine exploded. The *Nevada* took many other direct hits and was run aground to save her sinking and blocking the main channel, but *Pennsylvania* although superficially damaged, was not fatally hurt.

The bombs carried by the dive-bombers could demolish upperworks but not penetrate the big ships' armoured decks to their vitals. Abe's dive-bombers, bringing up the rear, on sighting no carriers, went for the cruisers as instructed. He described his attack in great detail:

'With my eyes glued to the bombsight it seemed that the fiery, candy-coloured tracers were being funnelled directly into my eye but, seemingly at the last moment, they passed by the side of the plane. My other eight bombers were diving close behind me in a single line, but I was too intent to be aware of them.

'I found my target, a big cruiser, squarely in the middle of the range scale of my sight. Saito began to call the range while a strong north wind began to blow the plane to the left. I corrected it for the drift was we fell toward the target, which drew nearer and nearer until it almost filled my bombsight. "800 metres" Saito called, "Ready ... release!" I toggled, and at the same time pulled back on the stick. I almost blacked out for a moment, but pulled out at 150 metres (492ft) to the sound of Saito's voice on the intercom calling out the results of our bombing.

'"Formation leader: short. Second pane: short. Third pane: hit! Adjustment correct. Second Echelon successful!" I later identified our target as an *Omaha* class cruiser, the *Raleigh*.'

The first wave had lost only one solitary Val but Egusa's men, as expected, took the brunt of the alerted firepower and no less than fifteen Aichis failed to return to their carriers. Against this the dive-bombers had halted the *Nevada's* dash for freedom and caused her to be grounded; had blown up the destroyers *Cassin*, *Downes* and *Shaw*, and caused damage to the battleship *Pennsylvania*. They had also damaged the light cruisers *Raleigh* and *Honolulu*, destroyer *Cummings* as well as the auxiliaries *Curtiss* (hit by doomed Val crashing into her) and *Rigel* and near-missed the cruiser *New Orleans*. Their hit rate was between 26 percent and 27 percent, mainly in the face of intense return fire while diving through smoke from the earlier attacks.

The assault on *Nevada* was particularly effective. Splitting into two sections, the Vals, led by Lieutenant Saburo Makino, came in from the south west and south east at 0900hrs to split the defensive fire. Three direct hits were scored on her fo'c'sle and forward deck to port, causing fierce fires and the flooding of main and second deck compartments. A second wave led by Lieutenant Yamada followed them down at 0907hrs, almost immediately scoring three further direct hits in her 'midships superstructure and further dangerous fires in her starboard gun casemate. Realising she was settling and would block the main channel, the *Nevada* was deliberately run aground on Hospital Point at 0910hrs. This act caused the most damage, as mud blocked her intakes.[147]

The US battleship *Nevada* received many direct hits from Egusa's dive-bombers and had to be beached to prevent her from sinking in the narrow channel, which would have blocked the entrance to Pearl Harbor for a long period. *(US National Archives, Washington D C)*

After this assault, Egusa gathered his surviving aircraft about him and set course for the long trip back to the waiting Task Force. He could confirm that the American battle fleet had been dealt a heavy blow, but that the shore installations, workshops and oil storage tanks on which subsequent American fleets would rely, were still largely intact. More importantly to Egusa, was the fact that the enemy carriers had not yet been located and sunk. Despite his desperate tiredness, Egusa tried to put over his viewpoint via *Sōryū's* commander, but the commander-in-chief, Vice-Admiral Chuichi Nagumo, turned down the appeal. Despite the acclaim he received as leader of the great carrier Task Force, he was not a carrier man at heart and was much concerned with the vulnerability of his ships, a concern which was later proven to be well founded. He weighed up the pros and cons and, much to the fury of the young airmen, decided he had done enough. The great carriers turned their bows about and headed toward home. Behind them, it is true, they left the shattered remains of the American Pacific Fleet, but they also left a legacy of hate and revenge. More pertinently, the US carriers remained intact and free.

Egusa's continued anguish about his failure to find, and destroy, the American aircraft carriers, and of failing to convince Nagumo of the importance of this omission, never left him. Kiyoko remembered how, almost a year later, while they were living in the historic city of Kamakura, about thirty minutes by train from Yokosuka Air Station, the mask slipped for an instant. Kamakura faces the sea and its beach is very quiet and beautiful. The two were walking along the beach, when Takashige suddenly stopped to pick up a piece of stick and started to draw. Kiyoko watched as he drew an outline map of the Hawaiian islands in the sand. She was totally surprised and did not know what to make of it. Her husband said softly: 'I strongly recommended to my higher officers that we had not achieved the right war result yet from the attacks we had made. We had not yet sunk the enemy carriers. I guessed the enemy carriers were surely somewhere in the vicinity of the islands. I said, 'Let us find them and strike them' when I returned to *Sōryū* from the attack on Pearl Harbor.'

Then, just as suddenly Takashige stopped talking, as if regretting he had spoken at all. Kiyoko felt very seriously that her husband's mortification about this lapse was something very profound, because he had never before spoken to her about the war at all. It seemed to Kiyoko that he felt seriously at fault for not finding the American carriers at Hawaii for he felt it was quite possible for them to work out where they were. The superior officers whom Takashige spoke on returning to *Sōryū* would have been the Commander of Carrier Division 2, Rear Admiral Tamon Yamaguchi, Yamaguchi's Staff Officers, the Commanding Officer of the *Sōryū*, Captain Ryusaku Yanagimoto and the Flight Operations Officer, Commander Ikuto Kusumoto, because they were all aboard the *Sōryū*. Egusa would have directly recommended a search for the carriers to Rear Admiral Yamaguchi, because the latter made the same recommendation to the Commander of the *Kidū Butai*, Vice Admiral Chuichi Nagumo. But Nagumo shelved it, and ordered the *Kidū Butai* to return to Japan.[148]

Takashige's recommendation to hunt down the American carriers off Pearl Harbor was confirmed by Lieutenant Commander Toshiro Akagi to the historian Mitsuharu Uehara.[149] Kiyoko, who knew nothing of the battle or the circumstances, thought that her husband might well have located the enemy carriers, even though the *Enterprise* was some 200 miles west of Oahu and *Lexington* 420 miles to the south-west of Midway. Both ships could have been caught and easily dealt with by the *Kidū Butai*.[150] Kiyoko speculated that her husband had a kind of inbuilt sixth sense in such matters. 'He had an insight into battle because he was unselfish in thought and deed.'[151]

CHAPTER NINE

Through the Southern Oceans

'Attaining 100 victories in 100 battles is *not* the pinnacle of excellence.' *Sun Tzu – The Art of War.*

The Hawaiian operation, as the Japanese termed the Pearl Harbor attack, was but one of the many assaults throughout the Pacific Theatre. Others were taking place against the Philippines, Malaya, Hong Kong and Wake Island. Most were devastatingly successful, the last-named were not and the Japanese invasion force sent to crack this small nut was bloodily repulsed. Grumman F4 Wildcat fighters and the 5in shore batteries, valiantly manned by the US Marines, not only repelled the invasion force but sank two Japanese destroyers, *Hayate* and *Kisaragi*, in the process.

The Japanese force withdrew and regrouped. The destroyers *Asanagi* and *Yunagi* replaced the lost pair. A powerful heavy cruiser squadron, *Aoba, Furutaka, Kako* and *Kinugasa*, which had recently assisted the conquest of Guam, were sent to lend their batteries of 8in guns to the bombarding force, and the seaplane carrier *Kiyokawa Maru* was added to the second invasion force, under the command of Rear Admiral Kajioka, which sailed from the Marshall Islands on the morning of 21 December. The converted destroyers used as landing ships had their complement of 225 assault troops apiece increased to 250 with the addition of seasoned veterans of the Guam assault. These troops had conducted landing exercises at Kwajalein to stiffen them up in readiness for a seriously defended landing before embarking.

As if all this was not enough firepower to soften up the island for a second attempt, Vice Admiral Shigyoshi Inoue, Commander, South Seas Force (Fourth Fleet) appealed for further support. As a result Nagumo was ordered by Admiral Yamamoto, to detach *Hiryū* and *Sōryū*, escorted by the heavy cruisers *Chikuma* and *Tone*, and screened by the destroyers *Tanikaze* and *Urakaze*, all under the command of Rear Admiral Hiroaki Abe, commander 8th Cruiser Division, to proceed as the Wake Island Reinforcement Force. Their softening-up attacks had been scheduled to start on 22 December, but two days earlier intelligence reports indicated that the Americans were flying in fresh aircraft to Wake. In order to catch these aircraft as they arrived, Abe was ordered to move this date forward to the 21st and his force increased speed to thirty knots to comply.

The Japanese carriers arrived within striking distance of Wake Island early on 21 December and, at 0700hrs, Egusa led a force of eighteen D3A1s against the island's airstrip. However, in this and subsequent missions, low cloud and a 200 metre ceiling, hindered the skill of the dive-bombers and made target selection difficult. No fresh US patrol aircraft were sighted at 0800hrs and so, at altitudes that varied from 50 to 200 metres, Egusa's Vals circled to find targets of opportunity, mainly concentrating their attacks on shore installations. Egusa reported that defending anti-aircraft fire was 'very slight' causing little inconvenience. This was in such marked contrast to the reception they had received over Pearl Harbor that Abe opined: 'The enemy seemed to lose their fighting spirit.' Such guns as did fire were subsequently silenced, mainly by bombing and strafing by the accompanying Zero fighters. The one serviceable Wildcat, piloted by Major Putnam did not get airborne until after Egusa's formation had broken off the attack to return to their carriers. Not a single Japanese aircraft had been so much as damaged.

Further attacks followed the next day, once Abe's force had closed to within 200 miles of Wake, and were repeated on 21 December. This time targets included the deadly 5in coastal gun batteries with which the US Marines had inflicted humiliating losses on the first invasion force. These dive-bombing attacks proved effective, so that, by the time the second invasion attempt was made, most of the Marines' heavy weapons had been destroyed and the island fell. For example 'L' battery on Wilkes islet, when trying to engage the transport and landing craft of the second invasion, found that one gun had been immobilised and was unable to train on the target, while the second had her recoil cylinders damaged and rendered inoperable. Deploying as infantry to engage the Japanese small craft dive-bombing caused the final Marine casualty of the action when Private 1st Class Robert L Stevens was killed, long after all his compatriots had long since surrendered.

Rear Admiral Yamaguchi's 2nd Carrier Division then returned to Japan to refit in preparation for further assaults. Already the Japanese were swarming over south-east Asia, crushing such feeble resistance as they found and moving with speed and skill into Borneo, Celebes, Malaya, Singapore, Sumatra, Java, Timor and New Guinea, each step forward being a consolidation for the next.

Egusa had little time with his family, now safely through their own ordeals, before *Sōryū* and her companions were on the move once more, standing southward. Their initial objective was to provide air support for the invasion of the island of Ambon (previously Ceram) in the Northern Banda Sea, to the east of the Celebes. A mixed Dutch/Australian garrison consisting of 2,000 troops, hastily reinforced, attempted to stem the onward surge of the Japanese toward Australia.

The Royal Australian Air Force had based Lockheed Hudson medium bombers of 13 Squadron on the island since the first day of the Pacific War. The bombers were based at the established airfield of Laha on the Hitu Peninsula. They were followed by ground troops, in the form of 2/21 Battalion commanded by Colonel L N Roach, which had disembarked on Ambon on 17 December 1941, following the decision of 5 December, after talks with the local Dutch commanders based at Bandung. Known as 'Gull Force' Roach also had a detachment of construction engineers, 2/11 Field Company; some anti-tank guns of 'C' Troop 18th Anti-Tank Battery; and a few bren-gun carriers at his disposal, in total some 1,170 officers and men. Urgent requests for heavier weapons, including 25lb field guns, mortars, anti-aircraft guns and more anti-tank weapons, as well as more infantry, all fell on deaf ears, and instead Roach was replaced on 16 January by Major Scott. These Australians reinforced the existing Dutch garrison of 2,800 troops, including native soldiers with Dutch officers, all under the overall command of Lieutenant-Colonel J R L Kapitz.

In addition to the RAAF Hudsons there were some Dutch medium bombers, three Dutch Brewster Buffalo fighter aircraft, (one other had crashed during the flight from Java, and one of the remaining trio was damaged), as well as American and Dutch flying boats based at Namlea. The Bay of Ambon was mined by the Dutch minelayer *Gouden Leeuw* before she left. This resulted in the sinking of the Japanese minesweeper *W-9*, and damage to the *W-11* and *W-12* later but there was no naval defence whatsoever apart from two requisitioned motor boats, the *Singkil* and *Kwandang*. The first Japanese bombing took place as early as 6 January, destroying one of the fighters and two of the Hudsons as well as damaging installations. Further air attacks on the 13th resulted in the two remaining Buffalo fighters being destroyed in air-to-air combat with ten Zero fighters, both pilots parachuting to safety, and more Hudson's. Most of the flying boats were also put out of action and the survivors withdrew.

Originally, the Japanese had planned to assault this base on 6 February, but their unexpectedly easy conquests to date, enabled them to bring this date forward. By 21 January 1942, a first-class fleet anchorage had been obtained by the Japanese at Staring Bay, south of Kendari in the Celebes, and from here, the carriers *Sōryū* and *Hiryū* sailed to carry out their softening-up attacks. Two strikes were made, totalling thirty-five aircraft, against Ambon by the dive-bombers on 24 January, the same day as their troops stormed ashore at Kendari. Allied opposition was negligible and much damage was done. Egusa's Vals made further air attacks the next day.

Air reports of seventeen Japanese transports escorted by five warships were received on the 29th. In fact the Kure 31st Japanese Special Naval Landing Force, commanded by Rear Admiral Kouichiro Hatakeyama, and the 228th Infantry Regiment, veterans of Hong Kong, were moved in ten transports, escorted by the light cruiser *Jintsu*, flagship of Rear Admiral Raizo Tanaka, with destroyers *Asashio*, *Oshio*, *Arashio*, *Michishio*, *Natsushio*, *Kuroshio*, *Oyashio*, *Hayashio*, *Amatsukaze*, *Hatsukaze*, *Yukikaze* and *Tokitsukaze*, minesweepers *W-7*, *W-8*, *W-9*, *W-11* and *W-12* and submarine-chasers *Ch-1*, *Ch-2* and *Ch-3*. There was also an Air Group with the seaplane tenders *Chitose* and *Mizuho* equipped with Mitsubishi F1M2 'Pete' floatplane fighters. If this was not enough, the two heavy cruisers *Nachi* and *Haguro* of the 5th Cruiser Squadron, escorted by destroyers *Ikazuchi*, *Ushio* and *Sazanami* were in support, under Rear Admiral Takeo Takagi if required.

Despite these reports, when the Japanese troops landed on the night of 30 January, they achieved local surprise, and quickly overran the coastal defences. Further fighting was intense but could only have one outcome and by 3 February, this strategically-important island soon joined the long list of Allied defeats.

Nagumo regrouped his forces at Davao on Mindanao in the Philippines and, with the same carriers that had hit Pearl Harbor (less *Shokaku* and *Zuikaku*), refuelled at Staring Bay and entered the Timor Sea. Their target for this strike was the northern Australian port of Darwin, the only sizeable harbour in reach of the threatened area and the main staging post for troops and supplies being rushed up toward the battle zone by the Allies.

On 19 February, Nagumo ordered a weather reconnaissance aircraft to overfly the port and she duly reached Darwin at 0730hrs

that morning. The weather was fine and the harbour was packed
with shipping, but as the aircraft's radio was unserviceable, she was
of absolutely no use to Egusa or his fellow strike force fellow
commanders. Nonetheless, Nagumo order the strike to go-ahead.
Since the early hours the Task Force had positioned itself some 350
kilometres north-west of the target and, by 0845hrs, 188 aircraft had
been launched under the overall command of Commander Mitsuo
Fuchida once more. There were seventy-one dive-bombers,
including eighteen Aichi D3A Vals under Egusa from *Sōryū*; eighty-
one Yokosuka B5N Kate attack bombers and thirty-six Mitsubishi
A6M2 Zero fighters. Co-operating in the assault were a further fifty-
four land-based, twin-engined, naval bombers of the *Takao Kokutai*
23rd *Koku Sentai*, from Kendari, Celebes with twenty-seven
Mitsubishi G4M1 Betty bombers, and the same number of
Mitsubishi G3M1 Nell bombers from Ambon Island.

Again, the Japanese caught the Allies completely off guard. A
US Navy Catalina flying boat from VP 22 was surprised by the
fighter escort and quickly shot down into the sea off the northern
end of Bathurst Island before she could raise the alarm. Two shore
based observers transmitted sighting reports but neither reached the
proper authorities.

Egusa's dive-bombers crossed the coast at Koolpinyah before
turning north-west over Noonamah for Darwin. A force of nine
USAAF Curtiss P-40 Kittyhawks from the 33 Pursuit Squadron
(Provisional) attempted to intercept but were likewise quickly dealt
with, all being destroyed by the Zeros and four of the pilots killed
including their Commanding Officer, Major Pell. Three more
Catalinas were sunk at their moorings in the harbour and eleven
RAAF aircraft were summarily destroyed

This left Egusa's dive-bombers free to concentrate on the massed
shipping in the crowded harbour while the fighters and altitude
bombers eliminated the opposition defences and hit shore targets.
The Vals found ample targets to occupy their attention for forty-six
ships were present. Of these twenty-one were sunk and two more
were put down off Bathurst Island. In the harbour seven large
transports and tankers, totalling 43,429 tons, had been sunk, as well
as many small craft, while the Australian sloop *Swan*, the US
seaplane tender *William B Preston*, nine large freighters and many
small ships had been badly damaged. This effectively finished
Darwin as a threat for the rest of the invasion period.

The attack on Port Darwin. Egusa's dive-bombers created mayhem among the assembled shipping at this vital port and staging post for the Australian forces fighting in New Guinea. Among the ships hit, set ablaze and sunk by the Vals were the tanker *British Motorist* (left) and the American destroyer USS *Peary* (right). *(Australian War Memorial, Canberra ACT)*

Particularly effective was Egusa's dive-bombers demolition of the ammunition ship *Neptuna*. Her demise typified the whole debacle. She was originally a German-built cruise ship. She had been converted to a troopship-cum-ammunition hauler for the Australians and had taken reinforcements to Hong Kong just before the war started. She had subsequently evacuated refugees from Rabaul, Madang, Lae and Salamaua in the face of the Japanese advance, on her way home. She carried a crew of eighteen Australian officers, four cadets and 125 Chinese deckhands, stokers and the like. She had loaded another military cargo at Sydney, NSW, troops; supplies and vehicles, plus 200 depth-charges and anti-aircraft shells for the Navy. On arrival at Darwin on 12 February, she had been berthed at the main wharf. While offloading some of her ammunition into the sloop HMAS *Swan*, the Australian dockyard labourers threatened to stop work, despite this being vital war work in the midst of conflict. In the middle of a confrontation between these malcontents and the naval personnel, Egusa's dive-bombers arrived unannounced to reinforce the point!

There were shouts of 'The Yanks have arrived' and 'they are dropping leaflets', and then the first bomb hit the wharf just forward of the ship. While the Vals screamed down, the *Swan* cast off and backed out to gain sea room, opening fire with her guns and the newly-transferred shells. Meanwhile *Neptuna* had been holed below the waterline and began to fill with water. As she listed another bomb scored a direct hit which demolished much of her upper works, mortally wounding her Master, Captain W Michie and starting a fierce fire. The oil storage tanks ashore close by had also been hit and blazing oil was spewing into the harbour area close by. Another very near miss followed almost immediately. 'Abandon ship' was ordered by Third Officer B Deburca, the senior surviving officer, and most of the crew managed to clear the ship as she heeled over. Then the blaze spread aft to the No 3 and 4 hatches where the depth-charges were stowed. With a shocking explosion and a huge column of fire and smoke, the *Neptuna* tore herself apart. With her went three senior officers, three engineers, three radio officers a young cadet, R Stobo, and forty-five of her Chinese crew.[152]

Ship	Type	Result
Admiral Halstead	Freighter	Damaged
Barossa	Freighter	Sunk
Benjamin Franklin	Norwegian Tanker	Damaged
British Motorist	Tanker	Sunk
Coongoola	Motor Boat	Sunk
Deloraine	HMAS Minesweeping Sloop	Damaged
Don Isidro	Filipino freighter	Sunk
Florence Dee	US Freighter	Sunk
Gunbar	Water carrier	Damaged
Kangaroo	HMAS Boom Defence Vessel	Damage
Kara Kara	HMAS Boom Defence Vessel	Slight damage
Katoomba	HMAS Minesweeping sloop	Damage
Kelat	Coal Hulk	Sunk
Kookaburra	HMAS Boom Defence Vessel	Slight Damage
Manunda	Hospital Ship	Sunk
Mauna Loa	Freighter	Sunk
Mavie	HMAS Patrol Boat	Sunk
Meigs	US Army Transport	Sunk
Tulagi	MV	Beached
Neptunia	Ammunition Ship	Blown Up
Peary	US Destroyer	Sunk
Platypus	HMAS Submarine Depot Ship	Damaged
Port Mar	US Freighter	Beached
Southern Cross	HMAS Examination Vessel	Damaged
Swan	HMAS Sloop	Damaged
Tulagi	Cargo Ship	Hit and beached
Warrego	HMAS Minesweeping Sloop	Slight Damage
Warnambool	HMAS Minesweeping Sloop	Slight Damage
William B Preston	Freighter	Damaged
Zealandia	Freighter	Sunk

The Australian Official Report commented:

'All the evidence concurred that the bombing of the Japanese, especially the dive bombing, was extremely accurate. The high level bombing did not achieve the same degree of accuracy, but was moderately accurate and caused a great deal of damage. Air Force officers, however, expressed the view that there were no novel tactics displayed and that the performance of the Japanese aircraft was not beyond their expectations. All these officers insisted that the accuracy was due to lack of effective opposition by our own forces, rather than to any specially high qualities displayed by the Japanese.'

This is a typical response, slavishly following the long-established RAF line, of always and without exception disparaging the accuracy of dive-bombing, and the results achieved, whether conducted by German, Japanese or indeed any air force, because it did not fit their own myopic view of air power.

While the Australian anti-aircraft gunners and Lieutenant Bob Oestricher between them claimed a Zero and three Vals shot down, in truth only two Japanese aircraft failed to return to their carriers. The dive-bomber concerned was that of Warrant Officer Katsuyoshi Tsuru with his backseat man NAP I/C Musashi Uchikado, from the *Kaga*. Their assigned target was the West Point base and, at 0830hrs, he dive-bombed an aircraft hangar there, scoring a direct hit. This not only badly damaged the hangar building but also a Lockheed Hudson bomber inside. Six other RAAF Hudsons and a USAAF Consolidated Liberator at the base were also destroyed. However, on turning back out over the harbour Tsuru's aircraft was hit by flak in the petrol tank, killing Uchikado and setting the aircraft on fire.

The report continued:

'The 14th Anti-aircraft Battery put their guns on to independent control. The dive-bombers were attacking the larger ships and the fighter aircraft were strafing the smaller vessels. The 14th's guns were too slow to engage the Japanese aircraft at such short range. The only strategy they could adopt was to put up a shield of fire above the ships in the harbour. The shortest recommended fuse setting was 2 seconds. They selected 1.5 seconds as the fuse setting to reduce the range before the shell would explode. Eventually one of the shells exploded near the nose of one of the dive-bombers. The damaged Japanese dive-bomber side slipped into the harbour The Val dive bomber crashed in the sea, north of East point after it was hit by a cone of gunfire from the town defences.'

One of his wingmen, Shoichi Ogawa, recorded that Tsuru apparently could have baled out, but failed to do so and the Val hit the water at 0846hrs some 2000 metres east of the military airfield. He also stated he saw flames 40 metres high as Tsuru's aircraft burned on the water. Tsuru's body was recovered and buried at Darwin but was later removed to the Japanese war cemetery at Cowra, New South Wales.

By 21 February, the Nagumo Task Force had slipped silently away and was back at Staring Bay. Here they replenished and rested while Java was invaded. At the beginning of March, they again sailed for the waters south of that island, along with the 3rd Battleship Division (*Hiei* and *Kirishima*) and 8th Cruiser Division (heavy cruisers *Tone* and *Chikuma*) of Admiral Kondo's Main Body, Southern Force, for the mopping-up of any survivors trying to escape by sea. Among these were the US destroyer *Edsall* (DD-219) (Lieutenant Joshua J Nix). She had earlier been damaged by the explosion of one of her own depth-charges but, on 26 February, had sailed from Tjilatjap to rendezvous with the American aircraft transport *Langley* along with the destroyer *Whipple*.

The *Langley* (11,050 tons) had been the first American aircraft carrier converted from a collier, but, in February 1937, she had been reconverted to serve as a seaplane tender, being reclassified as the AV-3 in April of that year. In her new configuration, she had only about two-thirds of her original deck landing area, the forepart being replaced by a wheelhouse for navigation, and so she was unable to fly off aircraft any more. This left space for thirty-two fully assembled Curtiss P-40E Warhawk single-engined fighter aircraft from the 33rd Provisional Squadron and 13th Provisional Squadron USAAF, to be parked aft for transportation to Tjilatjap, Java, the last remaining port relatively undamaged, even though there was no airfield in the area. The *Langley* had left Port Darwin on 17 February as part of convoy MS-5 bound for Karachi via Singapore, and had been detached on 23 February, while in the vicinity of the Cocos Islands. So desperate had the situation ashore become, that serious consideration was given to beaching the *Langley* and lowering her deck cargo of aircraft for them to subsequently make take-offs from the beach. However, this all proved irrelevant.

However, early on 27th, while still some seventy-five miles short of their destination, the force was brought under attack by nine twin-engined Japanese bombers who attacked in three waves of three. The first and second waves failed to do anything other than bracket the slow-moving transport, but the third trio made much better practice. No less than five bombs hit or near-missed the old vessel, damaging her engines and opening her hull below water, and she quickly took on a ten-degree list. Her deck cargo of fighters hit by the blasts, ignited and were soon being swept by flames and fire. Soon *Langley* had slid to a halt and, at 1332hrs, 'abandon ship' was ordered. Once the crew and passengers had been embarked aboard the escorting warships, the two destroyers aided her to the bottom with nine 4in shells and two torpedoes to prevent her being salvaged by the Japanese.

Edsall had rescued 177 survivors. The destroyer then met the fleet oiler *Pecos* off Flying Fish Cove, Christmas Island, on 28 February to transfer the rescued sailors to that ship, including two wounded P-30 pilots. This was done while under air attack, and the task was completed by 1 March. *Edsall* herself took aboard thirty-two fit Army pilots and engineers from the *Whipple*, whom she was to transport to Tjilatjap, where it was thought they might be able to operate a further batch of P-40E's *en route* aboard another US Navy transport ship, the *Sea Witch*. With these airmen embarked, she sailed back to Tjilatjap, but never got there. Orders were sent telling all ships to retire back to Australia, but it is unknown whether *Edsall* ever picked up this signal. On the afternoon of 1 March, some 250 miles SSE of Christmas Island, *Edsall* ran smack into Admiral Kondo's heavy ships. Despite attempts at concealment, the lone American ship was sighted by the *Tone* at 1718hrs at a range of fifteen miles, and twelve minutes later the *Chikuma* also had her in sight, and opened fire at 21,000 metres (eleven nautical miles). There was no escape, for in her crippled state she could not outrun the lithe cruisers.

There followed an epic struggle. Alone and unaided *Edsall* fought her last battle with grim tenacity, laying a smokescreen and twisting and turning at the best speed her little hull and straining old engines could manage. They both gave the best performance of her long career. For an hour or more, aided by a passing rain squall, she bore a charmed life. Lieutenant-Commander Nix's tactics were to watch for the flash of the enemy guns and turn the ship violently, up to 360 degrees, and vary the speed from the maximum and stop to throw off the Japanese rangefinders. As well as the heavy cruisers *Tone* and

Chikuma, she was taken under fire at 27,000 metres range by the 14in main batteries of the *Hiei* and *Kirishima* from 1747 onward. Japanese accounts state that some 1268 rounds of 14in, 8in, 6in and 5in shell were fired at her altogether. During the initial long-range period of this unequal struggle, only two shells struck their target. The *Hiei* hit her at 1824hrs and, nine minutes later, an 8in round from *Tone* also hammered home, but somehow *Edsall* evaded all the rest and kept moving. For a time it almost looked as if she might get clean away. In frustration, Kondo called up the *Kidū Butai* to slow her down.

Between 1827 and 1850 eight aircraft launched from *Akagi*, followed by nine more from *Sōryū*, led by *Egusa*, made dive-bombing attacks on the elusive *Edsall* as she made smoke yet again. Initially, *Edsall* managed to avoid the first Val assaults, but then took several direct hits, which rapidly started uncontrollable fires (*Kasai* – raging conflagration – in Japanese reports).[153]

The crippled destroyer immediately veered round out of control, steering *toward* her tormentors, then slowed down to become a sitting duck. The *Chikuma* was able to bring her fast-firing secondary batteries into play to pound her into scrap, blowing her stern off, and she finally sank about 430 miles south of Java, in 13° 45' South, 106°, 47' East. Very few of her crew survived to be picked up by the *Chikuma*, (accounts vary from five to eight), and they eventually ended up in a POW camp at Kendari, in the Celebes, None of these unfortunates survived the war (again, some accounts claim they were beheaded by their captors). No word ever came from her or her 150-man crew and it was not until the spring of 1952 that the Americans found out her fate.

Nor did other ships long survive her; *Pecos* herself was destroyed on the same afternoon. Japanese accounts started that Egusa and one wingman from *Sōryū* carried out this mission, but it is now known that this was not the case. Instead, Egusa ordered a section of Vals from *Kaga* to perform this simple task. The last aircraft of that section scored a direct hit on the little ship. One of the pilots, Shinsaku Yamakawa, later described the attack, which was, initially at least, one of the less successful dive-bombing sorties ever mounted by the Japanese:[154]

'The mission was to be carried out by two sections of *Kaga's* dive-bombers squadron, according to the set sequence of sorties. The commander of the nine aircraft was Lieutenant

Watanabe, whose pilot was Chief F/Sgt Hiwatari. The third section, to which I belonged, was not included. However, I heard that NAP1/c 155 of the second section was in the sickbay and informed my company commander of this. He replied, "Then you go on the mission". My navigator was NA1/c Nakata as usual. So as an extra, like a canteen dangling from a knapsack, we joined in and headed for the naval oiler *Pecos* of the US Asiatic Fleet. We sighted the *Pecos* soon after take-off. Our formation had attained an altitude of 5000m. Although they were some cloud patches, it was a fine day for dive-bombing.

'We broke formation and began our dive approach run. The enemy flak was heavy but it did not trouble us. Our commander's aircraft led the attack, with his No 1 and 2 following him down. My aircraft would be the very last one of the nine to attack, as we were guests of the unit. We expected to be only observers of their attack, as I assumed they would sink her easily and would not need us. As I watched, the leading aircraft and the next astern increased the angles into their attack dives. The enemy vessel turned towards them. By now all the aircraft save ourselves, had committed themselves to their attack dive approach. The light anti-aircraft guns of the ship continued to fire continually. In a short time the leading aircraft dropped her bomb and pulled her nose up. The *Pecos* was turning to starboard leaving a long white wake astern. The wake drew a long white arc and a huge column of water sprouted up off her port bow.

'Then the second dive-bomber also missed, her bomb making a splash of her port bow as the vessel twisted desperately. Her wake showed a 45-degree turn as the third aircraft released the bomb. The ship had a heavy list as she turned and that bomb also missed. If only her steering had been slower, or the aircraft had anticipated her turn sufficiently, we would have got her, but she was doing an excellent job. Her captain must have been very able to so dodge our bombs.

'When the fourth and fifth aircraft dropped their bombs, the ship was still steering hard to starboard and had already made a 90-degree plus turn. Both these bombs detonated about 10m off her port bow, to our chagrin, and merely produced big columns of water. A praiseworthy job. On our side, the sixth and seventh attacks were made in succession on her. Usually we released our bombs at a height of 450m. We had never missed in our aim like this previously. I was still just watching and wondering why. I examined her wake and the points where our bombs had fallen, thinking they would be sure to hit her this time, but the ripples caused by the bombs paralleled her wake; the sixth, seventh and eight aircraft all completely missed.

'Finally, it was our turn. We were given the chance to attack. When I opened up the dive-bombing sight, I muttered "damn". I had been admiring her excellent steering and had neglected my own position up until then. Now I noticed that an oil leak on the windshield of my aircraft made it hard to use the sight. Since we only carried a single bomb each, it was now a serious task for me to hit her with the last one. We commenced our dive, diving down through 4,000m, 3,000m, 2,000m... The enemy's machine-guns were still firing intensely. Although she had had done well in evading eight bombs so far, I sensed some slackness in her manoeuvring at that moment. Then I released my bomb as I blacked out. I pulled the control stick hard back out of the dive and rolled the aircraft slightly at the same time. The whole ship's hull reared up as I watched, and a fierce blaze of fire and smoke erupted from amidships, close by an anti-aircraft gun position. "I've got her." I was incomparably joyous. "On the return I strafe them". I tried to turn my aircraft to port. Maybe I pulled the stick so fiercely that I blacked out for an instant, but I soon saw clearly again. I felt a heavy thud as my plane banked at 90-degrees. I saw a large hole in the engine cowling just in front of me. As I realised we had been hit, I looked back at her and saw her stern anti-aircraft guns still shooting at me fiercely, with pretty accurate aim. I had pulled back the stick hard after my attack dive and lost speed, as well as rolling sideways, and, in that instant I had almost been stationary in the air. We had been hit.

'It had been strictly forbidden to strafe ships after dive-bombing in this way. I got hit because I broke the rule. However, I thought the guns crews were admirable for continuing to fire back persistently from a sinking ship.'

Despite the heavy flak strike, and the fact he could not see out of his oil-covered wind-shield but had to stick his head out of the side of the canopy, Yamakawa got his Val (named 'All Japan Schoolgirl's offering to the Nation' after the subscriptions that had paid for her) back on *Kaga's* flight deck without further accident. The other dive bombers allowing him to get down first. The *Pecos* had meanwhile finally heeled over and sunk.

Egusa subsequently harangued the aircrew for their lack of accuracy, and this shaming again soon achieved the desired effect. On 5 March, Egusa led a 180-plane strike against Tjilatjap itself, which was packed with shipping, repeating the Darwin devastation. Further attacks were made on the survivors south of that port that were fleeing to safety. In total, three merchant ships were sunk *Woolgar* (3,060 tons), *Kidoel* (775 tons) and *Manipi* (536 tons) the latter pair of which were later salvaged and used by the Japanese themselves. Fourteen others including the *Alfoer* (473 tons), *Madras* (134 tons), *Overijssel* (395 tons), *Dayak* (174 tons), *Mambang* (764 tons), *Nias* (75 tons), *Pasir* (1,187 tons), *Poelau Bras* (9,278 tons), *Poseidon* (696 tons), *Reteh* (513 tons), *Rokan* (563 tons), *Sipirok* (1,787 tons), *Sipora* (1,594 tons), *Tohiti* (982 tons) plus the whaler *Gemas* (207 tons), were so damaged that they were scuttled before the port fell to the advancing Japanese Army.

The case of the *Poelau Bras* (Captain P G Crietee) was particularly poignant. Unlike the majority of the ships mentioned previously she had cleared safely from Tjilatjap on 28 February and thought she was safe, but the Dutch authorities recalled her in order to embark some high civilian officials, including top brass from the Shell Oil company with their families, who urgently wanted out. There were also some important Army and Navy personnel from the Wijnkoopsbaai including Rear-Admiral J A van Staveren, second-in-command of the Royal Netherlands Navy in the Dutch East Indies. One of the eighty or so Dutch naval passengers was Frans J Zantvoort, who had earlier escaped the Tjilatjap, (which he described as 'a madhouse') but had been sent to join the *Poelau Bras* on 6 March, then anchored in Pelabuhan Ratu Bay. In all some 150 evacuees were ferried out to her and, as there was only accommodation for twelve passengers, things aboard were chaotic. People found spaces below and up on deck wherever they could. One of those who joined was an American journalist William H McDougall, Jr who later wrote a book on his experience.

The heavily-laden freighter finally put to sea that night and headed south at her maximum speed of fifteen knots under cover of darkness. At dawn this headlong flight had to be modified as they steered a precautionary zigzag course as it was feared Japanese submarines were patrolling the area. At 0900hrs the following morning, their hopes of making it were dashed when a scout plane sighted them. They knew they were doomed but had little choice but to try to steam to safety. They thought that they would beyond range of Japanese shore-based aircraft by noon, but they had forgotten the Japanese had aircraft carriers. Two hours later, around 1100hrs, a force of ten dive-bombers from the *Sōryū* located them and commenced attacks. The ship was quickly hit, with large numbers of casualties among the passengers and began to sink. The few survivors abandoned the ship, and only a handful, including Zantvoort and McDougall, finally made landfall at Kroe (now known as Crui), where the local natives handed them over to the Japanese Army.

The *Woolgar* had also escaped the carnage in the port and was some 150 miles south-west of Tjilatjap when caught by *Sōryū's* Vals. The few survivors finally landed at Port Blair in the Andaman Islands after enduring eighty-eight days in a ship's lifeboat, only to find the Japanese already established there. A few other ships, were more fortunate, the RAF Auxiliary, the 549-ton coaster *Tung Song*, was the last ship out, with RAF evacuees, but five thousand other RAF personnel were left behind and became prisoners-of-war.[156]

By now, Egusa's victories were becoming legendary and his accuracy a byword in the fleet. To his crews he was inspirational. One Japanese officer told me that he was called the 'god of dive-bombing.' His group always achieved an incredible percentage of bomb hits. Yet, despite the tempo of operations thus far, Egusa's best work was still to come.

CHAPTER TEN

Carnage in the Indian Ocean

'One who knows neither the enemy nor himself will invariably be defeated in every engagement.' *Sun Tzu – The Art of War.*

On completion of the Java mopping-up operations Nagumo took his carriers back to Kendari and here *Shokaku* and *Zuikaku* replaced *Kaga* once more. On 26 March the force put to sea again, steering south to pass north of Timor and then west, south of the Java and Sumatra barrier, to enter the Indian Ocean on 2 April. Their objective was to engage and destroy a scratch fleet hastily assembled by the Royal Navy under Admiral Sir James Somerville to defend the Indian subcontinent. On paper, the British had a formidable force with five battleships, three carriers and numerous cruisers and destroyers. In practice, the ships were a hotch-potch, many dating from the First World War, while the aircraft on the British carriers were hopelessly outdated and outclassed by the Japanese. The British were still using biplanes at this late stage of the war (Fairey Albacore torpedo bombers), and, amazingly, had no dive-bombers at all serving in front-line units, (although both the Blackburn Skua and Vought Chesapeake, monoplane dive-bombers, were being used back in the UK as target tugs); while the British fighter aircraft, three-seater Fairey Fulmars, were one hundred miles an hour slower than the IJN's incomparable Mitsubishi Zero-Sen. The Admirals, Arbuthnot, Somerville with the fleet and Sir Geoffrey Layton in Ceylon[157] contributed risky decisions during the course of the battle, which split their forces and left them open to attack piecemeal.

The first Japanese strike was launched on 5 April against Colombo in Ceylon (now Sri Lanka), and included thirty-six Vals. The RAF was alerted and had fighter aircraft in the air waiting for them. Enormous claims of casualties inflicted were subsequently made, and repeated by Churchill in Parliament, (and repeated *ad naseum* since the war by those who should know better).[158] The Japanese lost just seven aircraft in total. The British, by contrast, lost twenty-seven, including fifteen Hawker Hurricanes and four Fairey Fulmars. The Japanese naval airmen hit and sank the destroyer *Tenedos* and the Armed Merchant

The *Sōryū* prepares to sortie into the Indian Ocean against the British Eastern Fleet under Admiral Sir James Somerville. This fleet was based at Addu Atoll in the Indian Ocean, south of Ceylon (now known as Sri Lanka), and consisted of five battleships, three aircraft carriers, two heavy cruisers as well as light cruisers and destroyers. It could not be left to operate on the Japanese flank and needed to be eliminated or neutralised. The base itself was unknown to the Japanese who searched for the British force without success but who attacked the known ports of Colombo and Trincomalee, causing great damage. *(Kaijinsha, Tokyo)*

Cruiser *Hector*, and inflicted damage on other ships and naval base facilities, including submarine workshops.[159]

After casting about blindly in the hope of making a dusk torpedo bomber attack on his Japanese opponent's fleet, Somerville had prematurely detached part of his force for other duties. When news came in of the Colombo strike he belatedly attempted to reconcentrate them but it was then too late. Two heavy cruisers, *Cornwall* and *Dorsetshire,* were recalled, but, soon after midday on 5 April, they were sighted by a scout plane from the Nagumo fleet, which reported them at first as destroyers. At once Egusa was despatched with a full force of eight Vals from *Akagi, Hiryū* and *Sōryū,* to hunt them down. A corrected sighting was received reclassifying these isolated ships as cruisers.[160]

The British ships had intercepted these reports and knew that they were in trouble. They increased speed to twenty-seven knots, their maximum, and went on to full alert. At 1338hrs Egusa spotted their long wakes in the clear visibility. The two ships began a desperate zigzag but this only served to throw the gun crews off their aim. Approaching from up-sun and astern to mask the main anti-aircraft batteries, Egusa led in against *Dorsetshire* and scored a direct hit with his first bomb. Egusa's terse radio orders were intercepted on the Japanese flagship's bridge and the nineteen-minute assault was recorded for posterity in his own words:

> 'Sighted enemy vessels. Get ready to go in. Air Group, 1 CarDiv, take the first ship; Air Group, 2 CarDiv, take the second ship.
> [There was a brief pause]
> 'Ship No 1 has stopped, dead in water. Listing heavily. Ship No 2 is aflame.
> 'Ship No 1 has sunk.
> 'Ship No 2 has sunk.'[161]

Dorsetshire, the ship that had torpedoed the *Bismarck* and sent her to the bottom of the North Atlantic a year earlier, was hit in quick succession on her aircraft catapult, her W/T office, on her bridge, and in her engine and boiler rooms. Her rudder was jammed to starboard and she careered around taking further hits, including one, which penetrated a magazine. In just eight minutes she had gone. *Cornwall* took something like fifteen bombs into her in seven minutes. She heeled over and sank bows up. One survivor wrote:

> 'The Japs by this time had formed up in squadrons and flew past in perfect formation, thirty or forty of them and, much to our relief flew away. We were quite expecting to be machine-gunned in the water.'

Two Royal Navy heavy cruisers, the *Dorsetshire* and *Cornwall*, were caught detached from the main British fleet and Egusa's dive bombers sank them both within minutes, scoring a unique number of direct hits which put both ships on the bottom in short order. Here the *Dorsetshire* is heavily hit. *(Zenji Abe)*

The British heavy cruiser *Cornwall's* bows rear into the sky as she takes her last
plunge to the bottom of the Indian Ocean after Egusa's dive-bombers had
smothered her with direct hits. *(Zenji Abe)*

Smothered in bomb hits from Egusa's Aichi Vals, the British heavy cruiser *Dorchester*
heels over moments before following her sister ship to the bottom of the sea.
(Japanese Official)

However, Egusa did not fight that way, nor did he allow his men to do so. Quite the contrary, on the way back to their carrier they passed over a British hospital ship, and directed her to the survivors struggling in the shark-filled waters. After they landed back on board an analysis of the attack followed in the usual way. It concluded that this attack had achieved an all-time high record for accuracy in dive-bombing for the Japanese (or anyone else for that matter). It was calculated that just about every bomb dropped had been a direct hit or a very near miss: 'So thick were the explosions from the rain of bombs that many plane crews could not determine whether they had actually released their missiles. Only after all our planes had assembled in formation and the pilots could visually check the racks of other planes could we tell whether or not several planes were still armed.'

After refuelling, Nagumo took his carriers back to Ceylon on 9 April and launched another strike, this time against Trincomalee harbour. Events were almost an exact repeat of the first raid. Again, the British fighters got a mauling, ships were sunk in the anchorage and others damaged. RAF Bristol Blenheim bombers mounted a counter-attack, the first time Allied eyes had even seen the Nagumo Task Force ships since the Pacific War had started, but, although they achieved tactical surprise, which ought to have given the Japanese much pause for thought, they were as inaccurate as ever, and subsequently most of them were destroyed by the pursuing Zeros. This again did not prevent huge claims of victory being made over this failure back in Britain.

Yet another massive blunder was made by the British Admiral Arbuthnot, when all the available ships in harbour were hurried away to sea without any fighter protection whatsoever. This gave Egusa his longed-for opportunity to destroy an enemy aircraft carrier. It was not the big US carriers he had been hoping for, just the small and elderly British carrier *Hermes*, but it *was* an operation aircraft carrier, albeit without any aircraft embarked.[162] She had an escort of a solitary Australian destroyer, HMAS *Vampire*, of even greater vintage. Once more ninety Aichis roared off from the Japanese carrier's flight decks and headed west. Scanning the shallow waters off Trincomalee, the first wave sighted the flat-top at 1035hrs and began his attack. Within ten minutes, *Hermes* was on her way to the bottom of the Indian Ocean, literally smothered by the deluge of direct hits. An eyewitness recalled:

The Indian Ocean Operation. Death plunge of HMS *Hermes*. Caught without air cover by the Val dive-bombers of Egusa's team, operating at the peak of their powers and delighted to finally to have an aircraft-carrier in their sights, the *Hermes* was pulverised in short order, along with accompanying vessels. *(Zenji Abe)*

'The Japanese came in so low that, after dropping their bombs, they were in serious danger of being blown to bits by blasts of their own making. Those in the look-out positions in the fighting top, some 120ft above the flight-deck, remarked later that some planes swept in below their level.'

By the time Egusa arrived, it was all over.

With *Hermes* rapidly eliminated, the following waves of Japanese dive-bombers turned their attentions to the other vessels in the vicinity. First, the destroyer *Vampire*, then the corvette *Hollyhock* followed the carrier to the seabed, along with some auxiliary vessels and oil tankers. Not a single Val was so much as hit, let alone damaged, while inflicting this carnage.

One of Egusa's victims was the tanker *Athelstane, en route* to Colombo from Trincomalee with a cargo of 7,000 tons of Admiralty fuel oil for the fleet. She had been cleared out of Trincomalee at 0100hrs on 9 April, escorted by the corvette *Hollyhock*. She had a single LA 4-inch gun in charge of a RAN naval gunner, A Goodman, and two PAC rockets[163] as her total defensive armament. At 0900hrs,

The first aircraft carrier of any nation to be sunk outright by dive-bombing, the Royal Navy carrier *Hermes* heels over hit by numerous bombs from Egusa's Vals. She had been hurried to sea with no aircraft to defend herself, and the promised RAF protection failed to materialise. As such, she was a sitting duck for the elite dive-bombing teams from the Nagumo Task Force. *(Zenji Abe)*

they were in sight of the carrier *Hermes*, the *Vampire* and the tanker *British Sergeant*, who were some miles distant, and they witnessed their easy destruction. At 1100hrs about twenty-nine Japanese aircraft flew overhead having completed their attack and returning to the carriers. These had no bombs left for the two ships, (who mistakenly described them as 'monoplane aero-fighters [*sic*])' but instead reported them to Egusa's follow-up team, who found them an hour later.

Her master, Captain Moore, later gave this account of his ship's final moments:

'We proceeded at nine knots steering a southerly course, weather was fine with good visibility, smooth sea with light airs. The sun was directly overhead when, at 1207hrs ATS on the 9 April, in position 7 degrees 31 minutes North, 82 degrees East, we sighted a large number of planes approaching them from the south, that is from directly ahead. They were Zero fighters (*sic*) about twenty-nine of them as far as I could count, then I noticed nine planes in a V-formation making toward us, flying a height of about 10,000ft.

'I ordered the crew to take cover behind the sandbags, as we had no AA armament, and as I did so the planes formed into single line astern and dived one after the other in rotation in a fore and aft line over the ship. Each plane carried one bomb, which was released at a height of 800ft, the aircraft pulling out of its dive at 400ft. We fired the PAC rockets but one jammed in its box, and the other fouled the wireless aerial.

'A large number of bombs fell around us; we received five direct hits and two near misses. The first bomb struck the fore deck between Nos 1 and 2 tanks, the second in almost the same position, the third on No 3 tank, the fourth fell into No 3 tank, exploded the oil, which was thrown up, smothering everything, and blew a hole in the starboard side shell plating.

'The fifth bomb, which fell on the aft deck, apparently failed to explode properly, as there was no damage to the deck, the only effect being to throw the gunner at the 4in gun up into the air. One near miss fell off the starboard side, doing no damage, but the other fell off the port side abreast of the engine room amidships, smashing the steering gear out of action.

'The whole attack lasted about five minutes, during which another formation of enemy aircraft was attacking HMS *Hollyhock*. The first bomb fell close alongside her; the second struck her near the funnel, probably exploding in her magazine, as she immediately blew up, disintegrating, and sank at 1217hrs.'[164]

Captain Moore waited until the attackers had flown off and then gave orders to lower the boats and abandon ship, which was done by 1222hrs without loss. They rescued two officers and twelve ratings from the *Hollyhock* and finally rowed ashore at Kalamani, Ceylon, some eight miles from the scene of the attack. *Athelstane* finally foundered at 1430hrs, almost two-and-a-half hours after being hit.

The RAF had been ordered to send fighters to protect all these ships, but they never took off. Some Fleet Air Fulmars finally arrived on the scene, far too late to affect the issue as Egusa's men were already of their way back to their ships.

Good as these results had been, an even bigger prize awaited Egusa's men, if only fortune had favoured them. Search aircraft were sent off from the Japanese ships looking for Somervilles's main force. They ploughed diligent furrows across the empty ocean on 6 and 8 of April. These searches were concentrated to the south and south-east of Ceylon, but were unrewarded. Why was this? Rather belatedly it had finally dawned on the worried British admiral that, far from being scared to take him on, the Japanese were actively seeking to do so. It also was now rather obvious that, should they find him, the British fleet was likely to suffer a heavy defeat.

Somerville had two carriers against the five Japanese ships. Moreover, against the three hundred sleek Japanese monoplanes, the Royal Navy could only field about four-dozen Fairey Albacore torpedo bombers and biplanes which were incredibly slow. They would have stood no chance, even in a dusk attack and would have shared the fate of the Fairey Swordfish squadron off Ceylon earlier. In response, although the British carriers were equipped with armoured flight decks, and, (as the Stuka attack on *Illustrious* the year before off Malta had shown), were no pushovers to dive-bombing, their defences would have been swamped, thus enabling the Kate torpedo bombers to finish them off. While the five old British battleships were heavily protected, with the carriers gone they would have no air defence whatsoever and with top speeds of nineteen knots at best, would have been subjected to attack after attack by aircraft from the swifter pursuing Japanese carriers. Any British ship damaged and left behind would have been easily sunk by Nagumo's four accompanying fast battleships.

As it was, Somerville was beating a hasty retreat to Mombasa on the east coast of Africa and as the gap between the two forces widened, Japanese search planes increasingly flew futile sorties. As Captain S W Roskill recorded: 'We must be thankful that they never found him.'[165] This view was put even more forthrightly by Captain Russell Grenfell:

'One British Eastern fleet had been destroyed by the Japanese in December, and Mr Churchill has recorded that it gave him the worst shock of the war. Had a second and much larger British Eastern fleet been similarly disposed of in April, the shock not only to him but his countrymen would have been much more than twice as heavy; so severe, in fact, that Mr Churchill's political credit could hardly have survived it. The British Minister of Defence may or may not have known on 6 April 1942, that his office, his future, and his place in history were that day waiting on the toss of a heavenly coin whether or not the many questing Japanese aircraft would catch a glimpse of the British fleet.'[166]

But it was not to be, and eventually Nagumo's force turned back eastward and then steered for home waters. They had another agenda than the final elimination of British influence in eastern waters.

As for the accuracy of Egusa's Indian Ocean attacks, one source summed it up:

'Shortly after the Indian Ocean operation in which Egusa figured so prominently, we were able to have a reunion in Japan. I was preparing for the Midway and Aleutian Operations; I asked my old friend how his planes had sunk the British warships. Egusa looked at me and shrugged: "It was much simpler than bombing the *Settsu* [Japan's old target battleship].[167] That's all."'

As well as enjoying the reunion with his old comrade, Egusa used the opportunity of the fleet's return to home waters, where they arrived on 22/23 April 1942, to rejoin his extended family at last, following his second son Yoshimasa's difficult birth on 20 December 1941. He also received a hero's welcome, as was to be expected. For six months, the dive-bomber pilots had struck from the Nagumo Task Force like phantoms, leaving a trail of destruction behind them unequalled in naval warfare. Little wonder then, that the Japanese considered that the tide of destiny was with them.

This leave period was the happiest Egusa was to know, never again were things to be so perfect in every sphere. However, the time soon passed and it was back into training for the 'big operation', the final reckoning with the Americans, the MI Operation; Midway.

The Indian Ocean sortie had marked the high point of Egusa's career. Such an outstanding hit-rate in wartime conditions would be almost impossible to equal, let alone surpass, no matter what the odds. Nevertheless, Egusa knew that destroying the British warships, with their antiquated concept of modern sea warfare, was a very different proposition to taking on the United States Navy's aircraft carriers. These, all still intact six months after Pearl Harbor, were the elusive prizes that he sought most eagerly. Would he hunt them down, or would they do the hunting?

How to lure these carriers into a set-piece battle and destroy them, leaving Japan master of the Pacific, was the principal problem to which her navy leaders now applied themselves. Their deliberations resulted in the Midway and Aleutian operations. By occupying both these strategic places simultaneously, Yamamoto reasoned, the enemy would be forced to come out and fight on ground chosen by the Japanese and so with the odds heavily in the latter's favour. In theory, this was an admirable idea, and indeed, initially it worked perfectly. However, unknown to the Japanese planners, everything they decided upon was ultimately compromised due to the cracking of the secret naval codes, and the fact that the Americans could read their every move in advance. The assumption that the Americans would have no choice but to play by Japanese rules in the forthcoming battle was very flawed.

Admiral Nagumo was to write in his estimate of the situation: 'Although the enemy lacks the will to fight, it is likely that he will counterattack if our occupation operations proceed satisfactorily.' This may have been fairly accurate, but he then went on to state: 'The enemy is not aware of our plans', which was about as wrong as wrong could be! The Japanese reasoning was encapsulated by Nagumo: 'After attacking Midway by air and destroying the enemy's shore based air strength to facilitate our landing operations, we would still be able to destroy any enemy task force which may choose to counterattack.'

In underestimating the American will to fight, the Japanese compounded their error by assuming all along that the *Yorktown* had been sunk at the Battle of the Coral Sea. This vessel therefore never appeared in any of their evaluations of the possible strength that could be deployed against them. They knew that *Enterprise* and *Hornet* were definitely in the Pacific; that *Lexington* had almost certainly been sunk, or, if not, was under repair and unavailable, and that the *Ranger* was in the Atlantic. Their only doubt was the location of the *Wasp* (she was not in the Pacific at this time). Nor do they mention the *Saratoga*.

The very ease by which the Japanese conquests across the whole of south-east Asia had been achieved against the hitherto invincible white races, led to a nation-wide euphoria, retrospectively labelled 'victory fever' by historians. This led her to disperse her forces over a vast area instead of concentrating them for the killer blow, as they should have done. Conflict between the Army and Navy, the former having greater influence with the Government, also played its part. The Navy wished to push down the Solomon Islands chain and on to

New Caledonia, Fiji and Samoa thus cutting the only link between Australia, dangerously exposed now, and the United States. The Japanese had already captured the vital Rabaul base on New Britain, as well as Lae and Salamua on the northern coast of Papua.

The Navy, by contrast, was so enthusiastic that they even committed three of their vital aircraft carriers to support this plan, during which they planned to occupy Port Moresby on Papua's southern coast facing Australia, on which the Army remained, at best, luke-warm.[168] In the resulting Battle of the Coral Sea, they lost one carrier, the *Shoho*, and had one of the other two, the *Shokaku* damaged. As her sister ship had her air group decimated in the battle, even though the carrier itself was untouched, it meant that all three Japanese carriers were then unavailable for the next, and far more important, battle.[169]

Even so, the Japanese still retained an overall superiority in numbers of aircraft carriers, but again, they dissipated this, some being sent to cover the Aleutian Islands operation far to the north, others being split between the various Midway Task Forces. Thus it came about that, in the final analysis, four Japanese carriers, *Akagi*, *Kaga*, *Hiryū* and *Sōryū*, faced three American carriers *Hornet*, *Yorktown* and *Enterprise*, but plus what was in fact a fourth, and unsinkable aircraft-carrier packed with all manner of warplanes, Midway itself, to reinforce them. Overconfidence had reduced the odds quite needlessly from a ratio of 10:3 to a mere 4:3 in carriers, but actually 4:4 in terms of air-launch platforms.[170] The conflicting needs of having to attack both the island airstrip and the American carriers further split the Japanese air striking forces, as different types of bomb-loads were required for each target. The result was that, this time, it was the Japanese who were caught flat-footed and between two stools at the crucial time. During the Battle of Midway, the American Navy dive-bomber pilots did not waste their opportunities, they acted brilliantly and single-handedly won the battle when all other types of attack had failed dismally and totally. This time it became the Japanese who felt the weight of dive-bombing on exposed carrier decks. The result was equally devastating.

CHAPTER ELEVEN

The Biter Bit – Midway

'One who, fully prepared, awaits the unprepared will be victorious.' *Sun Tzu – The Art of War.*

When the big carriers had returned to their Japanese home ports at the end of April, they had immediately been taken in hand for urgent repair and maintenance to ready them for the next mission. Likewise, their air complements undertook training programmes at various shore bases, in the case of *Sōryū's* group, at Kasanohara. The various bomber leaders underwent their programme separately at Iwakuni. The results, in general, were very hard to swallow after such a string of successes in action.

Nagumo recorded:

'Although the flight training programme was conducted without any major incident, there had been a considerable turnover in personnel, so practically no one got beyond the point of basic training. Inexperienced fliers barely got to the point where they could make daytime landings on carriers. It was found that even some of the more seasoned fliers had lost some of their skill. No opportunity was available to carry out joint training, which, of course made impossible any co-ordinated action...'

The value of this training period for dive-bomber units was largely negated by the fact that the target ship *Settsu*, was confined to the waters of Naikai Seibu (the Western Inland Sea). This meant that the Val aircrew had to waste valuable time traversing from their bases to that area and back. This reduced the programme to just one dive-bombing practice per day without seriously interfering with their basic training. Even this modest effort was compromised because the men were kept occupied with maintenance work. This limitation of time on training extended to the surface ships also, and Nagumo was to ruminate bitterly after the battle that:

'Added to this, we had practically no intelligence concerning the enemy. We never knew to the end where or how many enemy carriers there were. In other words, we participated in this operation with meagre training and without knowing the enemy.'[171]

If the man in command had grave doubts, he kept them to himself and the nation at large was certainly not privy to any such considerations. While *Sōryū* herself was undergoing repairs, the Flag of CarDiv 2 was transferred to the *Hiryū* at Sasebo early in May and she later became the permanent flagship.[172] Gradually the various squadrons of warships assembled at Hashirajima, but not until the end of May, just a few days before they sortied out to the battle, did all the units concentrate there. The Air Groups finally re-embarked aboard their respective carriers on 24 May, ready or not.

Overconfidence may have been the prevailing mood among the civilians at home and in some elements at naval headquarters or in the Army, but Egusa himself was under no illusion as *Sōryū* put to sea once more from Hashirajima, at 0400hrs on 27 May 1942, with the reduced strength *Kidū Butai*. She was just one of no less than seventy-one Japanese warships, including the whole battleship strength, converging on the tiny atoll of Midway for what was hoped would be the final showdown.

Let us consider the composition of the Japanese air-striking forces as they were organised at this stage of the war. A product of the 1934 Second Replenishment Programme, *Sōryū* herself[173] was a typical Japanese aircraft carrier. Displacing 15,900 tons, she could steam at 28 knots and carry a total of seventy-one aircraft, sixty-three operational and eight in reserve. She had been completed in December 1937. Her appearance was far from conventional to western eyes, she had a small 'island' bridge structure on her starboard side, and two smoke-vents discharged almost horizontally from the same side, leaving her 711ft planked wooden flight-deck clear and unobstructed for operating for aircraft. Like contemporary American aircraft carriers, but unlike equivalent British carriers, this deck was unarmoured. The theory was that instead of being built to stand up to hits by large bombs, as were the new British carriers, the Japanese and American idea was to embark the maximum possible number of aircraft in order to both strike hard and to defend herself from the air, rather than absorb punishment. She was therefore, comparatively vulnerable and relied heavily on her own fighter and gun defences to stop her being hit in the first place.

At this period of the war, Japanese aircraft carriers had

numerous fuelling points positioned around two large hangars, so that her aircraft could be fuelled below decks and then be brought up later ready to go. This certainly made for speedier operation of her air group compared to British carriers with their tiny complements of planes, but it meant that under that flimsy flight-deck they were wide open to bomb hits.

Each hangar had two decks, which were each almost completely sealed and isolated from the rest of the vessel. Ventilation systems changed the air at ten-minute intervals, but any fumes from leaks could build up dangerously in that confined space. In the event of a major fire, the hangar crews could not escape easily, or get rid of flammable material, while the ship's own fire-fighting teams could not gain instant access inside, and nor could other ships help very much to contain the spread of flames. However, up that time, hardly any enemy aircraft and no ships at all, had so much as sighted them, let along made a serious attack, and little concern was therefore felt on these points.

As originally built, *Sōryū* lacked sheer in the bows, a fault, which was rectified in her later sisters by the addition of further, decks forward. This profile made her notoriously 'wet' and she would dip her prow into every sea and throw spray back over the flight-deck in sheets. No catapults were carried to launch her aircraft, the heavily-laden bombers taking off against the wind without such assistance. A smoke-discharger forward gave wind direction and the carrier thus had to steer into the prevailing breeze when launching. This again, made her vulnerable, as she had to maintain a steady course during this and landing operations. Once the aircraft had been fuelled and armed below decks in the large enclosed hangars, they were brought up on the one of the three lifts and 'spotted' on the wood plank flight-deck[174] in readiness for launch as described earlier.

The *Hikochū* (Air Operations Officer) controlled events from the bridge with the aid of two other officers, while the *Seibiin* (Flight Deck Controller) was responsible for arranging the aircraft on the deck. Once the order was given to launch, the *Hikochū* raised a white flag from his position in the bridge wings, and the aircraft flew off one by one at about 20 second intervals until all had become airborne, whereupon the flag was lowered. Destroyers were allocated to each carrier in the usual manner as 'plane-guards' to rescue any aircrew forced to ditch. Once airborne the various groups formed up on the leaders before heading off to the target.

Landing operations were almost as basic. Returning planes (priority being given to damaged aircraft of course) flew some 500m from the carrier waiting for the *Seibiin* to signal by lamp that the flight deck was clear. Abreast of the bridge structure, the aircraft turned at a height of some 200m and positioned itself astern.

He then used his own judgement, but was aided by the IJN's unique *Chakkan Shidoto* (Landing Guidance Light) landing aid.[175] Invented initially as a method of reducing the dangers of carrier night landings, which itself was later largely abandoned by the IJN, this device, was developed and perfected by Kasumigura in 1932.

On either side of the flight deck aft, ahead of the forward lift, a set of adjustable red and a matching set of fixed green 1kw variable intensity datum reference lights were located at deck level, with a gap of approximately 10 to 15 metres between them. Each light was equipped with a refracting mirror, which could be adjusted to give a cone of light, and the separation angle of the two coloured beams could be managed. The resulting glide path indication varied by aircraft type between 4 and 6 degrees. By keeping both sets of lights in view during his approach, the pilot knew he was centrally placed on the flight deck. Similarly, if the blue or green light was directly above the red, the pilot knew his approach height was spot on. Too low an approach and he would only be able to see the red light, and could adjust accordingly, so red alone meant, pull up. Too high an approach and the other light would appear superimposed on the red.[176]

The first carrier to have this apparatus fitted was the *Hosho* a year later for sea trials and it became commonplace on all Japanese flat tops from *Sōryū* onward.

The pilot was also assisted in positioning himself correctly by the trapezoidal outriggers located on each side of the flight deck and red and white painted stripes, both of helped him position where he was in relation to the after deck or 'round-down.' A bad approach would result in a 'red flag' signal from the *Hikochū* as an order to abort the attempt and go round again for a retry.

Nine *Kure* Type 4 arrestor wires, two located in front of the crash barriers and seven abaft, normally lowered, would be raised to a height of between 100-150mm across the rear portion of the deck. So many options normally ensured that at least one engaged the tail hook of the aircraft and brought the 8,378lb (3,800kg) Val to a halt in under 40 metres. These wires each had their ends affixed to sturdy cables, which in turn were spooled around an induction-coil drum beneath the deck. The sturdy, fixed undercarriage of the Val militated against the effects of too hard touchdown, when more fragile types with retractable gear got into trouble in most British and American navies. It took just twelve seconds for the wire to be retrieved electrically after each operation.

A pair of flexible, six-feet high, triple-wired, hydraulically-raised *Kusho* Type 3 crash barrier was positioned forward to block any aircraft that bounced the wires or otherwise failed to connect with her tail hook, as a last ditch protection against the demolition of any aircraft parked forward. These barriers could stop a Val within 7 metres. *Sōryū* also had two mobile crash barriers to supplement the fixed ones, and they could be installed between the two lifts. There was also a hydraulically-raised propeller blast screen located ahead of the foremost lift.

In the event of the worst-case scenario, a large 4-ton retractable crane and foam fire-fighting apparatus stood ready on the deck platforms for any cripples or mistakes by novices. No bomber was allowed to land with a bomb intact for obvious reasons, not than many of Egusa's skilled and proud pilots would contemplate bringing home his weapon while an enemy ship was still available as a target. It was a point of honour among these veterans to make every bomb count. As each Val landed safely on, she would be wheeled forward over the lowered barrier to the deck park, and the barrier would then be raised ready for the next aircraft. When all the formation had got down safely, the sweating deck crew would wheel the parked aircraft aft to the lifts to be struck down into the hangars for refuelling, rearming or maintenance. Not until this cycle had been completed could the next strike be brought up onto the flight deck in turn for their launch. After earlier experimentation, the Japanese largely avoided the use of catapults on their carriers, considering such a method as being too slow.

The Second *Koku Sentai* under Rear Admiral Tamon Yamaguchi aboard *Hiryū*, comprised that ship and *Sōryū*, commanded by Captain Ryusaku Yanagimito. Both *Hiryū* and *Sōryū* carried almost identical aircraft complements: twenty-one A6M5 (Zero or Zeke) *Sentoki* (fighters); twenty-one B5N2 (Kate) *Kogekiki* (torpedo or attack-bombers) and twenty-one D3A2 (Val) *Kyukoka Bakugerkiki* (dive-bombers). Lieutenant Masahiro Ikeda commanded the latter, while Egusa flew from the same aircraft carrier in his distinctively marked Val as overall Flight Leader and Attack Co-ordinator for the whole strike force. There were also two of the brand-new Yokosuka D4Y *Comet* dive-bombers (codenamed Judy by the Allies) aboard *Sōryū*. They were very new, in fact, they were the third and fourth prototypes. Fast, sleek and powerful as these new aircraft were, they were *not* being employed in their designed role as there were problems, but the intention was to use them in their scouting configuration, as fast reconnaissance aircraft so the Val was to remain as the mainstay of the dive-bomber forces for this battle.

The normal bomb load for attacking ship targets with the Val was a single 250kg armour-piercing bomb, but SAP (semi-armour piercing) and 242kg HE (high-explosive) bombs were available when required, as were oil bombs for fire-raising on enemy carriers and small fragmentation bombs designed to scythe down anti-aircraft gunners in their nests or infantry ashore. The defensive armament of the dive-bomber consisted of two 7·7mm machine-guns in each wing and one flexible mounting of the same calibre operated by the wireless operator seated in tandem behind the pilot. The aircraft themselves were slow and relied on their own fighter protection for their immunity of the flight out to the target and back again. Once committed to their 60-degree dives, only a direct hit by a large calibre shell (3in or 5in) could deflect them and this was not easy to achieve, even by experienced gunners willing to stand up to a screaming dive-bomber heading straight at them. Smaller calibre weapons in barrages would score hits and eventually disable a dive-bomber in approach or during the breakaway but by then the bomb would have been released and on its way to the target regardless of what happened to the delivery vehicle and her crew.

The aircrew complement aboard each carrier was approximately one-tenth of the entire ships' company, but they were the principals on whose achievements all the others depended and whom they served. As *Sōryū* sailed to battle, the majority of her *Kyukoka Bakugerkiki* aircrew were veterans, the *crème de la crème*, with only the slightest leavening of new recruits among them.[177] However, as we have seen, the hitherto shining sword had lost some of its edge, even though losses hitherto had been minimal. Each man thirsted for the sight of a 'Yankee' flat top in his dive-bombing sights, and most were convinced that, when the opportunity arose, they would deal with it as positively as they had done with the *Hermes*.

It was fated not to be. The American SBD Dauntless dive-bombers were to find the Nagumo Task Force with all its bombers still rearming and awaiting free-deck space so that they could be brought up in readiness to launch. However, initially, all seemed to be proceeding according to the Japanese plan. Strict radio and silence was maintained as the ships steamed eastward to the destinies, with a tight anti-submarine screen around them. The big carriers pushed on toward an area to the north-west of Midway Island, and refuelled on 1st and 2nd of June. They were shielded in the approach by a thick fog, which descended from about 1000hrs on the 2nd and thickening continually all night until the ships were navigating blindly without visual signals. Not until 1030hrs did this fog lift and then visibility steadily increased.

The layout and disposition of the Japanese force was as follows:

Disposition

1st Div. (CV)	2nd Div. (CV)	
Akagi (F)	*Hiryū* (F)	
Kaga	*Sōryū*	
BB	CA	CL
Kirishima (F)	*Tone* (F)	*Nagara*
Haruna	*Chikuma*	
About 10 DD's		

Various reports of sighting of enemy aircraft were received during the 4 and 5 June, and on one occasion, fighters were scrambled from *Akagi* to intercept them, but no contact was made. However, from 0830hrs on the 5th, American reconnaissance aircraft were in continuous contact with the Japanese Task Force, so no surprise was to be achieved.[178] The force was steering a course of 130 degrees at twenty knots in screen cruising disposition No 1. As the morning developed speed was increased, firstly to 24, then to 26 and ultimately to 28 knots, as *Tone's* seaplane reported two enemy submarines on the surface some eighty miles distant. Meanwhile the Japanese carriers had despatched a 108-plane strike, including eighteen of *Sōryū's* Kate's led by Lieutenant Heijirū Abe, and nine of her Zero's under Lieutenant Masaharu Suganami, designed to hit the Midway Island airfield and defences at first light. Meanwhile the *Akagi* and *Kaga*, the battleship *Haruna* and the heavy cruisers *Chikuma* and *Tone* all launched search planes to seek out any possible American forces to the south and east of them.

From 0700hrs until 1030hrs, a succession of American air attacks developed against the Nagumo force. From the decks of the *Sōryū*, Egusa witnessed wave after wave of the enemy's air power dashed itself in vain against the defending Zero fighters and the wall of steel from the fleet's anti-aircraft guns. All types of tactics were employed, altitude bombing from B-17 Flying Fortresses, (a totally useless exercise); glide bombing by Marine Vindicators; dive-bombing, torpedo bombing by Catalina flying boats, B-26 Marauder twin-engined army bombers and naval carrier-borne aircraft. Not a single hit was made and, in return, the attacking aircraft were decimated.

Egusa, watching from the *Sōryū*, could only grandstand. With her own personal anti-aircraft guard ship, the heavy cruiser *Chikuma*, keeping close watch, she manoeuvred through this mayhem to land back aboard one of her scouting aircraft at 0739hrs, a dangerous moment as it took her away from the protection of the main fleet. At 0748hrs, from six to nine enemy aircraft were sighted bearing 320 degrees, and *Chikuma* laid down a three-minute concentrated barrage against this threatening group. Many aircraft braved this and carried out dives against *Sōryū*, some nine or ten bombs being aimed at her, but there were no hits. The *Sōryū's* commander also reported that, 'fourteen enemy twin-engined (*sic*) planes, had over-flown her at 270 degrees at an altitude of 30,000 metres (*sic*).'

The recovery of her scout was safely accomplished and *Sōryū* turned to rejoin her companions, but she was still isolated and a tempting target for a while and, at 0800hrs she briefly made smoke to shield her. Four minutes later *Chikuma* reported another group of American aircraft bearing 30 degrees to port and, at 0806hrs, amplified this to report that these were carrier-based aircraft, the first seen, heading for the main force. All the fleets' guns opened up against these incoming assailants, which proved to be single-engined torpedo-bombers. At 0807hrs *Sōryū* reported three heavy bombers overhead and a minute later ten torpedo bombers were seen approaching her at low altitude.

The pace was now hot. *Chikuma* shot one of the torpedo bombers to pieces at a range of 200 metres at 0809hrs and a minute later a solitary enemy aircraft dived on *Sōryū* as they came round to a course of 140 degrees. Both ships held their fire now as three Zero fighters from *Akagi* closed with this force and a deadly air combat developed during which the remaining attackers were all destroyed. At 0819hrs, Egusa witnessed a whole cascade of heavy bombs exploding in the close vicinity of his ship, but again none hit, and she and *Hiryū* replied with every gun that would bear. The sea was boiling with the explosions and spray and near-misses and, at 0829, *Chikuma* was engaging three more enemy torpedo bombers crossing over from 15 degrees to port to starboard, increasing speed to thirty knots as she did so. These were all destroyed and the immediate danger passed.

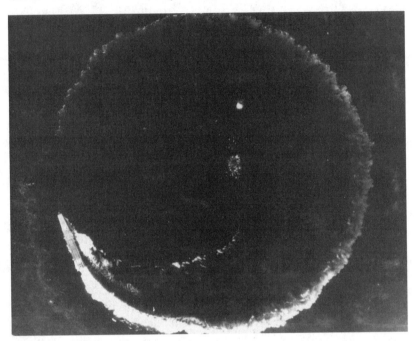

The Nagumo Task Force was charged with both neutralising the island base itself and its air power, and defeating any American fleet that ventured out to its rescue. Yamamoto's plan assumed that there would be ample time to complete one task before turning to the other, but, thanks to pre-knowledge of the Japanese plans, the Americans were fully ready and caught the Japanese carriers with most of their aircraft below decks. Here the *Sōryū* is turning a full circle while under ineffectual attack from the USAAF heavy bombers. The only aircraft that can be seen on her deck appears to be a Zero fighter ready to take off to reinforce her defensive Combat Air Patrol. Egusa's Val dive-bombers are still all struck down in the hangar decks being readied prepared for their own strike. Their fleeting opportunity never arose. *(US National Archives, Washington D C)*

Very few of the attacking American aircraft returned to their base, which the *Hiryū's* and *Sōryū's* teams had hit heavily, returned to their base. For the loss of only two Zeros, three Kates and just a single Val (incredibly the Americans claimed to have shot down more than a dozen of them), the island's installations had been pounded. At 0700hrs, *Hiryū* signalled: 'There is a necessity for carrying out a second attack.'

This was a fateful signal. Nagumo had signalled Organisation 4 to his other three carriers, which meant that the Kates had been armed with torpedoes for use against ship targets should an enemy Task Force put in an appearance. None had, and now a second strike was thought necessary against Midway. He pondered a while, and then ordered the Kates to replace their torpedoes with bombs suitable for use against land targets. This involved striking them all down on the carrier lifts again for the changeover. Egusa's dive-bombers were not affected by this, but still sat parked in their hangars below, leaving the flight deck above clear for defending fighters to take off and land to rearm and refuel as they dealt with successive incoming American attacks. Egusa and his young dive-bomber crews could only wait, impotent and chafing at the bit.

Then, at 0800hrs,[179] came another signal, this one from one of the float planes from the heavy cruiser *Tone*.

'Sighted what appears to be the enemy composed of ten [ships] bearing 10 degrees, distance 240 miles from Midway, on course 150 degrees, speed 20 knots. (0728hrs).'

Two more signals from the same aircraft followed without adding any amplifying detail and Nagumo was forced to prompt the airmen with a signal of his own: 'Advise ship types.'

Finally, at 0830hrs, a fourth signal, time ten minutes earlier, put the cat among the pigeons in no uncertain manner.

'The enemy is accompanied by what appears to be a carrier in a position to the rear of the others.'

Nagumo was now in a real dilemma. The Kate torpedo-bombers were still in the middle of being rearmed with Type 80 land target bombs (805kg) so could not be sent off to attack, even though Nagumo had signalled to Yamamoto that the enemy fleet had been sighted, adding: 'We are heading for it.'

Aboard *Sōryū* earlier, Egusa had watched with professional interest as the one remaining D4Y (coded BI-201 the other had been written off in an accident earlier) was prepared and then launched to take over from *Tone's* aircraft. As this machine droned away over the horizon, there was an expectant pause.[180]

Nagumo had determined in his own mind that, rather than despatch his air striking forces piecemeal, flying off those like

Egusa's dive-bombers that could be got ready quickly, and following them later with the again rearmed Kates, he would wait and make what he termed a 'a grand scale attack' with every aircraft at his disposal. So the Vals remained chained to the carrier and, instead, at 0905hrs, Nagumo instructed: 'After taking on the returning planes, we shall proceed north to contact and destroy the enemy task force.'

He also instructed: 'Prepare to carry out attacks on enemy fleet units. Leave torpedoes on those attack planes which have not as yet been changed to bombs.'

CarDiv1 advised that its aircraft would be ready for take-off at 0730hrs and CarDiv2 that it would be ready between 1030hrs and 1100hrs. The planned attack force that would be despatched was to be *Akagi* – three fighters and eighteen bombers; *Kaga* – three fighters and twenty-seven bombers; *Hiryū* – three fighters and eighteen dive-bombers and *Sōryū*, three fighters and eighteen dive-bombers. The paucity of the fighter escorts was marked, due to their continuous deployment in defence of the fleet and the need to maintain a continuing air umbrella, as well as keeping a reserve force for escort to a second striking force.

There was other information, which, had Nagumo been aware of it, might have brought about a more urgent reaction. Aboard the *Sōryū* were two of the new, experimental Yokosuka D4Y (Type 13) dive-bombers, faster and with much greater range than the Vals.[181] One of these dive-bombers had been despatched as a scout. She had sighted an additional American Task Force containing two further carriers to the north of the first group. Due to radio failure, she was unable to communicate this vital information and until she landed back aboard *Sōryū*, Nagumo was in blissful ignorance of this powerful force.

So, Lieutenant Abe's attack bombers had been struck down to be rearmed for a second strike against Midway Island itself. The elite crews of Egusa's unit, eighteen Vals each aboard the *Hiryū* and *Sōryū*, remained chained on hold, as they had been for a long period. However, a third of them were equipped with instantaneous-fuse HE bombs and not the more suitable anti-carrier SAP bombs, and thus needed rearming as well.[182] Egusa and his men were eager to be off but in order to mount his 'grand scale' attack, Nagumo had no time to spare, let alone unleash them. They remained in their central hangar, now rearmed and fuelled but chained impotently as the vital minutes ticked by.

One can only imagine the effect this was having on Egusa himself. He had trained long and hard with the focused aim of destroying the American aircraft carriers, bringing his dive-bomber team to an unequalled pitch of efficiency. This supreme weapon had been thwarted at Pearl because the American carriers were not present. Egusa had urged a search for them, which had been denied to him. Now, once more the target he yearned for was seemingly within his grasp, temptingly just over the horizon, and *still* he was unable to go. The constant American attacks, with their resulting effect on the movements of the carriers in taking avoiding action and the constant despatch and recovery of defending Zeros to maintain the CAP, negated any time window sufficient to bring up Egusa's Vals and send them away.

Twice the commanding officer of the Second Carrier Division, Rear Admiral Tamon Yamaguchi, had signalled to the flagship suggesting that the aircraft be launched immediately, armed with whatever they had. One wonders whether Egusa's relayed urgings, as at Pearl, were behind these frustrated taps on the shoulder from Yamaguchi to his superior. This author strongly suspects they were. The first signal was duly acknowledged but nothing happened because nothing could happen, the enemy attacks were almost continuous and unrelenting. Several of the eyewitnesses have since blamed the influence of Commander Minoru Genda, First Air Fleet Staff Officer. As far as air operations went, what he advised Nagumo, Nagumo did; at least that is the perceived wisdom of these officers. But striking forces could not be brought up, whatever their current weapons loading, spotted and launched while the ships were heeling over, alternately heading into, at right angles to, and away from the wind, and while the Zeros were taking off and landing?

Yet further attacks by land-based aircraft had been repeatedly beaten off by the fleet's fighters and guns, but, at 1024hrs on 4 June, well before the launch could finally be initiated[183] ready for the Vals to brought up on deck, fate struck a cruel blow. The great carrier had turned to the north, course 350, into the wind in readiness to launch further Zeros to reinforce the CAP, many of which were still 'down on the deck' finishing off the torpedo bomber remnants, while others duelled with Lieutenant-Commander John S. Thatch's F4F Wildcats.[184]

Undetected in the general mêlée, powerful American dive-bomber forces arrived over the Japanese carriers and commenced their final attack. Lieutenant-Commander Maxwell Franklin Leslie,

leading VB-3 from *Yorktown*, related that: 'At about 1223hrs[185] my
radioman reported that the carrier which was my target was
launching planes.' At 1225hrs he gave the order to attack. This is
firmly backed up by Lieutenant DeWitt Wood Shumway, who
related how he witnessed VB-3 start their attack on a very large
carrier (in fact *Sōryū*). He stated quite clearly that: 'Its flight deck
was covered with planes spotted aft. Upon sighting our aircraft the
objective turned left 90 degrees to the north in order to launch planes
and the sides of the ship tuned into a veritable ring of flame. Diving
from the north, all pilots had a steady dive along the fore and aft line
of the target.' This, of course, agrees with the account given by
Fuchida, but that is now being seriously questioned.

While Egusa's and his pilots waited in vain aboard the *Sōryū* for the signal to take
off and attack the American aircraft-carriers, American Douglas SBD Dauntless
dive-bombers from the carrier USS *Yorktown* arrived unheralded and commenced
started their dives on the *Sōryū* . Hit by three heavy bombs, which wrecked her
flight deck, damaged her engines and caused internal explosions among her packed
aircraft hangars, the Japanese carrier was mortally wounded. Egusa was blown into
the ocean by one detonation, but survived to be rescued by the destroyer *Isokaze*.
This is a diorama of the fatal dive-bombing attack. The *Sōryū* sank several hours
later with most of her aircraft. *(US National Archives, Washington D C)*

Other American dive-bomber pilots give different views, some maintaining that very few Japanese aircraft were visible on the flight decks as the SBD's homed in. This author recently interviewed four surviving Japanese veterans who were at Midway, serving on each of the doomed aircraft carriers. All of them, without exception, were vehement that *none* of the dive- or torpedo-bomber groups had been brought up on deck.

There were a total of seventeen SBD's from VB-3 in the strike force, but only thirteen were carrying ordnance. From the carrier they counted at least twelve Dauntless dive-bombers diving on the ship from bow-to-stern, which seem to have included three of the unarmed aircraft. The latter dive-bombers made diversionary attacks against screening warships, two taking on the battleship *Haruna* and the other three going for the *Sōryū's* guard ship astern, the destroyer *Isokaze*. At the same time other American dive-bombers were diving on other Japanese carriers, although a fortuitous rain-squall shielded the *Hiryū* and she escaped their attention.

Within a few minutes *Akagi*, *Kaga* and *Sōryū* had been hit by a number of bombs which penetrated their frail decks, carved through to the hangar decks, and exploded with devastating results inside the hangars among the packed aircraft, fuel tanks, bomb and torpedo arsenals. It was a moment of utter devastation and with this one attack; the bulk of the elite air mechanics and servicing team of the Japanese dive-bomber forces was annihilated, even if the aircrew up on the flight deck were largely spared their fate.

An estimated thirteen Douglas SDB Dauntless dive-bombers hurtled down on *Sōryū* and the carrier received three direct hits immediately, at 1025hrs, 1026hrs and 1028hrs. One 500lb missile struck the flight-deck forward of the main lift, right on the great red 'meatball' of the nationality marking painted there, the other two on each side of the amidships lift, the latter smack in the centre. They penetrated down into the crowded hangar decks. The fuel from the pulverised aircraft ignited and spread instantly through the hangar decks. Bombs and torpedoes exploded in their storage rooms. The anti-aircraft and machine-gun ammunition rooms as well as the aviation fuel storage also cooked off? The resulting chain reaction spread like wildfire through the great vessel's innards. Soon the heat was so intense that the very metal of the vessel started to melt. Both engines stopped at 1040hrs.

Egusa himself, like many of his companions, had been forced to congregate on the deck by the spreading flames.[186] They hardly had time to realise the attack was taking place before an enormous explosion blew him violently overboard and into the sea. He was still alive but the searing agony of multiple burns was barely eased by his contact with the warm salt water of the sea. He survived the explosion, the catapulting into the sea from the flight-deck and the flames, and was finally pulled out, breathing but in a very bad way, when the destroyers *Hamakaze* and *Isokaze* moved in among the wreckage and the survivors to retrieve whoever they could from the carnage. The *Chikuma* also lowered her ship's cutter with her Pharmacist's mate and eight crew, to lend a hand. The intention was to put survivors back aboard *Sōryū* on her still intact forward deck so medical help could be administered to them, but this could not be done. This cutter was eventually left behind and her crew taken aboard the *Isokaze* and later rejoined their own ship. Meanwhile *Sōryū's* engines came to a halt at 1040hrs and three minutes later, her steering useless, she was a floating, blazing hulk. Captain Yanagimito had ordered 'abandon ship' at 1045hrs, within twenty minutes of the first detonation, but he remained aboard in the bridge signal tower until the end.

At 1655hrs, Nagumo ordered the destroyer *Hamakaze* to, 'join *Isokaze* in screening *Sōryū* and at the same time retire to the north-west.' There was still hope of saving her and getting her home. The Commander of DesDiv 4 signalled to *Isokaze* at 1732hrs, 'stand by in the vicinity of the *Sōryū* until otherwise ordered. Would she be operational if her fires were brought under control?' Although the fires aboard the stricken ship had somewhat abated by 1900hrs, and the air officer who was acting commander organised fire fighters in the hope of reboarding her, the *Sōryū* herself was doomed. The *Isokaze*, where Egusa was undergoing what sparse medical treatment there was with so many injured on such a small vessel, replied at 1802hrs: 'There is no hope of her navigating under her own power. All survivors have been taken aboard this ship.' The uncompromising response came at 1830hrs: 'Each ship will stand by the carrier assigned to her and screen her from enemy submarines and task forces. Should the enemy task force approach, engage him in hit-and-run tactics and destroy him.'

The *Sōryū* finally went down at 1913hrs, in position 32°42.5' N, 178° 37.5'W, along with approximately 718 of her complement, (35 officers and 683 Petty officers and men)[187] and her boilers exploded underwater seven minutes later. The destroyer *Hamakaze* radioed to Nagumo, who had earlier transferred to the cruiser *Nagara*, '*Sōryū* has sunk.'

Egusa was hardly recognisable when taken aboard the rescuing destroyer, with severe burns to his face and left hand arm and body, but prompt medical care soon restored him to a painful fitness during the long voyage back home to Japan. Incredible as it may seem, it has been calculated that only ten of *Sōryū's* aircrew were killed in this battle, six in the air and four aboard the carrier when she was hit.[188]

CHAPTER TWELVE

The Last Sortie

'Being unconquerable lies with yourself, being conquerable
lies with the enemy.' *Sun Tzu – The Art of War.*

It was a sad homecoming for the hitherto conquering hero. His
burns were bad enough to ensure a short period of hospitalisation,
but Egusa was indomitable. Along with other wounded from the
battle, Egusa was tended to at the large, sprawling IJN Naval
Hospital at Yokosuka. Rebuilt in 1931 after the original 1881
complex had been largely destroyed by the Great Kanto earthquake,
this was a modern hospital with twelve two-storey wings. According
to some accounts, the wounded and injured were landed from the
rescue ships at night and in greatest secrecy, lest the scale of the
Midway defeat leaked out to the general public and these men were
treated almost as pariahs by the Government.[189] Whether or not this is
so, or somewhat exaggerated, the treatment that Egusa received at the
hands of the medical staff at Yokosuka was first-class.

This did not prevent Takashige's stubborn temperament from
taking over again, for he soon became bored with the hospital and
enforced idleness and yearned to see Kiyoko, who, like all the other
wives of the killed and wounded, had still not been informed of their
husbands' fates. The result was predictable. Kiyoko was to recall how,
one day in the summer of 1942, she returned home after visiting a
friend nearby only to find that, to her astonishment, her husband was
there. Her pleasure at seeing him was marred by the fact that his
whole face was wound round with bandages except for his eyes, and
his left arm, which hung limply at his side, was also heavily bandaged.
He briefly explained that he had been flipped into the air by a bomb
explosion and burned, but received few other details. His injuries had
not yet healed up, but he was determined to see her and his family.

Takashige had faced a narrow escape from death, and was
determined to make the utmost time with his loved ones, for he
knew he would be returning to the battle front before too long. He
may have wanted to fight, but he was not yet fully fit. Not only did
he recover quickly from his injuries but, once he was up and around
again, he was campaigning to fly once more. Within a month, he was

given his wish, but not with a front-line unit. On 10 July 1942, he was back once more working as an instructor with the Yokosuka *Kokutai*. The family moved home to Kamakura and he continued to gain strength, but was not yet able to fly. His brain, however, was as sharp and determined as ever.

With the loss and injury of some of her finest and experienced aircrew, most of them without any opportunity to strike back at the enemy, Japan's position was a very serious one. True, actual numbers of pilots killed was very small, and true, the Aleutians were occupied, but this had little relevance. The Americans were soon landing on Guadalcanal in the Solomons as the first stage of their long fight back. The loss of the aircraft carriers was grievous, the loss of so many frontline aircraft was sad, but these could be replaced. The 110 veteran aircrew who died was a setback, but the loss of more than 2,500 experienced aircraft maintenance crewmen who went down with their ships at Midway would never be made good. From this moment on Japan was fighting a losing battle.

There was obviously a clear need for the training of large numbers of replacements, and veterans such as Egusa, became doubly valuable in this role, much as they may have wished otherwise. Somehow, he had to impart his special skills and expertise to the new arrivals, knowing that when they faced the enemy the odds against them would have increased enormously. In fact the rest of the Pacific War was to see the ever more frantic training of fresh batches of young airmen, and their subsequent wholesale squandering in operation after operation without a decisive result. As their training period grew shorter and shorter due to lack of fuel and the urgent need to get them to the front line, so their ability to inflict meaningful damage upon the Americans lessened. It was a wasting return of talent and bravery. With an enormous industrial base behind them, the first fleet of the United States doubled and quadrupled in a short period and never again did the Japanese have the advantage of numbers over their opponents as they could (and *should*) have done at Midway.

New aircraft were now on the drawing boards in Japan to replace the standard models. A powerful new dive-bomber for carrier work, the Yokosuka D4Y 'Judy', showed great promise in both speed and range, but suffered numerous teething problems, which delayed its entry into service. New aircraft carriers were laid down or converted from oilers and the like, but for every one Japan commissioned, the

United States commissioned three, four or five. With her ring of island bases forming a series of bulwarks across the Pacific, the Japanese husbanded their naval strength while seeking to rebuild their air arm. This gave the United States the breathing space she required to steadily outbuild the Japanese and then begin her assaults with overwhelming force.

One of the conversions carried out to bring Japan's carrier strength back up to strength, was that of the Submarine Depot Ship *Taigei*. She had been completed as recently as March 1935, but was taken in hand for conversion to an aircraft carrier in 1941, and renamed as *Ryūhō*. She was stripped down and given a 607ft flight deck. Her former diesel motors were taken out and replaced by 2-shaft geared turbines and four destroyer–type boilers developing 52,000hp, which still only gave her a top speed of 26.5 knots. She was armed with four twin 5-in, 40 calibre dual-purpose guns and 38 25mm anti-aircraft guns. She had a single hangar, which was served by two lifts, and could carry just 31 aircraft, and in her new role displaced 13,360 tons. In fact, she was too small and slow for the job of fleet carrier, nor was the work carried out done very well. Her hull was too weak and had inferior internal sub-division, making her very vulnerable, and while her flight deck was later lengthened and armament increased, she was always destined to be a second-class unit.

Egusa received his assignment to *Taigei* on 15 October 1942, before her conversion, and she made a final voyage to Truk atoll carrying military stores, supplies, equipment and personnel before reconstruction took place. Egusa stood by her while this was done, and on 1 February 1943 was assigned to serve aboard the *Ryūhō* in her new role. In the event his orders were soon changed, not once but twice.

As Japanese carriers were at a premium, the Imperial Navy called for a fast, land-based dive-bomber to equip the island bases destined to be attacked by the American drive through the central Pacific. The Yokosuka design and development team was headed up by Professor Ryoichi Nakagawa, a noted aeronautical design engineer. Dr Nakagawa had majored in mechanical engineering at Tokyo University (Class of 1936) and had then joined the Nakajima Aircraft company. He had made his name as chief engineer developing the *Sakae* double radial 14-cylinder air-cooled engine that was the mainstay of the famous Mitsubishi A6M1 (Zero) fighter aircraft, all at the tender age of twenty-three.[190]

After hospitalisation and a well-earned leave, Egusa resumed his duties as an experienced instructor at Yokosuka before being assigned the role of testing and training new aircrews for a brand-new twin engined, land-based dive- and torpedo-bomber, and assumed flight command of the 521st *Kokutai*.
(Dr Toshimasa Egusa via Mitsuharu Uehara)

The principal designer was Dr Commander (Technical) Masao Yamana, (who was also responsible for the advanced single-engined, carrier based dive bomber, the D4Y2 *Suisei (Judy)* and the Rocket propelled *Ohka* MXY-7). Dr Yamana had joined the Imperial Navy after graduating from the Tokyo Imperial University, having majored in aeronautical engineering in 1929. By July 1943, he concurrently assumed the post of professor of aeronautical engineering at the university and retained that post until the end of the war.[191]

Development at the Naval Aeronautical Engineering Yard in Yokosuka, was under Lieutenant Commander (Technical) Tadanao Miki. Miki had also attended Tokyo Imperial University, (Class of 1933) and majored in shipbuilding engineering. He entered the navy as a Technical Officer.[192]

This strong team duly produced a powerful new twin-engined attack bomber, the NK9B, based on the outstanding German dive-bomber the Junkers Ju 88, for use from their island airstrips. It was thus hoped that these, working from their 'unsinkable aircraft carriers', would inflict enough damage on the attacking American Task Groups to so weaken them that the Japanese fleet would be able to tackle them on something like level terms. This new bomber was the Yokosuka P1Y *Ginga* (Milky Way), which the Allies later code-named 'Frances.' Taking the versatile Junkers Ju. 88 as an ideal, the Navy *15-Shi* specification of 1940, called for the aircraft to act as a fast strike bomber, torpedo and dive-bomber. Powered by two Nakajima Homare 12, Model NK9-B double radial engines each of 1,825 PS at take-off; the first *Ginga* made her operational debut in August in 1943 and achieved speeds of almost 300mph. It could carry an internal bomb-load of two 1,100lb or two 550kg bombs or a single 1,764lb (800kg) torpedo or a single 1,870lb torpedo, internally at 354mph and had a 3,000-mile range. It had a crew of three. In total 1,000 *Gingas* were produced at Nakajima and a further 100 came out of Kawanishi.

Egusa was one of the first of the Navy's more experienced veterans to fly the *Ginga* as a test pilot. On 30 November 1942, he had been assigned to the training carrier *Hosho* to again teach deck landings, take-offs and other techniques, but, on 1 February 1943, he returned once more to Yokoshuka. His job now was to test and evaluate the *Ginga* ready for combat use. The need was now urgent with the Americans everywhere on the advance and the latest batch of trained naval aircrew wasted in Yamamoto's abortive and costly

An extremely rare aerial view of Egusa's new aircraft the Yokosuka P1Y1 twin-engined, land-based dive- and torpedo bomber, the *Ginga*, code-named by the Allies as the *Frances*. It was designed by an elite Japanese naval team, and based on the general design of the German Junkers Ju 88. It was one of the fastest of the new breed of IJN aircraft which, it was hoped, would help keep the growing might of the US fast Carrier Task Forces at bay. Egusa was placed in command of the 521st *Kokutai*, the first experimental unit to be equipped with this new machine, and commenced intense training in readiness for combat in defence of the Japanese central Pacific island bases. *(Authors collection)*

I-Go operation, which was hailed as a great success but which achieved little or nothing. Numerous design changes were required as the test programme continued; in particular, although it was found to be an excellent aircraft in the air, the P1Y1 was a difficult and temperamental aircraft to keep operational. This fact was discovered during training, and it was realised that ground crews at the more primitive airstrips out in the atolls where they were to be based would experience even greater difficulties.

Despite this, so confident were the aircraft's manufacturers of the machine's ultimate potential, that large numbers of *Gingas* were ordered straight off the drawing board. Although designed by the *Kaigun koku gijutsu-sho* (abbreviated to *Kugisho*, Navy Aviation Technical Workshop) it was hoped to mass-produce the various components of the bomber at dispersed workshops, then bring them together for final assembly. Yoichi Nakagawa, design engineer and senior technical manager at the Nissan Motor Company, oversaw this development. Unfortunately the *Ginga*, being of a high specification, proved that it was not suited to mass-production by the smaller Japanese sub-contractors as hoped. They did not have sufficient expertise to make the higher-standard parts for such an aircraft and so, although a magnificent machine, it was produced in 'penny-packets.' The total number that were finally completed included several variants, including a fighter version designed to combat the high-flying Boeing B-17's.

The engines were changed, the defensive armament increased and a host of other modifications all complicated production, but, contrary to what has been hitherto written about this aircraft, the *Ginga* soon saw combat. The Americans were at anytime expected to make their next major move and it had been decided to meet this thrust with every available ship and aircraft. In anticipation of this, experienced instructors such as Egusa, were withdrawn from basic training and thrown into the fight. Thus, on 15 August 1943, Egusa was given command of the 521 *Kokutai*, the first complete unit of P1Y1's. With a select team, he was ordered to develop suitable bombing and torpedo attack tactics in anticipation of imminent combat. They trained at the Kisarazu air base, in Chiba Prefecture, east of Tokyo Bay, with flight course training under Captain Akira Kōno.

Just one month after receiving this important assignment, the Egusas were blessed with their third child, a daughter, whom they named Haruko. Now Takashige's life was full, he had a daughter, whom Kiyoko says, he loved very much indeed. Whenever he returned home from the base and his training with the new aircraft, he would eat his supper always cradling Haruko on his lap as he did so, as if making every possible minute he spent with his young family count. Then it was back to his new command to ready them for the stern test that faced them.

Why was Egusa, the Navy's premier dive-bomber pilot, chosen to lead a torpedo-bomber unit? Still taking the Junkers Ju 88 as an example, this high-speed German dive-bomber had been found to be the perfect vehicle for carrying a pair of aerial torpedoes when the Luftwaffe belatedly adopted this weapon on a large scale in 1942, in order to attack convoys of Allied aid on their way to North Russia.[193] However, the aircraft was versatile to be used in both roles and so both dive and torpedo-bombing were part-and-parcel of the *Ginga's* remit and Egusa's men practised both. Remember also that Egusa had received early training in the basics of aerial torpedo attack when a young trainee and thus was not a total novice. The decision to opt for the torpedo bomber attack was due to the fact that the growing efficiency of both the US Navy's fighter defence, with the appearance of the Grumman Hellcat in mass; and the adoption of the close-proximity AA fuse by the USA, made any daylight attack a high-attrition tactic. Dive-bombing continued to be the most accurate method of attack, but only torpedoes could guarantee to sink heavy ships outright. There was also another factor, as Vice-Admiral Jisaburo Ozawa, the Commander-in-Chief of the Japanese fleet during the Philippine Sea battle, later revealed. This was that, while the American strengths lay in the widespread use of radar, radio intercepts and their results on defence, the American weakness was perceived to be: 'the slowness, the lack of manoeuvrability in case of torpedo attacks.'[194]

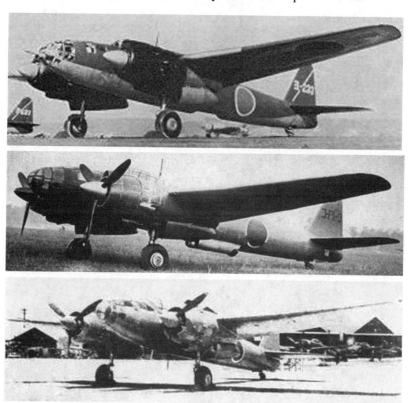

Examples of the Yokosuka P1Y1 twin-engined, land-based dive and torpedo bomber, the *Ginga*, codenamed by the Allies as the Francis. It was designed by an elite Japanese naval team, and based on the general design of the German Junkers Ju 88. It was one of the fastest of the new breed of IJN aircraft which, it was hoped, would help keep the growing might of the US fast Carrier Task Forces at bay. Egusa was put n command of the 521st Kokutai, the first experimental unit to be equipped with this new machine, and started intense training in readiness for combat in defence of the Japanese central Pacific island bases. *(Authors collection)*

Lieutenant-Commander Egusa seen relaxing during the period he was busy preparing the newly-formed 521 Air Group equipped with the new Yokosuka P1Y1 for combat. His facial burns and wounds have all healed up fully but his face shows the mental stress he was under knowing, as he did, the odds his new unit was to face. The photo was taken just two months before Egusa left Japan for the final time for his operational war base in the central Pacific. *(Dr Toshimasa Egusa via Mitsuharu Uehara)*

As Ozawa later revealed, the Japanese considered that the American fleet would either move up from New Guinea to attack Palau. Only as a secondary consideration did an assault on the Marianas seem imminent. Nevertheless, this scenario was confirmed when the Japanese received a signal from Saipan that Palau was to be the target.[195]

The 521 *Kokutai* formed part of the re-organised 1 Air Fleet of land-based aircraft under the command of Vice-Admiral Kakuji Kakuta. This was built up over the next year to a strength of 1,000 aircraft and was therefore, on paper, a formidable force. By the spring of 1944, wind of the next American assault against the Marianas was received and Kakuta moved his units forward into the combat area in anticipation, setting up his headquarters on Tinian Island and distributing his forces across airfields on in the Marianas, Carolines, Iwo Jima and Truk, from where they could island-hop to reinforce the threatened area once the American attack had been committed. On 18 April 1944, Egusa led the advance element of the 521st (named *Ootori Butai*, the 'Phoenix Force', having risen from the ashes of the Midway defeat, but also called *The Scattering Bloom* unit) from Kisarazu on the long flight to Miyajima (as the Japanese called Guam) and the newly constructed Tomioka airfield there. The rest of the force followed at intervals throughout the next few weeks.

The crews of the 521 *Kokutai* line up on Kisarazu Air Base on 18th April 1944, when the advance group left for Guam. Egusa salutes his commander and Captain Kamei returns it from the podium. Such was the speed of the American advance that the Japanese were given insufficient time to train up enough crews to cover every option, and Egusa's unit was among many hustled off to plug the gaps as attack followed attack. *(Professor T Kamei, Ph D)*

What proved a terrible blunder for the Japanese was that they allowed a large proportion of these aircraft to be withdrawn from this area and redeployed down to New Guinea for the Biak operation. Not only were large numbers thus destroyed there fruitlessly, but also a number of aircrew were lost through malaria. This deployment proved a grave mistake, for when the pre-emptive American carrier strikes began to hit the island airstrips in the Marianas on 13 June, half the Japanese force, which should have met it, had already been thrown away. The main US assault went in against Saipan at 0840hrs on 15 June 1944, by which time Kakuta's remaining air strength had been further decimated in heavy air fighting.

The original Japanese plan, Operation *A-Go*, had called for the land-based aircraft to co-ordinate their attacks with Vice-Admiral Jisaburo Ozawa's powerful main fleet, which had been rebuilt around no less than nine aircraft carriers. This latter force was based at Lingga and in the homeland, and was to rendezvous at Tawi Tawi, then move to the north-east of Palau and standby to meet the United States fleet in direct combat. By that time it was hoped that Kakuta's land-based aircraft, reinforced from Palau and elsewhere, would already have inflicted severe damage on the enemy. This plan was made by Admiral Toyoda back at Combined Fleet Headquarters in Tokyo. Although the land-based and carrier-based aircraft were to carry it out jointly, there was *no* conference between Toyoda and Ozawa prior to the battle. It was physically impossible as Ozawa was with his fleet at Singapore in April-May when the plan was issued as an order. Even worse, the land-based aircraft remained under the *direct* command Toyoda. Ozawa also said: 'The First Air Fleet Headquarters was at Tinian, and the C-in-C of the First Air Fleet had the direction of the air force of all land-based planes.'[196] Specifically, the land-based units were to attack the American carriers. However, although the attacks were said to be co-ordinated, Ozawa later revealed that the aircraft rendezvoused as individual squadrons, 'and every squadron was assigned its own individual target.'[197]

Word about the approach of the American task Force was received on 9 June and immediately what was left of the Biak diversion force was hastily ordered back. Unfortunately for the Japanese these units had by this time suffered high losses, from both combat and aircrew illness in the tropics which reduced their combat efficiency enormously. Only a fraction of the diverted aircraft managed to return to their original bases, and most of the few that did return had to operate from just any field they could fight their way into. Other reinforcements were later sent in from the homeland and via Iwo Jima.[198]

At the Yokosuka Naval Air Station, there remained some 120-130 miscellaneous naval aircraft of all types, one-third only of the pilots being experienced, the rest novices. These too were to be thrown into the battle. However, by then, it was too late. Heavy fighter sweeps were mounted from the twelve large carriers of Admiral Raymond A Spruance's Task Groups and so destroyed Kakuta's units both in the air and on the ground, that the latter were unable to make any effective reply. Within two or three days almost all these aircraft were wiped out and, far from whittling down the odds for Ozawa, they had inflicted no damage whatsoever on the American fleet.[199]

The start of the assault, which the Americans code-named FORAGER was to lead to what was later to become known as the Battle of the Philippine Sea. Egusa's unit was based at No 2 Airfield (Wasile) on Guam Island and he had about thirty *Gingas* on his operational strength, along with seventeen Yokosuka *Suisei* dive-bombers from 523 Ku, of whom twelve were operational. There were also fifty-nine Zero fighters from 261 and 265 Ku's, of whom forty-nine were operational. A further pair of *Gingas* were at Yap. The *Gingas* had undergone further training at Guam and Yap prior to the final deployment, but it was all fruitless. With the overwhelming numbers of the new Grumman Hellcat fighter at the Americans' disposal and the huge concentration of anti-aircraft firepower mounted by the massive array of warships in the American Task Force, Egusa knew that he stood as little a chance in a straightforward daytime attack as would Somerville's antiquated biplanes have had against the Nagumo Task Force back in 1942. Like Somerville then, Egusa knew that his only hope of even getting close to the American carriers – which over and over again were reiterated as the No 1 and only worthwhile target for all Japanese flyers in the islands – was by a low-level dusk approach under their radar cover. To inflict the most damage by such methods dive-bombing was rejected, shallow bombing was not considered decisive enough and so the adaptable *Ginga* was equipped for torpedo attack.

The airfield they used on Guam, Tomioka,[200] had been built by the Japanese 321st Naval Air Force (Moonlight) unit under Flight Captain Shimoda in 1943, along the Orote peninsula. It was additional to the old US Marine Patrol Squadron Naval Air Base (Airfield No 1 in

Japanese parlance) which lay near to Sumay village, and which had been deserted since 1931. Tomioka, (known as Airfield No 2) had the main runway running from north-west to south-east, and housed the sixty *Gingas*, led by Egusa and under the overall command of the former veteran Navy pilot Captain The Count Yoshio Kamei,[201] and who was now captain commanding the Marianas naval air defence. They practised and practised against the clock.

Count and Captain (posthumously Rear-Admiral) Yoshio Kamei, commander of the Air Flotilla at Miyajima (Guam) under whose command the 521st *Ootoributai*, was placed for the defence of the Marianas.
(Professor T Kamei, Ph D)

Even before they could mount this planned assault, the unit suffered grievous losses as the American naval fighter aircraft swarmed over Guam throughout the daylight hours, bombing and machine-gunning everything and anything that moved on the tiny airstrips. Their tormentors were the fliers of Task Group 58.1 under Rear-Admiral J J Clark with the carriers *Hornet (II)*, *Yorktown (II)*, *Belleau Wood* and *Bataan*, with four cruisers and twelve destroyers. On 12 June, this force mounted 468 sorties against the two Guam airfields and Rota, although the Japanese were not using the latter. The American fliers lost fifteen aircraft and claimed to have destroyed a total of forty Japanese aircraft. The next day 339 sorties were made, with the loss of four aircraft and claimed the destruction of even more Japanese planes. On 14 June Task Group 58.2 under Rear Admiral A E Montgomery, took over. He had the carriers *Bunker Hill*, *Wasp (II)*, *Monterey* and *Cabot*, with a similar screen. They launched eighty sorties and claimed a further thirteen Japanese aircraft shot down for the loss of just two of their own machines.

Switched south from the Marianas to protect the Marshalls, the surviving aircraft of the 521st were again re-deployed back to Guam when word was received of the impending American assault. The master plan was for the land-based aircraft to attack the US Task Groups, especially their carriers, and so inflict such damage on them that the Japanese Fleet fleet would be able to crush them in a final battle in the Philippine Sea. It did not work out that way, the fleet was late in sailing, and meantime the American Navy aircraft ranged over the Japanese bases causing enormous damage and losses. Here the 521st *Kokutai's* main base, the north airfield at Guam, is seen under heavy air attack by US carrier planes.
(U S National Archives, Washington DC)

It was obviously futile for the men of 521 *Kokutai* to sit and endure any more of this slaughter. They were being annihilated piecemeal and, if they waited for Ozawa to come up as planned, there would be no aircraft left to co-operate with his carrier bomber force anyway. Twice before the American carriers had seemed to be almost within Egusa's grasp, and twice before he had been denied. This time he was determined to attack.

Egusa decided to launch his attack that evening while he still had some planes left intact to do so. All-in-all, it was a pathetic attack group he was able to muster on the afternoon of 15 June; a few D4Y dive-bombers and just ten *Gingas* were still airworthy. All along Egusa had known that his next battle might well be his last – a forlorn hope against the burgeoning strength of the US Navy. Long gone were the halcyon days of 1942. In his last conversation with his wife, just before he left homeland Japan for Tinian in May, he told her: 'This is *Minato-gawa*.' *Minato-gawa* means that one has made up one's mind to go out fighting despite the certain knowledge that one is to be killed in defeat.[202]

Although Egusa had not avoided being wracked by the inevitable diseases found on Pacific Islands, he was upbeat. He conveyed no sense of despair at the vastness of the daunting task he faced in the last letter that he wrote to Kiyoko. Instead he was full of care for her.

> 'I am told that you were not well the other day. I have been worrying about you since then. As for myself, set your mind at ease because I've become acclimatised to conditions here. My bowels are now recovered, just the same as I was in the interior of Japan. I am in very high spirits. You told me (in your letter) that Hiroyuki and Toshimasa were making merry. I can visualise them clearly. I am pleased to hear that you had begun to wean Haruko. Even in the rainy season here, we are getting on well. The morale of all our men is very high. I've recovered my health completely after the dysentery attack the other day. Set your mind at ease about it. I'm full of vitality. Remember me to everybody.'

Two years on from Egusa's great victories, the Japanese air attacks now seemed as puny as spear against armoured plate. But, enough of the old skill remained to ensure that even this tiny force was to give the Americans the only real fright they had in this one-sided battle. The aircraft took off just before dusk, evading enemy air patrols and flew toward the hidden enemy Task Force.

Egusa had deployed his force in two groups. The first, ten 'Judys', the second a mixed group of another ten *Gingas*, three 'Judy' dive-bombers and six Zero fighters – all that remained. The *Gingas* were variously reported as 'Betty' navy bombers and 'Sally' army bombers in a few subsequent American reports and even in many later historical books,[203] although **NO** aircraft of either of these two types were in the islands at this time. Even the very existence of 521 *Kokutai* is not acknowledged in the definitive histories. Thus, Egusa's last mission has, hitherto, been totally misreported. However, there is no need for any of this inaccuracy, since the contemporary reports of both the Japanese and the American survivors give accurate and precise details.

The objective of Egusa's final mission turned out to be Task Group 58.3 under Rear Admiral J W Reeves with the carriers *Enterprise, Lexington (II), San Jacinto* and *Princeton*, with four cruises and nine destroyers. Part of Vice Admiral W A Lee's battle line Task Group 58.7, the battleship *North Carolina*, had rejoined Reeves carrier group at 1848hrs that evening, when Egusa's *Gingas* slid in softly out of the gathering dusk darkness toward them.

At last, after three long and frustrating years, Egusa had *finally* found the *Enterprise*.

He had studied every aspect of this carrier prior to the Pearl Harbor attack, his main target then, and she had eluded him; he had agonised that he had failed in his effort to persuade his superiors to seek her out then; he had witnessed her power at Midway. Now, at long last, after two-and-a-half years searching, there she was before him, her silhouette unmistakable compared to the accompanying *Essex* class ships.

The earlier raid had been plotted by radar and intercepted by the Combat Air Patrol from *San Jacinto* which shot down six of the D4Y dive-bombers from the force of ten (and wrongly identified them as 'Tonys'). These defenders had thus been drawn out and this enabled the *Gingas* to get in close enough to make a determined attack.

Lexington (II)'s report read:

'The USS *North Carolina* began firing to port at 1903hrs, and firing was seen on the horizon dead ahead. At 1907hrs lookouts reported ten low-flying multi-engine planes dead ahead at 10,000 yards. These planes were lost until at about 4,000 yards when they were reported coming in from dead ahead and on the port bow. All the ships of the Task Group began firing. During the next four minutes, a total of eight planes attacked this ship, and four were shot down in flames and one hit the water without burning. Five sure and two sure assists were claimed by the USS *Lexington (II)*. Four definite torpedo wakes and possibly a fifth were observed, two of which were within ten yards of the hull, running down each side. [The report goes on to state, perfectly correctly] It is the opinion of this ship that the attacking planes were "Milky Ways", new type enemy light bombers. This action with the enemy aircraft resulted in eighteen casualties, of which eleven were of a minor nature, and seven were considered serious enough for admission to the sick list. One man suffered a serious shrapnel wound in the chest, three suffered multiple shrapnel wounds, one had both eardrums ruptured, and two received flash burns to the face.'[204]

Rather than wait until they were completely annihilated on the ground, the few remnants of the Japanese land-based air units were sent off in penny-packets to try to inflict some damage on their tormentors, but were totally overwhelmed by the mass firepower of the American fleet. This is Egusa's final mission. As the *Ginga's* slipped in at dusk to try and to torpedo the American carriers of Task Group 58.4, the mass anti-aircraft fire from the battleship *North Carolina*, aircraft carriers *Enterprise*, *Lexington (II)*, *Belleau Wood*, and escorting cruisers and destroyed spread a lacework of death across the dark sky and Egusa's aircraft was among the many lost in this gallant sortie against all odds. Egusa was given a posthumous two-rank promotion in recognition of his achievements.
(*US National Archives, Washington D C*)

The *San Jacinto's* report makes similar reading:

> 'In spite of the success of the CAP (Combat Air Patrol) eight enemy aircraft reached the disposition and attempted torpedo attacks. Formation 5V was affected and OTC manoeuvred the group in a series of evasive turns while all ships opened fire. All eight enemy aircraft were shot down by ships' anti-aircraft fire and no damage was inflicted on any unit of the TG by the enemy, although a bomb was dropped off the port quarter of *Enterprise*, doing no damage. *San Jacinto* shot down one "Betty" *(sic)* making a turn by her port quarter with *Enterprise* as her apparent target. Enemy attacks all appeared to be concentrated on the two large carriers.'[205]

The *Enterprise* herself reported that she was 'vigorously attacked.' Radar had detected the Japanese aircraft at a distance of twenty-two miles from the ship and they were picked up by binoculars at a distance of 20,000 yards, the Mark 37 director tracking their approach speed at 250 knots. 'The group of seven VB (M) made a determined attack on our port bow, meeting a tremendous volume of fire from the Task Group, six planes going down in flames.'[206]

She also reported that, in the half-light of twilight, the Mk 14 gunnery sight with which her AA batteries were equipped, were ineffective, and this precluded the use of the main 5in guns. Also that the blinding effects of the tracers made observation of the attacker at more than 1,000 yards out, very difficult. The identification of the aircraft in such circumstances was considered doubtful, but they seemed to be of a new type, possible 'Frances' or 'Milky Ways.'[207]

She also reported that a bomb from an undetected plane, that was never seen, exploded in the water about 750 yards ahead on the port bow just before the torpedo planes reached that point. This was probably one of the accompanying *Suisei* dive-bombers making her attack.

And Egusa?

'One torpedo plane dropped a torpedo about 1,000 yards on the port bow, the torpedo running parallel to the ship at a distance of about fifty yards.'[208]

Was this Takashige's last shot? We will never know but if so, it would be an apt *finale*.

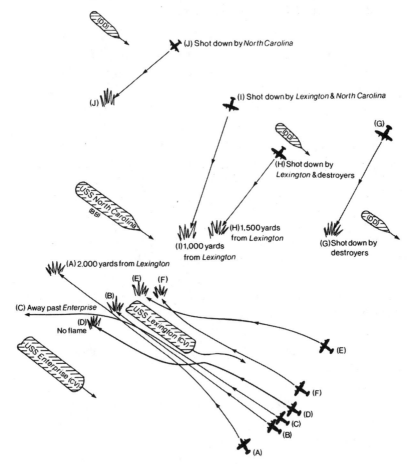

Egusa's Last Battle. The attack by the 521 *Kokutai* on Task Group 58.3 15 June 1944.

Surprise had been achieved but, despite their gallantry, Egusa's forlorn hope had been wiped out in vain. Thus passed, almost unnoticed by friend and foe alike, Japan's and, arguably, the world's leading naval dive-bomber pilot. He died in combat, as any good samurai should. His achievements remain unique and special in the annals of air/sea warfare. His passing typified the ultimate issue of the Pacific War: the age of the skilled warrior had been overtaken by the age of massed firepower.

Epilogue

'If our soldiers do not live long lives, it is not because they abhor longevity.' *Sun Tzu – The Art of War*.

Four days after these momentous events, back at home in Japan, Kiyoko lay sleeping and, as she later recounted, in her dream Takashige Egusa appeared to her to tell her of his fate. It was dawn on 19 June 1944. Several weeks were to pass before she received official confirmation that her husband had failed to return from his mission. He was given a most exceptional posthumous promotion, by two ranks, to Captain.

Eleven years later Kiyoko, by then a practitioner at the Kochi Medical College, was returning from the United States after a one-year study course at the University of California, Berkeley, when her ship passed close to the spot where her husband had fought his final battle. She dressed up in her national costume and, at the nearest point to Saipan, threw a wreath of flowers into the sea.[209] Takashige Egusa was not forgotten.

Finally, in February 1988, a permanent memorial was established at the Peace Park on Guam to honour the *Ootori Butai* group, thanks to Ootori-kai. Mrs Kiyoko Egusa was among the thirty-five bereaved families and survivors who attended the ceremony on 22 February that year. The inscription was the Group's Epitaph, written by Lieutenant Akira Kono, the former commander of the second company. It read simply:

'The 521st Air Group, *Ootori Butai*, a group of squadrons of the most advanced twin-engined dive-bomber, the *Ginga*, was first established in August 1943. With the ebbing of the Japanese tide, there were enormous expectations of this group, to try to annihilate the US Task Forces. After finishing training in Japan, the group started to move to the air base on Guam Island in April 1944. In anticipation of a decisive naval battle for the Palaus, the squadrons took up scattered positions around Peleliu and Halmahera.

'Suddenly and unexpectedly, on 11 June, US Task Forces attacked Saipan and Guam. We at *Ootori Butai*, led by Lieutenant Commander Takashige Egusa, although far inferior in numbers, made desperate efforts against the enemy in the Marianas. Also, all land units, headed by Captain Yoshio Kamei, fought to the death against the US invasion troops on Guam.

'This monument is here founded to remember the brave and valiant sailors who dedicated their lives to their country, and in that aim, that the absolutely pure spirits and sublimates may contribute toward an entire world peace forever.'

The Memorial to the 521 Air Group, the *Ootori Butai*, at the Peace Park, Guam dedicated on 22nd February 1988, with an epitaph written by the former leader of No. 1 Wing, Lieutenant Akira Kono. Among the thirty-five relatives and survivors was Mrs Kiyoko Egusa (wearing black dress and standing behind the memorial stone itself). *(Professor T Kamei, Ph D)*

Takashige's widow, Kiyoko, stands beside the memorial to the memory of Captain Takashige Egusa, which stands stop Fudeyama Hill in Kochi City. Alongside it stands the stone of his brother-in-law and friend, Motoharu Okamura. Kiyoko had become an English teacher of great skill post-war. She created a unique method of teaching the English language to the Japanese after spending time in the United States at various leading facilities. For her work, she became an honoured professor at Kochi University. She later wrote her own story, *Two Lives*, which recalled her life as a naval wife and her new life as an educationalist.
(Dr Toshimasa Egusa via Mitsuharu Uehara).

One more stone stands to Egusa's memory, and that is his tomb atop Fudeyama hill in Kochi City. Alongside it stands the tomb of Motoharu Okamura, the two great aviators, brothers-in-law and friends.

As one of Takshige's former Etajima classmates recorded: 'Their tombs are just like two aircraft flying side-by-side in close formation.'[210]

THE END

Footnotes

1: The previously given birth date of 10 October 1910 has been found to be incorrect. The present-day address is Shimoaruji Asahi-machi, Fukuyama City, Hiroshima Prefecture.

2: Mitsuharu Uehara, *Kambaku Taicho Egusa Takashige (Life of First Line Commander of Carrier-borne Dive Bombers)*, (Kojinsha, Tokyo, 1989).

3: Philip Wilkinson and Douglas Charing, *DK Encyclopaedia of Religion* (Dorling Kindersley, London, 2004).

4: Rev Shokai Kanai, *Introduction to the Lotus Sutra, Lectures*, Los Angeles, 2005.

5: Daikoku, besides being the god of wealth, also favoured farmers and so had been doubly relevant to the Egusa ancestors. His son, Ebisu, was the god of honest labour, which no doubt was not lost on the young Takashige as he helped his father on the land.

6: Hugh Cortazzi (Editor), *British Envoys in Japan, 1859-1972*, (Global Oriental Ltd, London, December 2003).

7: Peter Lowe (Editor), *Western Interactions with Japan: Expansion, the Armed Forces and Readjustment, 1859-1956* (Routledge Curzon, London, October 1990).

8: To know the man, you must know what formed the man. This is the story of a successful military leader, but in Japan, more than in many contemporary countries, the whole culture embraced and motivated him. This is no place to discuss in any great depth the full social and cultural mix that made Egusa what he was, but some aspects have to be understood. To get a fuller picture the reader is invited to turn to the Anglo-Japanese History Project – Professor Ian Nish – various contributors, *The History of Anglo-Japanese Relations, 1600-2000, Volume 5: Social and Cultural Perspectives*, (Palgrave Macmillan, London, November 2002). This is particularly relevant and covers the following periods – Part 1; Introduction; Part II – The Nineteenth Century and After; Part III – Twentieth-century Themes; Part IV – The Inter-War Years and Part V – The Postwar Era.

9: I would like here to acknowledge my fullest debt to the penultimate English instructor at Etajima, Cecil Bullock, for his detailed account of Etajima and how it worked, upon which I have drawn extensively. Bullock, Cecil, *Etajima: the Dartmouth of Japan*, (Sampson Low, Martson, London, 1942). Hereafter acknowledged as Bullock, *Etajima*.

10: Grenfell, Captain Russell, R N; *Main Fleet to Singapore* (London, 1951).

11: For a balanced and comprehensive biography of Admiral Togo readers should turn to: – R V C Bodley, *Admiral Togo: The Authorised Life of Admiral of the Fleet, Marquis Heihachiro Togo OM* (London, 1935). For a more personal view, H C Seppings Wright, *With Togo; the story of seven month's active service under his command* (Hurst & Blackett, London, 1905).

12: See Thomas Franklin Millard, *The ABC's of the twenty-one demands* (in *The Weekly Review of the Far East*, Shanghai, 1921) and *The Sino-Japanese negotiations, January-March 1915 and the treaties and notes signed in Peking 25 May 1915 official record and texts*. (*The National Review*, Shanghai, 1915).

13: This 'toleration' by the United States was of short duration, by 1921 Walter Broughton Pitkin was analysing often-expressed views in his book *Must we fight Japan?* (The Century Co, New York, 1921). Viscount Kikujiro and US Secretary of State Robert Lansing signed the agreement.

14: The United States also kept up pressure to have the Anglo-Japanese Alliance terminated as soon as possible, it being a long-running source of irritation in Washington D C. See G Zay Wood, *China, the United States and the Anglo-Japanese alliance* (F H Revell, New York, 1921), and *The Anglo-Japanese alliance*, (GPO, Washington, 1922).

15: See for example, Grenfell, Russell, *Main Fleet to Singapore*, (Faber & Faber, London, 1951), pages 40-41. 'Britain it was who lost on the deal. By accepting the main American ratios, she surrendered her long-standing sea supremacy among the nations of the world, she abandoned her ancient freedom to protect in the way she thought best her vital maritime communications, and she agreed to forgo her previous commanding lead over the Japanese.'

16: For full details of this mission's work see *The Journal of the Royal Aeronautical Society 1924*, pages 553 *et seq*, *The British Aviation Mission to the Imperial Japanese Navy* The Master of Sempill (London, 1925).

17: See *Kagetsurou, since 1889. The Kagetsuro 100th anniversary book*, presented to the author by the proprietor 1998.

18: Forbes-Sempill (he did not succeed to the peerage until February 1934, when he inherited the title Lord Sempill on the death of his father) was a distinguished linguist. He had links with Sweden and Norway, and had his own light aircraft. He made an early pioneering flight from Scotland to Norway, made a solo flight to Australia, served as an adviser to the Greek Government from March 1926, and was a President of the Royal Aeronautical Society, Chairman of the Anglo-Swedish Society and President of the British Gliding Association. During the Second World War, he wrote to Winston Churchill asking permission to rejoin the Fleet Air Arm and became a Commander dealing with aircraft equipment. (Churchill Papers 5 September 1939, CHAR 19/1/3-4).

Unfortunately, this, 'pillar of the British establishment' had earlier blotted his copybook on several occasions, being suspected by MI5 of passing secrets of 'Aeronautical Construction', in fact the *Iris* seaplane, by interrogating the constructor's staff. It was alleged he hoped to pass this information on to the Japanese Naval Attaché in London, Captain Teijiro Toyoda between 1924 and 1925. Circumstantial evidence was accumulated against him, according to Foreign Office files of that year (See MI5 Files KV 2/871-871 at the National Archives, Kew, London). This was done not for payment but for ideological motives as he had become very close to the Japanese while based there. It is alleged that the only reason he was not prosecuted by the DPP was because the British agency wanted to protect its secret monitoring of diplomatic files, which would have been revealed had a case been made. It was also thought that, as he was an adviser to the company and the employees he talked to may not have considered the subject secret, the case was weakened. Sempill suspected he was being watched and demanded, and received, a meeting with security chiefs, where they revealed what they knew. Sempill seemed to realise he had a close call. It may have been that incident, or his earlier work in Japan between 1921 and 1923, that earned him a personal letter from the Japanese Premier Tomosaburo Kato which thanked him for his work for the Japanese Navy, which was termed 'almost epoch-making' (see *British lord was spy for Japan* by Will Hollingworth, *The Japanese Times*, 5 January, 2002). It is also claimed that he became a member of Captain Archibald Ramsay's The Right Club, and listed in the notorious *Red Book* (Wiener Library, London), that further, he was secretly retired from his position at the Admiralty under Churchill's authorisation, again under suspicion of leaking information to the Japanese. [See for example allegations in Richard Griffiths, *Patriotism Perverted; Captain Ramsay, The Right Club and British Anti-Semitism, 1939-40* (Constable & Robinson, London, 1998) and same author, *Fellow travellers of the Right; British enthusiasts for Nazi Germany 1933-39*, (Constable, London, 1980). Also Antony Best, 'Lord Sempill (1893-1965) and Japan, 1921-41', in *Britain and Japan: Biographical Portraits, Vol IV* pages 375-382, (Edited by Professor H Cortazzi, London, Japan Library, 2002). Whatever the truth of this Lord Sempill went off to Canada, and later lectured on the post-war economic situation, working steadily to improve Anglo-Japanese relations in the post-war period. For this work, he was awarded the Order of the Rising Sun in 1961 for post-war efforts at Anglo-Japanese rapprochement.

19: Nihon Kaigun Kōkūshu Hensan Iinkai, editor, *Nihon kaigun Kōkūshu (The History of Japanese Naval Aviation – 4 Vols)*, (Jiji Tsushinsha, 1969) Vol. 1.

20: Wilkinson & Charing, *DK Encyclopaedia of Religion, op cit.*

21: *ibid.*

22: *ibid.*

23: Bullock, *Etajima, op cit*, comments that during his time, only two years after Egusa had passed through the college, the last group of entries 'had amongst their number an able seaman and two Imperial Princes, cousins of the Emperor.' This representative character of the cadet body is really very impressive.

24: However, Japanese serving sailors *could* apply to become Cadets at the age of twenty-three, sometimes younger, if they could prove they had the merit and intelligence.

25: Sadly, Sato, having passed through Etajima and graduated with Egusa, was refused naval officer duty because he was diagnosed, even at that late date, as short-sighted! This author, having been twice rejected by the Royal Navy at the ages of fifteen and seventeen for the same reason, (even in the age of radar) can only sympathise with Egusa's companion being tripped up by 'the system' well beyond the final fence.

26: The mountain has been recorded in some histories as a dormant volcano, but this is **NOT** the case.

27: The legend that these red bricks were original English-manufactured bricks especially imported for the job, soon gained currency, so much so that it has been frequently recorded as fact. However, during the author's visit to Etajima in September 2005, Rear-Admiral Sadayoshi Matsuoka, Commandant, Kure District, Japan Maritime Self-Defence Force, revealed that recent research by a recognised expert in the building field had conclusively proven that the bricks were, in truth, manufactured in Japan to the English specification. The rumour arose because the bricks were shipped in, which led to an incorrect assumption that they had come from England, and this rumour was never challenged.

28: Mitsuharu Uehara, *Kanbaku Taicho Egusa Takashige, op cit.*

29: There was also the fact that British ships were designed for long cruises in distant waters, up to three-year commissions and weather-worthiness, while Japanese warships were mainly intended to fight a limited ranges close to home on shorter lines of communication and there could be less 'liveable.' The tendency to cram in more guns certainly made the Japanese cruisers and destroyers, ship for ship, seem far more battle-worthy ships than their British counterparts, and so it proved in combat. However the other side of the coin was the capsizing in tropical storms of several 'top heavy' Japanese warships in the 1930's. Also, the effects on unexpected long sorties, like that undertaken into the Indian Ocean in 1942, had a marked effect on crew fatigue in Japanese ships.

30: Bullock, *Etajima, op cit*, cites a figure of 130 new entrants in 1932, and 250 three years later.

31: Bullock, *Etajima, op cit*.

32: Colonel S Hattori to the author, 8 March 2001.

33: *ibid*.

34: *ibid*.

35: Fellow graduates from this Class, included Captains Shigeharu Murata and Nobuyoshi Suetsugu, Commanders Masataka Chihaya, Yutaka Izawa, Minoru Kato, Isamu Miyazaki, Masatake Okumiya, Mamoru Seki, Shiheharu Murata, Yoshiro Shimose, Nobuyoshi Suetsugu, Jisuke Takenaga, Kennosuke Torisu, Jintaro Yamazaki, Manpei Shimokawa and Lieutenant-Commander Tadashi Nakajima, many of whom went on to equal fame in the Pacific War.

36: The naval college continued operations until 1945, when it was closed down. However, in 1956, with the formation of the Japanese Maritime Self-Defence Force, it was reopened as the First Service School (1 MSS) and the Officer Candidate Training School (MOCS) followed a year later. Most buildings are in use today, albeit to a very modified programme. There is now an educational museum displaying some 14,000 objects including letters and artefacts left by Kamikaze pilots. The author visited the establishment as the guest of Rear-Admiral Sadayoshi Matsuoka in November 2005, and can confirm it has been immaculately maintained and restored.

37: The Krupp guns were replaced by Japanese-built 8 inch/50 calibre weapons from 1930. She was to outlive all of her successors and even visited Pearl Harbour in October 1939. Somehow she survived the Pacific War, was finally decommissioned on 10th January 1945, but was not broken up until 1947.

38: *Izumo* was another old armoured-cruiser, later coast defence ship and then training vessel for engineering branch cadets. She was a 9,180-tonner, completed the same year as *Yakumo*, but, more traditionally, in a British shipyard, that of Sir W G Armstrong Whitworth. It should be noted that *Conway's All the World's Fighting Ships 1922-1946* (London, 1980) incorrectly states that she did not become a training ship until 1943.

39: Yoshida would later become Japanese Prime Minister, and it was he who finally signed the peace treaty with the allied powers in 1951.

40: As a young Lt, Kaneko Yozo had been one of original three naval Lieutenants sent to Paris to learn to fly in 1911.

41: Which in 1930 became the *Sōjū Renshūsei* (Pilot Training Scheme or *Sōren*).

42: The *Hikō Yoka Renshūsei*, (Flight Reserve Enlisted Trainee Scheme or *Hikō*).

43: The following is based upon a detailed description of IJN aviation training at that time entitled, *How our naval air officers were selected, educated and trained after graduation form the Etajima Naval Academy*, prepared especially for this book by

Lieutenant-Commander (Rtd) (Zenji Abe, 3 September 2004). I am most grateful to my friend for this detail.

44: Lieutenant-Commander Ryunosuke Kusaka (later to be Chief of Staff, First Air Fleet) boarded this airship at Kasumigaura for the leg to Los Angeles according to the *Kaigun Koku Nempyo* (Naval Chronological Table), edited by *Kaikukai* (Association of Sea and Sky), published by Hara Shobo, Tokyo, 1982.

45: Here, we must, yet again, place on record, that authorities like Mark R Peattie, *Sunburst: The Rise of Japanese Naval Air Power, 1909-1941*, (Naval Institute Press, Annapolis, 2001), page 36, are in error in stating that dive-bombing, 'was born in October 1926' by the United States Navy. It was in actually first carried out in full battle combat in 1917 by the British on the Western Front, and many detailed experiments were conducted in the 1918-20 period by the RAF, and are on record. Full documentary details of all these dive-bombing experiences have been listed by myself in books like *Dive Bomber!* (Naval Institute Press, Annapolis, 1982) and *The History of Dive Bombing* (Nautical & Aviation Publishing, Annapolis 1981) and *Dive Bombers in Action* (Sterling Publishing, New York, 1985). The true facts have therefore been on record for more than twenty years. Thomas Wildenberg, author of *Destined for Glory: Dive Bombing, Midway, and the Evolution of Carrier Airpower* (Naval Institute Press, Annapolis, 1998) covered precisely the same ground more than thirteen years later, but totally omitted *all* the detailed early RAF reports from 1917-1920, even though citing my above two books which contain them in his sources list.

46: Although Commander Masatake Okumiya, an aviator from Etajima 58th Class, maintains that Lieutenant Minoru Genda contrived to employ Helldivers from carriers rather than air bases.

47: Fitted with our 20lb under wing bombs, Fairey Flycatchers conducted mock 'converging' attacks on carrier targets in the Mediterranean and at the Orfordness Proving Grounds in Suffolk, from 1928 onward. See Owen Cathcart-Jones, *Aviation Memoirs*, (Hutchinson, London, 1934).

48: See Peter C Smith, *Dive Bomber!* (Moorland Publishing, Ashbourne & Naval Institute Press, Annapolis, 1982), pages 13-16.

49: Ōhama Tetsuya and Ozawa Ikurō, editors, *Teikoku rikukaigun jiten (Dictionary of the Imperial Japanese Army and Navy)*, (Dōseisha, Tokyo, 1995).

50: Peter C Smith, *Aichi D3A1/2* (Crowood, Ramsbury, 1999) pages 10–14 for the full story of the development of Japanese dive-bombers.

51: See Yoshihashi, T, *Conspiracy at Mukden*, 1963; and Young, Louise, *Japan's Total Empire: Manchuria and the Culture of Wartime Imperialism* (Los Angeles, 1998).

52: The Japanese viewpoint was expounded at the time in *Background of the Shanghai trouble* distributed in the United States by the Bureau of Information of the Japanese Chamber of Commerce of New York in 1932. But this largely fell on deaf ears in the States, both then and later. See also, Thomas Arthur Bisson, *American policy in the Far East, 1931-1940* (International Secretariat, Institute of Pacific Relations, New York, 1939).

53: It is important to note that these were armed sailors, and **NOT** the Japanese equivalent of the Royal or United States Navy's Marines, although frequently recorded as such in history books.

54: Even before the opening of the Washington Conference in 1921, Japan had been preparing her case, and had established the Propaganda Bureau as part of the Ministry of Foreign Affairs. (See Peter O'Connor (compiler), *Japanese Propaganda – Selected Readings. Series 1: Books 1872-1943* (ten volumes) with foreword by Professor Uchikawa Yoshimi, Edition Synapse, October 2003). See also Hosoya Chihiro and Saito Makato, *Wasinton taisei to Nihonn kankei (Japan's Participation in the Washington Treaty)*. (Tokyo daigakko shuppankai, Tokyo, 1967); and Asada Sadao, *Amerika no tai Nichikan to Washinton taisei (The Washington Conference and America's view of Japan)* see article in *Kokusai seiji*, Vol 2. pages 36-57, 1966.

55: Ishimaru, Lieutenant-Commander Tota, IJHN, *Japan must fight Britain*, translated by Instructor-Captain G V Rayment, CBE, RN, The Paternoster Library, No XI, (Hurst & Blackett, London, February 1936). The same point was taken as the basis for the first of Professor Arthur Marder's two volumes, *Old Friends, New Enemies: Royal Navy and the Imperial Japanese Navy, Vol 1 Strategic Illusions, 1936-41*, (Oxford University Press, Oxford, August 1981). See also, Antony Best, 'The Road to Anglo-Japanese Confrontation, 1931-41' in *The History of Anglo-Japanese Relations: The Political-diplomatic Dimension, Vol II*. Edited by I Nish and Y Kibata (Macmillan, London, 2000).

56: *ibid*.

57: Henry Berry, *Semper Fi, Mac: Living Memories of the US Marines in WWII*, (Perennial, New York, 1996).

58: Ian Cowman, *Dominion or Decline: Anglo-American Naval Relations in the Pacific, 1937-1941* (OUP, Oxford, 1996).

59: Cunningham of Hyndhope, *A Sailors Odyssey*, (Hutchinsons, London, 1951) and B B Schofield, *British Sea Power*, (Batsford, London, 1967). Even the First Lord of the Admiralty, Lord Alexander was forced to complain to Churchill how plans to equip the British Pacific Fleet's six aircraft-carriers with the American-built Curtiss SB2C Helldiver dive-bomber in 1945, had been wrecked by the refusal of Admiral King to allow the agreed allocated numbers to be transferred to the Fleet Air Arm. The spurious grounds given were that reserve non-combat US Navy squadrons in the USA had to be fully equipped first! See Peter C Smith, *The Curtiss SB2C Helldiver*, (Crowood Press, Ramsbury, 2004).

60: In all some twenty-one Navy and Army officers, plus twenty civilians were implicated. Some reports even allege that, originally, the legendary film star, Charlie Chaplin, who was then on a visit to Japan, was also on the hit list in the hope that his death would provoke an American response, but this part of the plan was dropped. One of the main conspirators was Dr Shumei Okawa, who had been involved in many plots and would continue to intrigue. He survived all this, and much more, only to be sentenced to be hung as a war criminal post-war. However, he was eventually certified insane and released.

61: This 'Special Mission' was the Liaison Office of the Japanese Garrison for the Japanese residents there, and similar missions served in several other cities in North China with large Japanese enclaves, like Tienchin, Tongzhou, Chingtao, Chinan. For more details of Colonel Matsui, see *Boeicho, Boeikenkyujo, Senshi-shitsu* (War History Room, National Institute for Defence Studies, Defence Agency, Tokyo, *Shina Jihen: Rikugun Sakusen* (The China Incident; The Army Operation), Vol I, *Senshi Sosho* series (War Histories Series), (Asagumo Shimbun, Tokyo, 1975).

62: There is also a conspiracy theory that Zhang Zhi-Zhong was a communist 'mole' planed in the Nationalist Army by Chou En-Lai. He was known to have been part of a communist group in his youth and was known as 'Red Teacher' at the Whampoa Military Academy. He wanted to join the CCP but was told he could do more for the cause by staying under-cover. He is alleged to have rigged this incident deliberately. Whether this scenario has any credence or not is, of course, debatable but possible, in any event it was certainly a relief to Stalin that the Japanese became embroiled in China as it averted any threat to their own southern Far Eastern borders. See Jung Chang & Jon Halliday, *Mao: The Unknown Story*, (Jonathan Cape, London, 2005). To further confuse things the commander of the 33rd Army Group had the same name.

63: Assistant Chief of Naval General Staff to Commanders in Chief Combined Second and Third Fleets, timed 2300hrs, 28 July.

64: Message dated 28 July.

65: Chief of the Navy Department of the Republic of China, Shao-Kuan Chen and Deputy Chief of the Military Affairs Department, Hao-Sen.

66: Sadao Seno to the author, 14 April 2005.

67: *Dai Toa Senso Eno Michi (En Route to the Great Asia War)* by Professor Akira Nakamura, Dokkyo University, Soka City, Tokyo. (Tendensha, Tokyo, 1990). See also *Nihhon Institute for Critical Science (NICS)*, Kadzuwo J. Shimidzu, 31 August 2004. From 1941 the Japanese referred to the combat period as The Great East Asia War, although post-1945 the war with the Americans and British in the Pacific only, came to be termed *Taiheiyo Senso* (Pacific War).

68: Businessman Tom Simmen who was present in Shanghai that day, found the images so shocking that they were destroyed, but his pregnant wife smuggled the prints out of China. His son, John, many years later decided they should be seen. See *Photos document brutality in Shanghai*, by Tom Mintier, (CNN, Bangkok, Thailand, 23 September 1996).

69: The light cruiser *Yubari* (Flag), 13th and 15th Destroyer Divisions, reinforced later by 5th and 29th Destroyer Divisions from Japan.

70: *Hishogumo (Flying Clouds)* by Sadamu Takahashi (Takahashi, Kawasaki, Kanagawa), April 1978.

71: *ibid.*

72: The Order of the Golden Kite was a leadership honour decoration awarded to Japanese soldiers who have been in combat. It had several classes.

73: *Hishogumo, op cit.*

74: *ibid.*

75: Uesugui Kenshin and Takeda Shingen were very famous military commanders from the ancient 'Age of Wars.'

76: *Hishogumo, op cit.*

77: *ibid.*

78: *ibid.*

79: *Kanbaku Taicho, op cit.*

80: *Kanbaku Taicho, op cit.*

81: The most comprehensive analysis of the 'Rape of Nanking' charges are contained in Takemoto, Tadao and Ohara, Yasuo, *The Alleged 'Nanking Massacre': Japan's rebuttal to China's forged claims*. (Meisei-sha Inc, Tokyo, 2000). This is a measured and detailed denial of the allegations, particularly those made in the book by Iris Chang, *The Rape of Nanking: The forgotten Holocaust of World War II (sic)*. Foreword by William C Kirby, (Basic Books, New York, 1998).

82: See Navy Press Room Release, *Report of findings of the Court of Inquiry on the bombing and sinking of USS Panay*, 24 December 1937.

83: See Morison, Professor Samuel Eliot, *History of United States Naval Operations in World War II: Volume 3: The Rising Sun in the Pacific*, pages 16-18.

84: *ibid*.

85: See Trevor K Plante, *Two Japans: Japanese expressions of sympathy and regret in the wake of the Panay Incident*, Prologue: Quarterly of the National Archives and Records Administration.

86: See George Atcheson Jr, Second Secretary US Embassy, report of Court of Enquiry under Admiral Yarnell aboard USS *Augusta*, 23rd December 1937. Foreign Relations, Japan, 1931-1941, pages 532-547.

87: See Commander Okumiya, 'How the *Panay* was sunk', *US Naval Institute Proceedings*, June 1953, pages 587-596. It should be observed that such incidents were not one-sided however, on 14 August 1937, the truculent American leader of the Chinese Air Force, Claire Chennault, had sent his bombers to attack Japanese warships off Shanghai. His airmen completely missed the Japanese targets, and instead directed their attacks against the British heavy cruiser HMS *Cumberland* at anchor there. They also deposited many bombs in the heart of the city, killing 1,700 innocent Chinese and injuring as many more.

88: *Hishogumo, op cit*. In recording this classic 'Black shoe' versus 'Brown shoe' exchange it should be recorded that, surprisingly, terms of respect were not used so often as in Western Navies. For example *Hai* (Yes), *Lie* (No), *Ryokai* (I or we've understood) and *Shochi shimashita* (All right, Sir, Very well, Sir and Certainly, Sir were usually used. Sadao Seno states that he has never heard any Japanese words corresponding to 'Aye Aye, Sir', 'Yes, Sir' or 'No, Sir' in his naval career.

89: The author had the great pleasure of meeting and talking with Commander Susumu Takaoka at his home in Zushi City in April 1998, shortly before his death and can confirm his memory was very clear and sharp on such matters.

90: This section is based upon the memoirs of various surviving members of the families, on Kiyoko's own memoirs, *op cit*, and on further information supplied by Sadao Seno from contemporary sources.

91: A marriage between a commoner bride and bridegroom had the *nakoudo* usually call first upon the bride's house to hand the *yuino* to her father or mother. He returned with the present from the bride to the bridegroom to hand it to his father or mother in the latter's home.

92: This airfield no longer exists. Post-war, after acting as an ammunition storage area for the Americans during the Korean conflict, the area covered by this airfield later became a huge housing development and suburb of Hyuga City.

93: A *Haiku*, unconverted, consists of just seventeen Chinese characters, and is the shortest form of formal Japanese poetry. Egusa used to carry his sketch book of landscapes, which included his poems, during his time in central China and later on his journeys with Kiyoko, but these were all lost with the *Sōryū* at Midway.

94: The precise poetic translation loses in translation to English but can be construed as: – 'Two butterflies leave a dream and fly out into the May sky.'

95: Tosa was the old name for Kochi Prefecture.

96: In olden-day Japan, a formal letter of divorce was traditionally written with just three and a half lines, a far more civilised proceeding that modern Western divorce lawyers can manage, (and much more economical to boot).

97: His fellow-pilots of the 12th dive-bomber unit in China had nicknamed him Takahige, 'Fine Moustache' Egusa because of his luxuriant growth.

98: The author visited the area recently and can personally endorse the many praises lavished on Hakone.

99: Anti-British sentiment in Japan, coupled with exasperation with their own Governments handling of the response, had been accentuated by the *Asama Maru* 'Incident' on 21 January 1940. This NYK liner was stopped thirty-fives miles off Najima Zaki, Chiba Prefecture, by a British cruiser and twenty-one German civilian passengers forcibly removed.

100: See *Circumstances which led the Japanese Navy to agree to the Tripartite Pact*, Notes on Conference with Admiral T Takata, former Chief of First Section, Navy Affairs Bureau, 17 February 1953. Appendix 5 of Japanese Navy Monographs.

101: Ott was the former Military Attaché, 'an old line military conservative' and very anti-Hitler, according to Karl Otto Braun, see *Reflections on German and American Foreign Policy, 1933-1945*, Paper presented to the Sixth International Revisionist Conference, reproduced in *The Journal for Historical Review*, Vol 6 No 1, Spring 1986. Cited hereafter as *Braun, op cit*. The German Naval Attaché at the Tokyo Embassy, Vice-Admiral Paul H Weneker, who worked with Ott, stated, post-war, that he had had 'a definite falling out with the Nazi regime in 1944.' See USSBS (Pacific), *Interrogations of Japanese Officials*, OPNAV-P-03-100, Naval Analysis Division, Washington DC Nav No 70.

102: Ernest L Presselsen, *Germany and Japan: A study in Totalitarian Diplomacy, 1933-1941*. (Fertie, New York, 1961).

103: *Braun, op cit*.

104: Chief among them being Oikawa himself, Vice Minister Teijiro Toyoda, Chief of the Bureau of Naval Affairs Vice-Admiral Kose Abe, Chief of the Naval General Staff Prince Fushimi, Deputy Chief of the Naval General Staff Nobutake Kondo and Chief of the Operational Bureau of the Naval Staff Admiral Matome Ugaki; with Abe and Ugaki being particularly reluctant.

105: See *Circumstances which led the Japanese Navy to agree to the Tripartite Pact*, Notes on Conference with Admiral Kondo, former Deputy Chief of the Naval Staff, 17 February 1953. Appendix 5 of Japanese Navy Monographs.

106: But not without some severe pressure from General Tojo, the Minister of War, and the Army, if the statement by Captain Toshikazu Ohmae, at the time a member of the Naval Affairs Bureau and responsible for the defence of Naval installations, is to be believed. He recalled how the Japanese Army 'began to insist upon the conclusion of the Tripartite Pact.' General Itagaki, Army Minister, strongly supported by the Army-dominated Premier Hiranuma, emphasised the Army's attitude at a Cabinet meeting in May. As Admiral Yonai, Navy Minister, was equally emphatic in his opposition to the Pact, no decision could be reached. Some Army circles regarded the Navy as public enemy No 1 and rumours were spread that an Army unit would attempt to occupy the Navy Department in an endeavour to bring about an early Cabinet decision to ratify the pact. Ohmae recalled the reaction to this: – 'One battalion of the Naval Land Combat Force was alerted at Yokosuka to be ready for immediate action and machine guns were installed in the Navy Department building. Guards stationed in the Department were armed with pistols and swords.' The frenzied atmosphere that prevailed between the Army and Navy at this time is almost unbelievable and explains a great deal. See the statement by Captain Toshikazu Ohmae, giving main points of conferences held with Admiral Kondo and Admiral T Takata; 17 February 1953 in *Japanese Navy Monographs, Appendix 5*.

107: *ibid.*

108: Starting with prohibiting the export of scrap iron in September 1940 and moving on steadily via the freezing of Japanese assets in the USA and the suspension of the 1911 Commercial Treaty, to the threat of a total embargo of oil, the nation's lifeblood.

109: Discussions had been underway between General Issaku Nishihara and the French Governors, initially General Georges Catroux and later, Vice-Admiral Jean Decoux for some time. Finally the French Ambassador in Japan, Charles Arsené-Henry agreed with Matsuoka for the Japanese forces to be given access to facilities and bases in the area of Indo-China bordering on southern China, and the Japan-French Indo-Chinese Agreement (the Henry-Matsuoka Pact) was concluded on 22 September 1940. See also Kirby S Woodburn, *The War Against Japan, Vo. 1. The loss of Singapore* (HMSO, London, 1957).

110: Okumiya & Horikoshi, *Zero, op cit.*

111: Antony Best, *British Intelligence and the Japanese Challenge in Asia, 1914-41* (Palgrave Macmillan, London, 2002). Hereafter cited as *British Intelligence, op cit.* However, a very different view is expressed in C M Bell, *The Royal Navy, Seapower Strategy between the Wars* (Macmillan/King's College, London, 2000).

112: As completed in December 1937, *Sōryū's* aircraft complement was 27 Aichi D1A2 dive-bombers, plus 9 reserve aircraft, 9 Nakajima C3N1 Type 97 Scout planes; 9 Nakajima B5N1 Type 97 torpedo bombers plus 3 reserve aircraft and 12 Mitsubishi A5M4 Type 96 fighters plus 4 reserve aircraft.

113: Christened long after the war by the American Historian Samuel Eliot Morison as the '*Long Lance*', a term the Japanese themselves rarely used, but which has since gained almost universal currency in the west.

114: Rear-Admiral G C Ross, unpublished papers, IWM, London and *Memoirs* page 218.

115: As recorded in Antony Best, *British Intelligence and the Japanese Challenge in Asia, 1914-1941, op cit*, pages 166-167. See also, Captain J G P Vivian, *Efficiency of the Japanese Navy*, Report to the Admiralty, 1935. Vivian was the British Naval Attaché in Tokyo and his report contains another remarkable under-estimation of the capabilities of the IJN's naval aviation.

116: Gordon W Prange, with Donald Goldstein and Katherine V Dillon, *At Dawn We Slept; The Untold Story of Pearl Harbor*, (Brasseys, New York, 1990).

117: Zenji Abe to the author, interview dated 22 April 1998, Tokyo.

118: For a comprehensive picture of the development of Japanese naval thinking on all fronts pre-war, the reader is recommended to Donald M Goldstein and Katherine V Dillon, editors, *The Pearl Harbor Papers: Inside the Japanese Plans*, (Dulles, Virginia, 1999). Also David Evans and Mark R Peattie, *Kaigun: Strategy, Tactics and Technology in the Imperial Japanese Navy, 1887-1941*, (Atlantic Books, 1997).

119: Nihon Kaigun Kōkūshi Hensan Iinkai, editor, *Nihon kaigun Kōkūshi (The History of Japanese Naval Aviation – 4 Vols)*, (Jiji Tsushinsha, 1969) Vol 1, pages 693-4.

120: But **not** 90% as Peattie has it, *Sunburst*, pp 141, *op cit*.

121: This was the old battleship *Settsu*, discarded from the active list under the terms of the Washington Treaty, she was converted and modified into a radio-controlled target ship and much work in the development of dive-bombing accuracy was done with her before and during the war.

122: Shimada, *Estimate of the Situation Prior to Outbreak of War*, contained in *Progress of Revision of the Wartime Naval Organization from November 1940 until the Outbreak of War*, *ibid* 152, Chapter 1. Cited hereafter as *Organisation, op cit*.

123: Nagano, Joint-Army-Navy Supreme Military Council meeting, presided over by Field Marshal Prince Kanin, in the presence of the Emperor, 4 November 1941, *National defence and the use of arms in implementing the national policy of Imperial Japan*, contained in *Organisation, op cit*.

124: Sugiyama, Imperial Conference, 5 November, contained in *Organization, op cit*.

125: Several revisionist books have appeared in recent years claiming elaborate conspiracy theories connected with Franklin D Roosevelt and Winston Churchill, but this author does not give them any credence. More interesting and worthwhile is Seishiro Sugihara's *Between Competence and Culpability: Assessing the Diplomacy of Japan's Foreign Ministry from Pearl Harbor to Potsdam* (University Press of America, Lanham, Maryland, 1997).

126: One of a series of IJN Naval Messages intercepted by US Navy intercept sites at Hawaii, Guam and Corregidor, that remained neither coded or translated until after September 1945, and subsequently found by Henry Schorreck, NSA Historian, before being passed to the Naval Archives in 1978-9. See *Pearl Harbor Revisited: United States Navy Communications Intelligence, 1924-1941*, Department of the Navy, Naval Historical Centre, Washington, Navy Yard, Washington DC. (Subsequently referred to as *Revisited, op cit*.)

127: *Revisited, op cit*., National Archives SRN – 116566.

128: No further ambitions were envisaged by the Japanese at that stage, despite much post-war western speculation of Japan joining up with German forces in Arabia, after conquering the Indian sub-continent (no small feat!). See John B Lundstrom; *First South Pacific Fleet Strategy, December 1941- June 1942*. (US Naval Institute Press, Annapolis, 1977). Though of course contacts were made with Indian malcontents like Subhas Chandra Bose and his ilk, to stir up as much trouble as possible, and the

Indian National Army was equipped accordingly. The subsequent Japanese attacks into Assam were a later decision, taken after Burma fell with such ease.

129: Extensive as was this programme, one historian has made claims that even the occupation of Hawaii itself was contemplated as part of the Midway operation; see Professor John J Stephan, *Hawaii under the Rising Sun,* (University of Hawaii Press, 1984).

130: It has been stated by David Aiken that Egusa actually had two separate personal aircraft, both of which were garishly painted. The one used at Pearl Harbour was *Jaja Uma,* but he is said to have had another, which he used in China, *Tora Moyo.* It was also stated Egusa's aircraft was named *Dora Neko.* However, as James F Lansdale noted, 'There are purported interviews with witnesses to these schemes, but to date, NO photos of same.'

131: This veneration was far more than sentimental, see Nobshige Hozumi, *Ancestor-worship and Japanese law*, (Maruzen Kabushiki-Kaisha, Tokyo, 1912).

132: Imperial Rescript; Issue to the Army and Navy on the fourth of January in the fifteenth year of Meiji. Guntai was translated as 'soldiers', there being no direct English translation, but was always meant to mean all fighting men, including the 'soldiers of the sea', or sailors of the IJN.

133: The Japanese viewpoint is given in Donald M Goldstein and Katherine V Dillon, with Masataka Chihaya translator; *Fading Victory: The Diary of Admiral Matome Ugaki – 1941-1945* (University of Pittsburgh Press, Pittsburgh, 1991). The same authors edit the Gordon W Prange Collection of related Japanese documents in *The Pearl Harbor Papers: Inside the Japanese Plans* (2nd Edition Brassey's, London, 1999).

134: *Revisited, op cit.*

135: Contrary to many accounts, the battleship *Nagato* flew the Admiral's flag at the start of the Pacific War, because the new *Yamato* did not fully enter commission until 16 December, nine days later.

136: It will be noted that the complements of *Hiryū* and *Sōryū* were slightly smaller than the other carriers. This is because their design was based on heavy cruiser hulls and machinery, rather than on the much larger battleship and battle-cruiser hulls of the *Akagi* and *Kaga.* As 'flight deck cruisers' this was a ploy designed to overcome the limitations of the naval treaties, but this subterfuge became irrelevant once these were abrogated by Japan shortly afterward. The *Sōryū* (18,448 tons (on her trials), 728 x 70 x 25 feet – 221.9 x 21.3 x 7.6 metres) was therefore a more cramped design in every respect, but still managed to carry a substantial air group, as did the slightly larger *Hiryū* (21,900 tons, 731.5 x 73 x 25.5 feet – 223 x 22.25 x 7.8 metres). Both ships featured dual hangars and full-length flight-decks along with small bridge islands on the starboard side of the ship.

137: There are several versions of Abe's account of the approach and the attack, the original of which was written by him for the Japanese Defence Force English Language School, Chiba Peninsular, 1953, including a version in *World War II presents: Pearl Harbor* in *Aviation History* magazine. I prefer my own translation.

138: But, and ultimately unfortunately for them, they did not adopt the other Royal Navy practice of having armoured steel flight-decks as part of their protection. This enabled British aircraft-carriers like the *Illustrious, Formidable* and *Indomitable* to survive several direct hits in dive-bombing attacks from German Junkers Ju 87 Stuka dive-bombers in the 1940-42 period, that would have sunk either Japanese or American aircraft carriers with their wooden flight decks in short order. (See Peter C Smith, *Junkers Ju 87 Stuka* (Crowood Press, Ramsbury, 1997). This protection came at the price of striking power, with only a half of the number of aircraft carried by British ships as against their Japanese and American opposite numbers.

139: Mark Peattie, *Sunburst, op cit*.

140: Whether the dive-bombers were 'bombed-up' on the flight-deck or in the hangar would be dependant on a number of variables:

1) Operational use of the flight deck, (landing on and taking off of other strike forces or the Combat Air Patrols (CAP) etc) and whether the lifts were in constant use.

2) The type of mission being undertaken; (which determined the actual bomb type to be carried *viz* the 240kg semi-armour piercing (SAP) anti-ship, or the 242kg high explosive (HE) anti-ground target weapons, which shared common aircraft fixing assemblies).

3) Weather conditions prevailing at the time. However, whichever venue was chosen, the armourers who did the loading of the ordnance could only be in one place at a time of course. In addition, there were only sufficient mobile bomb trolleys available to load about one-third of the dive-bomber force at any one time.

141: See *Boeicho Boeikenshujo Senshibu- Vol. 43, Middowei Kaisen,* (Official War History –Vol. 43, *Battle of Midway*), (Asagumo Shinbunsha, Tokyo, 1971), page 289.

142: According to Gordon Prange, *At Dawn We Slept, op cit,* pages 490-2.

143: But not, unfortunately for Hollywood, *Tora, Tora, Tora* (Tiger, Tiger, Tiger) but *To, To, To* (Attack initiated), *Ra, Ra, Ra* (Attack successful). (*50th Anniversary of Pearl Harbor Symposium*, Tokyo, 7 December 1991).

144: Commander Seno was at pains to emphasise this fact, which, he felt, had been deliberately ignored by western air historians of the battle. Seno to the author, 4 February 2005.

145: Kunio Kosemoto, *Gekito Kanbakutai* (Tokyo).

146: Lieutenant Commander Howard L Young, *Report* to CinCUS/CinCPac HQ, dated 8 December 1941. US National Archives, Washington DC.

147: For a detailed analysis of the bomb strikes on *Nevada* see, Peter C Smith, *Aichi D3A1/2 Val*, (Crowood Press, Ramsbury, 1999).

148: Kiyoko Egusa, *Two Lives, op cit*. Lack of sufficient bombs has been cited as one reason.

149: Mitsuharu Uehara, *Commander of the Carrier Dive Bombers Egusa Takashige*, Tokyo, 1989.

150: The third US carrier, *Saratoga*, would, of course, never have been found as she was on the way back from the States after refitting, and was sailed from Pearl Harbor just too late.

151: Kiyoko Egusa, *Two Lives, op cit*.

152: See *MV Neptuna*, in *Australian Merchant Navy* by Ron (Steve) Wylie, 2000 for further details.

153: Information supplied by Colonel Shogo Hattori of the National Institute for Defence Studies, Tokyo, letter to author dated 10 July 1998. See also deck logs of USS *Edsall*, January 20-21 1942, (National Archives; also The death of USS *Edsall*, article in *Shipmate* magazine, April 1980, based on notes from Rear-Admiral Edwin T Layton, USN from Japanese records. Also Dull, Paul, *Battle History of the Imperial Japanese Navy*, (Naval Institute Press, Annapolis, 1978).

154: See Yamakawa, Shinsaku, Hitting *the Target (Meichu)*, in *The Pacific War Documentary Vol 1 (Taiheiyo Senso Dokumentarii da 1 kan)*, (Tokyo, 1967). Later published as *The Dive-Bomber Squadron of a Japanese Carrier (NF-bunko of Kojin-sha)*, (Tokyo, 1994).

155: NAP 1/C = Naval Aviation Pilot, First Class (*Itto Hikohei*).

156: For conditions at Tjilatjap before it finally fell, see Hugh Campbell and Ron Lovell, *So Long Singapore*, (David Lumbard, North Berwick).

157: Admiral Layton made an extensive report of the failings of those he worked with, both in Malaya and Ceylon, which pulled no punches. For much of the fiasco he puts the blame squarely on his subordinate, Vice Admiral Geoffrey Schomburg Arbuthnot, CB, DSO at HMS *Lanka*. Layton wrote: 'Apart from the decision to clear the harbours of merchant shipping, naval movements during the period of the Japanese attacks were under the control of Admiral Somerville as Commander-in-Chief, Eastern Fleet, with Admiral Arbuthnot acting as his deputy at Colombo while *Warspite* was at sea. This applied to the movements, for example, of *Cornwall*, *Dorsetshire*, *Hermes* and *Vampire*, though in the case of the two first-mentioned I advised Arbuthnot to sail them on a course which would have taken them to the west of the Maldives and clear of the Japanese naval aircraft which sank them. As to the *Hermes* and *Vampire*, I was not aware that these vessels had been sailed until they had already gone.' Of Arbuthnot, Layton also stated that, although he had been a very brave officer, 'he seemed to have aged prematurely and was incapable of decisive action.' (See *The Layton Papers*, ADM 1472A and B, National Archives, London; Also Correspondence and papers of Admiral Sir Geoffrey Layton, relating to the naval war in the Far East, 1940-1945; British Library catalogue numbers 74796-74806 inclusive). However, Somerville, as overall C-in-C afloat, also bore some of the responsibility for splitting his command at such a vital juncture.

158: For example Michael Tomlinson, *The Most Dangerous Moment*, (William Kimber, London, 1976), written from an RAF viewpoint, with little or no understanding of naval warfare, the exaggerated claims of Japanese losses are repeated as facts despite the true figure being long known.

159: Tomlinson, as well as exaggerating Japanese losses and minimising British losses, dismisses the damage inflicted on the bases. By contrast the man on the spot, Admiral Sir Geoffrey Layton, was to record with regard to Trincomalee that: 'The air raid of 9 April did considerable damage to the dockyard involving much labour in rebuilding. The ss *Saigang*, sunk in the raid, is very badly damaged.' See *War Records of the Flag Office Ceylon – Part II* (ADM 199/13900).

160: For the most detailed account of the Indian Ocean Val operations see, Peter C Smith, *Aichi D3A1/2 Val*, (Crowood, Ramsbury, 1999).

161: As quoted in Masatake Okumiya, *et al, Zero! The history of the Japanese Naval Air Force 1937-1945*, (Cassell, London, 1958).

162: The *Hermes* and other ships had been ordered to sea by Rear-Admiral Arbuthnot in the mistaken belief that she would be safer away from harbour, and that the RAF would provide her with air cover; both assumptions proved totally illusory! Admiral Somerville offered to take the blame for this extraordinary blunder when Churchill raised incredulous questions. That and Somerville's equally unfortunate dispositions with regard the *Cornwall* and *Dorsetshire* certainly indicated that something was *very* wrong with British thinking at this time. Somerville had earlier written an upbeat letter to his wife stating that the Japanese had been scared to engage his ramshackle fleet, words which, his usually obsequious biographer was forced to admit, 'he may have later regretted.' (See Donald Macintyre, *Fighting Admiral*, (Evans, London, 1961). Somerville may have also suffered from what Peter Lowe asserted was 'the grave underestimation of the Japanese armed forces by both the British and the Americans', (Peter Lowe, *English Historical Review*, February 1999). If so, he was far from alone in this and Winston Churchill was, if anything, even more deluded and had been for many years. See Captain Stephen W Roskill, *Churchill and the Admirals*, (Collins, London, November 1977) for many instances going back from the 1930's, right up to the eve of the Pacific War, on the Premier's almost total blind spot about Japanese naval potential and fighting abilities. Of course the Premier and supreme war leader was far from being alone in this misconception, sharing with many what Antony West describes as, 'the commonly held racial assumptions about the inability of non-white nations to confront the modern Western states.' (*British Intelligence, op cit)*. However, Churchill was in such a powerful position, and interfered so much, that his misreading of the situation affected the outcome of events far more than most. Tanks and Hurricanes went to Stalin, who never asked for them, and never thanked us for them, while British Malaya and Burma had to make do with Brewster Buffaloes and bren-gun carriers.

163: The parachute and cable rocket (PAC) was probably the most useless anti-aircraft weapon ever installed by any Navy at any time. A solid fuel rocket propellant fired the missile to a pre-determined height, whereupon a time fuse separated the forward section, which contained three parachutes and 400ft of cabling with a tiny bomb fixed to it. The parachutes opened, the wires trailed down and enemy aircraft (if their aircrews had not died laughing) were supposed to fly into it. Its only success in the war, after a prodigious waste of time and effort building, installing it and training men to use it, was one 'probable' at Dover in June 1940. But it may well have contributed to the loss of the battle cruiser HMS *Hood*, being an exposed fire hazard on the ships upper decks.

164: Confidential Report of an Interview with Captain Moore, Master of ss *Athelstane*; Shipping Casualties Section – Trade Division, Admiralty. AIR 2 4221).

165: Captain S W Roskill; *The War at Sea, Vol 2 The Period of Balance*, (HMSO, London, 1956).

166: Captain Russell Grenfell, *Main Fleet to Singapore*, (Faber, London, 1951).

167: Okumiya, *Zero, op cit*.

168: That those pressing positively for the proposed push down the Solomon Islands chain and onward were the Navy and not the Army was established definitively by Colonel Shoho Hattori, the Director of Operations Division, Army General Staff, from October 1943 to February 1945, see Shoho Hattori, *Daitoa Senso Zenshi (The*

Complete History of the Great East Asia War), (Hara Shobo, Tokyo, 1965). After the various 'incidents' on the Manchurian-Soviet border between 1939 and 1940, which were localised wars and in which the Japanese had come off very much second-best, the Japanese Army was obsessed with the need to concentrate all available resources there rather than spread troops all over the Pacific. Nor could the Japanese mercantile marine have safely and adequately supported any large land forces, even if they had have been so committed.

169: The Japanese are frequently said to have won the Battle of the Coral Sea 'tactically' as they traded the small carrier *Sōhō*, for the big carrier *Lexington*, but losses of dive- and torpedo-bombers were heavy. They most certainly lost the battle 'strategically' as the easy invasion of Port Moresby by sea was called off and the troops had to fight their way south overland, a task which they ultimately failed.

170: Often overlooked also is the fact that a fourth American aircraft carrier, with a full and complete aircraft complement, was on its way to the scene of the action, the *Saratoga*. Had the battle continued for a few days more than it did, she would have provided a crucial, fresh air striking force just at the right moment.

171: This may certainly be true with regard to the unfortunate Nagumo himself, but recent studies seem to indicate that he was alone in his ignorance on that fateful day. On 20 May, Yamamoto had advised Nagumo, among others, that it was estimated that two or three American carriers were in the area of Hawaii. (See Fuchida & Okumiya, *Midway; the Battle that doomed Japan*, (London)). Nagumo's own official report (*Mobile Force's Detailed Battle Report 6*, transcribed as *The Japanese Story of the Battle of Midway*, OPNAV P32-100, Office of Naval Intelligence, Washington DC, 1947), confirmed that he assumed these would sortie out in response to the Midway attack, which of course, is exactly what Yamamoto's plan had hoped for as they could then be destroyed. However, subsequent information gleaned from inceptions made on 29 May by the flagship *Yamato* of greatly increased radio signals traffic from Hawaii, which in turn indicated that the Americans might be on the move already, were *not* passed on to Nagumo by Yamamoto. He assumed that this increase had already been picked up by Nagumo's own flagship. Nor was he told that a Japanese reconnaissance over Pearl Harbour had been cancelled.

The old adage that, 'no news is good news' probably applied here, if the 'two or three' American carriers had sailed, or were missing, he assumed he would have been informed. Even when the Naval Staff in Tokyo came to the firm conclusion, on 2 June, that the American's had rumbled their mission and sent the carriers out to ambush them, and radioed Yamamoto and Nagumo accordingly, the latter did not receive this warning and his C-in-C did not pass it on, although inclined to, due to the need to maintain radio silence. This latter requirement would seem to be superfluous if the information from Tokyo was true, but, nonetheless, no relay from *Yamato* to *Akagi* was carried out. As Professor Dallas Woodbury Isom has stated, 'it seems that almost everyone in the Japanese naval high command suspect that American carriers might be at Midway –everyone except Nagumo.' See Professor Dallas Woodbury Isom, *The Battle of Midway; Why the Japanese Lost*, Naval *War College Review*, Summer 2000, pages 20-21. This is a condensation of his projected book, *Midway Inquest*.

172: This change of flag has led some historians to claim that the 2nd Division's Carrier codes and the unit bands were changed accordingly. Using *Sōryū's* Detailed Action Report for the Battle of Midway, (Naval Historical Centre Microfilm Reel JD-

1), the respected historian Michael Wenger has refuted these claims. However, allegations that they were indeed altered continue. Apart from the time factor to enable this to be done, all is still speculation. Whether *Sōryū's* dive-bombers retained their No 1 *Hiko Daitai* code of BI followed by three numerals and the single fuselage band as before or not, continues to dominate the minds of a certain type of Internet modeller and war-gamer. The aircrews appear not to have changed carriers in any case, even if their mounts *were* repainted.

173: In fact written as *Sauriyuu* at the time, although pronounced *Sōryū*.

174: On *Sōryū*, the outer edges of this wooden deck were steel edged, and steel plating was also used at the fore and aft extremities.

175: This was similar, in its purpose at any rate, to the Mirror Landing Aid system that, thirty years later was claimed to have been invented by the Royal Navy in the 1950's.

176: The full description of this unique apparatus is given by Carl Snow, archivist of the Tailhook Association, in *Japanese Carrier Operations: How Did They Do It? The Hook*, (Annapolis, 1995).

177: Mike Wenger states that 75% of *Sōryū 's* aircrew that participated in the Midway strike were veterans of Pearl Harbour, a high percentage of veterans. Citing *Hawai Sakusen* and the *Sōryū, Detailed Action Report for Midway, op cit*, Wenger further broke this percentage down as twelve out of eighteen pilots, fourteen out of eighteen observers and fifteen out of eighteen radiomen.

178: Not surprisingly, for OP-20-G's, the US Navy Radio Intelligence Sections intercept station at Correigidor had identified the Japanese code name for Midway 'AF' as early as March 1942. See editorial comments to Henry F Schorreck's *The Role of COMINT in the Battle of Midway* (SRH-230).

179: The receipt time of this signal, sent by *Tone 4* search aircraft at 0728hrs, Isom maintains, is contentious. What is known as the Nagumo Report (*sic*) *op cit*, states it was received at 0800hrs, and that this time is confirmed by Ryunosuke Kusaka in *Rengo Kantai (Combined Fleet)*, published in *Mainichi Shimbun*, (Tokyo, April, 1952), page 84. Kusaka was Chief of Staff of the First Air Fleet and a former captain of the *Akagi*.

180: This machine at first failed to locate the US ships reported by *Tone's* scout, but, by following returning American aircraft back to their carrier soon had them in clear view. Frantic signals to Nagumo reporting this momentous sighting never reached him because the *Susei's* radio malfunctioned. By the time this aircraft returned to the fleet, landing back aboard the blazing, crippled *Sōryū* was out of the question and so they put down on *Hiryū* only to share her fate a few hours later.

181: Also embarked were three additional Mitsubishi A6M2 Zero's belonging to the 6th *Kokutai*, who were to be based on Midway after its capture.

182: Isom, *op cit* page 12.

183: Jonathan B Parshall, David D Dickson and Anthony P Tully; *Set and Drift; Doctrine Matters. Why the Japanese Lost at Midway, (Naval War College Review*, Summer 2001, maintain that 'Nagumo was nowhere near ready to launch by 1025; in fact, he had probably barely begun preparations to do so'. Professor Dallas Woodbury Isom's article, *The Battle of Midway: Why the Japanese Lost, (Naval War College Review*, Summer 2000, pages 60-100, maintains that *Sōryū's* after lift, being both larger and faster than the older carriers, could also have been utilised to have prepared the dive-bombers much faster than is assumed, and, moreover, the fact that at least some of the dive-bombers were up on the flight deck, is seemingly confirmed by the *Boeicho Boeikenshujo Senshibu- Midowei Kaisen, op cit.*

184: See John B Lundstrom, *The First Team: Pacific Naval Air Combat from Pearl Harbor to Midway*, (Naval Institute Press, Annapolis, 1984).

185: See Bombing Squadron Six, *Report of Action, June 4-6, 1942* (FVB-6/A16/nhn in ADM199/1302 *The Battle of Midway Island* (National Archives, Kew, London). American times were two hours in advance of Japanese times in their respective reports.

186: His fate and survival, with so many other pilots and observers, would seem to lend credence to the claim that hardly any of the Vals of the second strike were actually at that moment spotted on the flight deck aft, as Fuchida and Okumiya claimed as eyewitness facts. Recent studies by distinguished authorities in both the United States and London tend to dispute this claim (*Set and Drift; op cit*, pages 139-151). This is a sharp *critique* of Isom's article. It was in turn countered by Isom's response, *They would have found a way*; contained in *In My View*, the letters page of the same edition (*Naval War College Review*, summer 2002).

The gist of this exchange was that;

1) following what is known of Japanese naval aircraft operating procedures at this time, and the time it would take;

2) given the continuing need to clear the flight-deck to facilitate the operating and frequent re-arming of the Zero fighters during the intense Combat Air Patrol activity;

3) given the need to replace anti-ground target bombs loaded on the Vals with armour-piercing bombs to strike the American carriers;

the Val's of the second wave aboard *Sōryū and Hiryū* would have had to be struck down into the central hangars. It is thus contended, and Isom seems to (provisionally), have conceded this point, that they would not have had time to be brought up again on deck before the SBD's struck. This hypothesis is backed by photographic evidence from the USAAF Boeing B-17's taken shortly before then, which show only fighter aircraft on the carrier decks. Isom still contends that the standard operation procedure might have been ditched due to the circumstances. Another view is that if *all* the Vals had been spotted on the decks running up the radial engines, their aircrew would have been aboard their aircraft when the Dauntless bombs hit, and that very few, if any, would have survived this, they would have died in their planes. That this did *not* happen (just ten aircrew were lost from *Sōryū*) *would* seem to indicate that they had not yet manned their aircraft, which were, therefore, still in the hangars waiting to be brought up. However, although Parshall Dickson and Tully *cite* the *Boeicho Boeikenshujo Senshibu-Midowei Kaisen, op cit*, as stating that '*every* Japanese carrier had its *attack* aircraft in the hangars', it could be argued, if one was as pedantic as they are on Isom's points, that this might mean only the Kates and might well *exclude* the dive-bombers! Further startling revelations are promised in the same author's book *Shattered Sword* (Potomac), but, at the time of writing, this has not yet appeared.

187: Needless to say there is considerable controversy about the exact number of *Sōryū's* complement that day. Sawachi Hisae, *Middowei kaisen: Kiroku (The Naval Battle of Midway; A Record)*, (Bungei Shunjû, Tokyo, 1986) has the crew lists broken down by ranks and departments, but detailed as it is, these figures are now being questioned.

188: Mark R Peattie, *Sunburst, op cit.* (See footnote 17 Chapter 7, information complied by James Sawruk).

189: See *Midway, the battle that doomed Japan, op cit.* There is nothing unusual in Governments covering up defeats, the Churchill Government in Great Britain repeatedly hid the truth from its own citizens, especially in the first three years of the war which were mainly humiliating defeats. Cases like the loss of the British of the Highland Division at St. Valéry (due to Churchill's political policy of appeasing the disintegrating French), along with the enormous loss of life when the troopship *Lancashire* was bombed and sunk, and the sinking of the battleship *Barham*, are typical of many such instances.

190: For a long period after the war Dr Nakagawa was the Chief Engineer of engine development at Prince Motors and the Nissan Motor Company.

191: Dr Yamana was later reinstated as a professor at Tokyo University from 1956 until 1966. During his tenure of office, Yamana made tremendous contributions to aeronautical research and development. He finally resigned in 1966, when, as Chairman of the Investigations Committee into the Boeing 727 crash at Haneda in February of that year, his view and opinion of the true cause of the crash was deemed unacceptable by the Japanese Government and was not admitted.

192: Post-war, Miki joined the Technical Research Laboratory of Japanese National Railways and played a significantly major role in the development of the famous *Shinkansen*, the so-called 'Bullet Train.'

193: For a full account of the setting up and operational use of the Luftwaffe Ju.88 torpedo bomber units based in Norway in 1942 see, Smith, Peter C. *Arctic Victory* (Crecy, Manchester, 1998).

194: See US Strategic Bombing Survey (Pacific), Interrogation No USSBS 32- *The Battle of the Philippine Sea, 19-20 June 1944, Interrogation Nav No 3, Vice-Admiral Jisaburo Ozawa, IJN.* Microfilm reels in author's collection. Cited hereafter as *Ozawa, op cit.*

195: Ozawa, op cit.

196: *Ozawa, op cit.* However, the Admiral later contradicted himself by confirming that his fleet broke their radio silence in order to inform the land-based aircraft the location in which to attack the American task Forces, although he stated that the decision had already been made of when the attack was to occur. This seems to indicate that Ozawa must have thought that he had a measure of *tactical* control of these aircraft, at least during the battle. It should be noted that these aircraft were exclusively Navy, there were *no* Japanese Army aircraft involved.

197: *Ozawa, op cit.*

198: US Strategic Bombing Survey (Pacific), Interrogation No USSBS 434- *Shore-based Aircraft in the Marianas Campaign, Captain Akira Sasaki, IJN*, 23 November 1945, and US Strategic Bombing Survey (Pacific), Interrogation No USSSBS 448- *Shore-based Aircraft in the Marianas, Captain Mitsuo Fuchida, IJN, 25 November 1945.* Microfilm reels in author's collection.

199: Ozawa received *no* direct information from Toyoda on the results, real or imaginary, of these land-based air attacks. *Ozawa op cit.*

200: Nowadays, Guam International Airport. See History Series No 71, *Base*

Naval Barracks Section, Combined Fleet (5), National Defence Agency, National Defence College, History Room Tokyo, 1974. A memorial stone dedicated to the 521st Air Group, erected in February 1988, is today located in the South Pacific Memorial Park, at Yigo, on Guam.

201: Count Yoshio Kamei, descended from an ancient feudal lord family, had been one of the first trio of Japanese Navy pilots to actually land an aircraft aboard an aircraft carrier, the *Hosho*, in 1923. He died in action in August and was posthumously promoted to Rear-Admiral.

202: Minato-gawa is a shrine close to Kobe railway station, dedicated to the great warrior hero Masashige Kusunoki (1294-1336). At the Battle of Minatogawa, he was cut off with a small force and chose suicide rather than surrender. This act was celebrated as the ultimate loyalty to his Emperor (Go-Daigo) and represented a noble final sacrifice for any fighting man. This laying down of ones life in combat, soon to find its ultimate expression in the *Kamikaze* ideal, was deep-rooted in the Japanese psyche, see for example, Ivan Morris, *The Nobility of Failure: Tragic Heroes in the History of Japan,* (Secker & Warburg, London, 1975) and in some ways remains so, see *The Enigma of Japanese Power: People and Politics in a Stateless Nation* by Karel Van Wolferen (Pelgrave Macmillan, London, 1989).

203: For example, Rene J. Francillon, *Japanese Aircraft of the Pacific War,* (Putnam, London, 1972) has long been accepted as an irrefutable source. He stated the *Ginga* was never operational, and makes no mention of the 521st. The majority of subsequent 'historians', in books and on the Internet, have followed that line unquestioningly ever since.

204: See Commander Task Group 58.3, *Action Reports of Operations against Saipan, Tinian and Guam from units of Task Group Fifty-Eight point Three,* Office of Naval Records and Library, 151927, Washington, DC. Cited hereafter as *Action Reports TF58.3.*

205: *Action Reports TF58.3.*

206: From USS *Enterprise* (CV-6), Action Report 6-22 June 1944. (CV6/A16-3 (10-wn) Serial 0017, dated 3rd July 1944.

207: *ibid.*

208: *ibid.*

209: For more details see Kiyoko's own autobiography, Kiyoko Egusa, *Two Ages* (Kojinsha, Tokyo, 1983).

210: Mitsuharu Uehara, Kanbaku Taicho Egusa Takashiige, *op cit.*

Bibliography

Abe, Lieutenant-Commander (Rtd) Zenji, *How our naval air officers were selected, educated and trained after graduation from the Etajima Naval Academy,* article written for the author, Tokyo, 2005.

Agar, Augustus, *Footprints in the Sea,* Evans, London, 1959.

Asada, Sadao, *Amerika no tai Nichikan to Washington taisei (The Washington Conference and America's View of Japan),* article in *Kokusai seiji, Vol 2,* Tokyo, 1966.

Atcheson Jr, George, Second Secretary US Embassy. *Report* of Court of Enquiry under Admiral Yarnal aboard USS *Augusta* 23rd December 1937. Foreign Relations, Japan, 1931-1941. Washington, DC 1937.

Barnhart, Michael, *Japan Prepares for Total War: The Search for Economic Security, 1919-1941,* Cornell University Press, Ithaca, NY, 1987.

Bell, C M, *The Royal Navy, Seapower Strategy between the Wars,* Macmillan/Kings College, London, 2000

Berry, Henry, *Semper Fi, Mac: Living Memories of the US Marines in WWII,* Perennial, New York, 1996.

Best, Antony, *Lord Sempill (1893-1965) and Japan, 1921-41* entry in *Britain and Japan: Biographical Portraits, Vol IV,* Edited by Professor H Cortazzi, London, Japan Library, 2002.

Best, Antony, *The Road to Anglo-Japanese Confrontation, 1931-41,* in *The History of Anglo-Japanese Relations: The Political-Diplomatic Dimension, Vol II,* Edited by Nish, I and Kibata, Y, Macmillan, London, 2000.

Best, Antony, *British Intelligence and the Japanese Challenge in Asia, 1914-41,* Palgrave Macmillan, London, 2002.

Bisson, Thomas Arthur, *American Policy in the Far East, 1931-1940,* International Secretariat, Institute of Pacific Relations, New York, 1939.

Bodley, R V C, Admiral Togo: *The Authorised Life of Admiral of the Fleet, Marquis Heihachiro Togo, O M,* London, 1935.

Boyd, Carl, *Hitler's Japanese Confident: General Ōshima Hiroshi and Magic Intelligence 1941-1945,* University Press of Kansas, 1993.

Braun, Karl Otto, *Reflections on German and American Foreign Policy, 1933-1945,* Paper presented to the Sixth International Revisionist Conference, reproduced in *The Journal for Historical Review, Vol 6, No 1,* Spring, 1986. USSBS (Pacific), *Interrogations of Japanese Officials,* OPNAV-P-03-100, Naval Analysis Division, Washington DC, No70.

Brice, Martin H, *The Royal Navy and the Sino-Japanese Incident, 1937-41,* Ian Allan, Shepperton, 1973.

Bullock, Cecil, *Etajima: the Dartmouth of Japan,* Sampson Low, Marston, London, 1942.

Burdick, Charles B. *The Japanese Siege of Tsingtau: World War I in Asia,* Archon Books, Hamden, Conn, 1976.

Cathcart-Jones, Owen, *Aviation Memoirs,* Hutchinson, London, 1934.

Chang, Jung and Halliday, Jon, *Mao: The Unknown Story*, Jonathan Cape, London, 2005.

Chang, Iris, *The Rape of Nanking: The forgotten Holocaust of World War II*, Foreword by William C Kirby, Basic Books, New York, 1998.

Chihiro, Hosoya and Makato, Saito, *Washington taisei to Nihonn kankei*, *(Japan's Participation in the Washington Treaty)*, *by Tokyo daigakko shuppankai*, Tokyo, 1967.

Cortazzi, Hugh (Editor), *British Envoys in Japan, 1859-1972*, Global Oriental Ltd, London, December 2003.

Cowman, Ian, *Dominion or Decline: Anglo-American Naval Relations in the Pacific, 1937-1941*, Oxford University Press, Oxford, 1996.

Cunningham of Hyndhope, Admiral of the Fleet, *A Sailors Odyssey*, Hutchinson, London, 1951.

Dull, Paul, *Battle History of the Imperial Japanese Navy*, Naval Institute Press, Annapolis, 1978.

Egusa, Kiyoko, *Two Lives*, Kojinsha, Tokyo, 1983.

Ferris, John, *A British Unofficial Aviation Mission and Japanese Naval Developments, 1919-1929*, in *Journal of Strategic Studies*, Washington DC, September 1982.

Francillon, Rene J, *Japanese Aircraft of the Pacific War*, Putnam, London, 1972.

Fuchida, Mitsuo and Okumiya, Massatake, *Midway: the Battle that doomed Japan*, Hutchinson, London, 1956.

Grenfell, Captain Russell, RN, *Main Fleet to Singapore*, Faber & Faber, London, 1951.

Goldstein, Donald M and Dillon, Katherine V, (Editors), *The Pearl Harbor Papers: Inside the Japanese Plans*, Dulles, Virginia, 1999.

Goldstein, Donald M and Dillon, Katherine V, (Editors), with Chihaya, Masataka, translator, *Fading Victory: The Diary of Admiral Matome Ugaki – 1941-1945*, University of Pittsburgh Press, Pittsburgh, 1991.

Griffiths, Richard, *Patriotism Perverted; Captain Ramsay, The Right Club and British Anti-Semitism, 1939-40*, Constable & Robinson, London, 1989.

Griffiths, Richard, *Fellow Travellers of the Right; British enthusiasts for Nazi German 1933-39*, Constable, London, 1980.

Haggie, Paul, *Britannia at Bay: the Defence of the British Empire Against Japan 1931-1941*, Clarendon Press, Oxford, 1981.

Hattori, Takushiro, *Daitoa Senso Zenshi (The Complete History of the Great East Asia War)*, Hara Shobo, Tokyo, 1965.

Hisae, Sawachi, *Middowei kaisen: Kiroku (The Naval Battle of Midway: A Record)*, Bungei Shunjū, Tokyo, 1986.

Hozumu, Nobshige, *Ancestor-worship and Japanese law*, Maruzen Kabushiki-Kaisha, Tokyo, 1912.

Iinkai, Nihon Kaigun Kōkūshi, Editor, *Nihon kaigun Kōkūshi (The History of Japanese Naval Aviation) 4 vols*, Jiji Tsushinsha, 1969.

Isom, Professor Dallas Woodbury, *The Battle of Midway: Why the Japanese Lost*, in *Naval War College Review*, Annapolis, Summer, 2000.

Isom, Professor Dallas Woodbury, *They would have found a way*, in *Naval War College Review*, Annapolis, Summer, 2002.

Ito, Masanori, *The End of the Imperial Japanese Navy*, Weidenfeld & Nicolson, London, 1963.

Kagetsurou Ltd, *Kagetsurou, since 1889, the Kagetsuro 100th anniversary book*, Tokyo, 1989.

Kanai, Rev Shokai, *Introduction to the Lotus Sutra*, Los Angeles, 2005.

Kaikukai (Association of Sea and Sky), *Kaigun Koku Nempyo* (Naval Chronological Table), Hara Shobo, Tokyo, 1982.

Kirby, Woodburn S, *The War Against Japan, Vol 1: The loss of Singapore*, HMSO, London, 1957.

Kusaka, Ryunosuke, *Rengo Kantai (Combined Fleet)*, in *Mainichi Shimburn*, Tokyo, April 1952.

Lowe, Peter (Editor), *Western Interactions with Japan: Expansion, the Armed Forces and Readjustment, 1859-1956*, Routledge Curzon, London, October 1990

Lundstrom, John B, *First South Pacific Fleet Strategy, December 1941-June 1942*, Naval Institute Press, Annapolis, 1977.

Lundstrom, John B, *The First Team: Pacific Naval Air Combat from Pearl Harbor to Midway*, Naval Institute Press, Annapolis, 1984.

Macintyre, Donald, *Fighting Admiral*, Evans, London, 1961.

Marder, Arthur J, *Old Friends, New Enemies: Royal Navy and the Imperial Japanese Navy, Vol 1 Strategic Illusions, 1936-41*, Oxford University Press, Oxford, August 1981.

Millard, Thomas Franklin, *The ABC's of the Twenty-One Demands*, article in *The Weekly Review of the Far East*, Shanghai, 1921.

Millard, Thomas Franklin, *The Sino-Japanese negotiations, January-March 1915 and the treaties and notes signed in Peking 25th May 1915 official record and texts*, article in *The National Review*, Shanghai, 1915.

Morison, Professor Samuel Eliot, *History of the United States Naval Operations in World War II: (Volume 3): The Rising Sun in the Pacific*, Little Brown, Boston, 1947-62.

Morris, Ivan, *The Nobility of Failure: Tragic Heroes in the History of Japan*, Secker & Warburg, London, 1975.

Nakamura, Professor Akira, *Dai Toa Senso Eno Mich (En Route to the Great Asia War)*, Dokkyo University, Soka City, Tokyo, Tendensha, Tokyo, 1990.

Nihon, Kaigun Kōkūshi Iinkai, Editor, *Nihon kaigun Kōkūshi (A history of Japanese naval aviation) 4 vols*, Jiji Tsushinsha, 1969.

Nish, Professor Ian, *The History of Anglo-Japanese Relations 1600-2002, Volume 5: Social and Cultural Perspectives*, Palgrave Macmillan, London, November 2002.

O'Connor, Peter, Compiler, *Japanese Propaganda- Selected Readings. Series 1: Books 1872-1943 (10 vols)*, with Foreword by Professor Uchikawa Yoshimi, Editions Synapse, October 2003.

Okumiya, Commander, *How the Panay was sunk*, article in US Naval Institute *Proceedings*, June 1953, Annapolis, 1953.

Okumiya, Masatake, and Horikoshi, Jiro, with Caidin, Martin, *Zero!: The Story of the Japanese Navy Air Force 1937-1945*, Cassell, London, 1957.

Parshall, Jonathan B, Dickson, David D and Tully, Anthony P, *Set and Drift; Doctrine Matters: Why the Japanese Lost at Midway*, in Naval War College Review, Summer 2001.

Peattie, Mark R, *Sunburst: The Rise of Japanese Naval Air Power, 1909-1941*, Naval Institute Press, Annapolis, 2001.

Peattie, Mark R and Evans, David, *Kaigun: Strategy, Tactics and Technology in the Imperial Japanese Navy, 1887-1941*, Naval Institute Press, Annapolis, 1997.

Pitkin, Walter Broughton, *Must we fight Japan?*, The Century Co, New York, 1921.

Plante, Trevor K, *Two Japans: Japanese expressions of sympathy and regret in the wake of the Panay Incident*, Prologue: *Quarterly of the National Archives and Records Administration*, Washington, D C.

Prados, John, *Combined Fleet Decoded: The Secret History of American Intelligence and the Japanese Navy in World War II*, Random House, New York, 1995.

Prange, Gordon W, with Goldstein, Donald and Dillon, Katherine V, *At Dawn We Slept; The Untold Story of Pearl Habor*, Brasseys, New York, 1990.

Presselsen, *Germany and Japan: A study in Totalitarian Diplomacy, 1933-1941*, Fertie, New York, 1961.

Roskill, Stephen, *Churchill and the Admirals*, Collins, London, 1977.

Roskill, Captain S W, *The War at Sea (3 Vols in 4 Parts)*, HMSO, 1954-67.

Roskill, Stephen W, *Naval Policy between the Wars, (2 vols)*, Collins, London, 1968 & 1976.

Schofield, B B, *British Sea Power*, Batsford, London, 1967.

Seno, Commander Sadao, *A Chess Game with No Checkmate, Admiral Inoue and the Pacific War*, in Naval War College Review, 26 (January/February 1974).

Sempill, Master of, *The British Aviation Mission to the Imperial Japanese Navy*, article in *The Journal of the Royal Aeronautical Society 1924*, London, 1925.

Shimidzu, Kadzuwo J, Nihhon Institute for Critical Science (NICS), 31st August 2004.

Simpson, Michael, MA, M Ltt, FR HIST S, (Editor), *The Somerville Papers*, *Selections from the Private and Official Correspondence of Admiral of the Fleet Sir James Somerville, GCB, GBE, DSO*; with John Somerville, CB, CBE, Scolar Press for The Navy Records Society, London, 1995.

Smith, Peter C, *The History of Dive Bombing*, Nautical & Aviation Publishing, Annapolis, 1981.

Smith, Peter C, *Dive Bombers in Action*, Sterling Publishing, New York, 1985.

Smith, Peter C, *Dive Bomber! A Pictorial History*, Naval Institute Press, Annapolis, 1982.

Smith, Peter C, *Aichi D3A1/2 Val*, Crowood Press, Ramsbury, 1999.

Smith, Peter C, *The Curtiss SB2C Helldiver*, Crowood, Press, Ramsbury, 2004.

Smith, Peter C, *Junkers Ju 87 Stuka*, Crowood Press, Ramsbury, 1997.

Smith, Peter C, *Arctic Victory*, Crécy Publishing, Manchester, 1998.

Snow, Carl, *Japanese Carrier Operations: How Did They Do It?* article in *The Hook*, Tailhook Association, Annapolis, 1995.

Sonokawa, Kamerō, Editor, *Nihon kaigun kōkūtai (The Japanese naval air force*, Kōdansha, Tokyo, 1970.

Stephan, Professor John J, *Hawaii under the Rising Sun; Japan's Plans for Conquest after Pearl Harbor*, University of Hawaii Press, Honolulu,1984.

Sugihara, Seishiro, *Between Competence and Culpability: Assessing the Diplomacy of Japan's Foreign Ministry from Pearl Harbor to Potsdam*, University Press of America, Lanham, Maryland, 1997.

Takahashi, Sadamu, *Hishogumo (Flying Clouds)*, Takahashi, Kawasaki, Kanagawa, April 1978.

Takata, Admiral T, *Circumstances which led the Japanese Navy to agree to the Tripartite Pact, Notes on Conference*, Appendix 5 Japanese Monographs Navy Affairs Bureau, Tokyo, 17th February 1953.

Takemoto, Tadao and Ohara, Yasu, *The Alleged 'Nanking Massacre': Japan's rebuttal to China's forged claims*, Meisei-sha Inc, Tokyo, 2000.

Tetsuya, Öhama and Ikurō, Editors, *Teikoku rikukaigun jiten (Dictionary of the Imperial Japanese Army and Navy)*, Dōseisha, Tokyo, 1995.

Tomlinson, Michael, *The Most Dangerous Moment*, William Kimber, London, 1976.

Tota, Lieutenant-Commander Ishimaru, IJHN, *Japan must fight Britain*, translated by Instructor-Captain G V Rayment, CBE, RN, The Pasternoster Library, No XI, Hurst & Blackett, London, February 1936.

Vivian, Captain J G P, *Efficiency of the Japanese Navy, Report to Admiralty, 1935*, National Archives, London.

Wildenberg, Thomas, *Destined for Glory; Dive Bombing, Midway, and the Evolution of Carrier Airpower*, Naval Institute Press, Annapolis, 1998.

Wilkinson, Philip and Charing, Duncan, *DK Encyclopaedia of Religion*, Dorling Kindersley, London, 2004.

Index